9/29

W9-BYU-819

Six Degrees of Social Influence

SIX DEGREES OF SOCIAL INFLUENCE

Science, Application, and the Psychology of Robert Cialdini

EDITED BY

Douglas T. Kenrick

Noah J. Goldstein

Sanford L. Braver

OXFORD
UNIVERSITY PRESS

Oxford University Press, Inc., publishes works that further Oxford University's objective of excellence in research, scholarship, and education.

Oxford   New York
Auckland   Cape Town   Dar es Salaam   Hong Kong   Karachi   Kuala Lumpur   Madrid Melbourne
Mexico City   Nairobi   New Delhi   Shanghai   Taipei   Toronto

With offices in
Argentina   Austria   Brazil   Chile   Czech Republic   France   Greece   Guatemala   Hungary   Italy
Japan   Poland   Portugal   Singapore   South Korea   Switzerland   Thailand   Turkey   Ukraine
Vietnam

Published by Oxford University Press, Inc.
198 Madison Avenue, New York, New York 10016

Oxford is a registered trademark of Oxford University Press
Oxford University Press is a registered trademark of Oxford University Press, Inc.

Library of Congress Cataloging-in-Publication Data

Six degrees of social influence : science, application, and the psychology of Robert Cialdini / edited by Douglas T. Kenrick, Noah J. Goldstein, and Sanford L. Braver.
     p. cm.
Includes bibliographical references and index.
ISBN 978-0-19-974305-6 (hardcover)
   1. Cialdini, Robert B. 2. Persuasion (Psychology) 3. Influence (Psychology) 4. Social influence.
I. Kenrick, Douglas T. II. Goldstein, Noah J. III. Braver, Sanford L.
BF637.P4S59 2011
153.8'52092—dc22   2011009682

---

1 2 3 4 5 6 7 8 9

Printed in the United States of America on acid-free paper

FOREWORD

The capacity to persuade—to capture the audience, convince the undecided, convert the opposition—has always been a prized skill. But, thanks to relatively recent developments, it is no longer only an elusive *art*, the province of those with an intuitive grasp of how to time an argument or turn a phrase just so. For most of us, this is welcome news. After all, one problem with an art form is that only artists can truly manage it. But, what about the rest of us? Must we resign ourselves to fumbling away open opportunities to move others in our direction because we so frequently fail to say the right thing or, worse, say the right thing at the wrong time? Fortunately, no. As is evident in the pages of this book, the delicate art of personal persuasion has been transformed into a solid social science.[1]

There is now a substantial body of systematic research into how people can be moved to agree with a request. It is worth noting that the persuasive practices covered in this work rarely concern the merits of the request itself. Instead, they concern the ways in which the merits are presented. There is no question that having a strong case is crucial to success. But having a worthy argument or set of arguments is not enough, because other worthy (yet competing) arguments are likely to exist as well. So, although making a good case is important, it's the person who can make a good case *well* who will gain the lion's share of assent. For optimal persuasive effect, then, our focus should be on methods for communicating our case in the most effective manner. A reading of the chapters that follow offers a rich vein of information regarding precisely those methods.

---

1. In academic usage a distinction is often made between persuasion, which refers to change in a private attitude or belief resulting from the receipt of a message, and social influence, which refers to socially-induced change in *behavior* and which doesn't require that attitudes or beliefs be modified in the process. For the purposes of this essay, however, I employ the term "persuasion" more broadly, meaning it to include changes of mind, feelings, and/or behavior. Consequently, I use persuasion and social influence interchangeably.

Dangerous Fruit

Before encountering that information, though, a brief foray into the past is in order. The renowned scholar of social influence, William McGuire, determined that in the four millennia of recorded Western history, there have been only four scattered centuries in which the study of persuasion flourished as a craft. The first was the Periclean Age of ancient Athens; the second occurred during the years of the Roman Republic; the next appeared in the time of the European Renaissance; the last was the 20th century, which witnessed the advent of large scale advertising, information, and mass media campaigns (McGuire, 1985). Although this bit of background seems benign, it possesses an alarming side: Each of the three previous centuries of systematic persuasion study ended similarly when political authorities had the masters of persuasion killed.

A moment's reflection suggests why this should be. Information about the persuasion process was dangerous because it created a base of power entirely separate from those that the authorities of the times controlled. Persuasion is a way to move people that doesn't require coercion, intimidation, or brute strength. Eloquent communicators win the day by commissioning forces that heads of state have no monopoly over, such as cleverly crafted language, properly placed information, and, most importantly, psychological insight. To eliminate this rival source of influence, it was easiest for the rulers to eliminate those few individuals who truly understood how to engage the process.

One aspect of this history appears relevant to the achievement of modern influence goals. Because of a variety of factors that have emerged in commercial, educational, and social contexts (e.g., matrix-based organizational structures, egalitarian empowerment practices, globalization), hierarchically-organized command approaches to change are rapidly becoming outmoded. Increasingly in work settings, for example, individuals come together on a project from different arenas within the same organization. The heterogeneous make-up of these teams makes unclear who is in charge of whom. Similarly, members of one organization often partner with those of different, cooperating organizations on joint projects. Here, again, issues of line authority are inapplicable or obscured. Finally, savvy managers, educators, and government officials have always recognized the morale costs of playing the Because-I'm-the-Boss card. In each of these instances, where reliance on hierarchical lines of command seems inappropriate, impractical, or imprudent, some other form of influence is preferred. That is why a thoroughgoing knowledge of the process of persuasion can be so valuable. As the rulers of old recognized, persuasion moves people by means that don't depend on formal power structures. Quite simply, it can provide influence without authority.

Recall, however, that each of the first three centuries of systematic persuasion study ended in the same unsettling manner—with a purge of the reigning persuasion experts. Should the recent completion of the last such century alarm those who master the material in this book, out of justified fear that they might be included in an impending fourth era of annihilation? Not this time.

The Flowering of Science

Something revolutionary has happened to the study of persuasion during the past half-century. In the bargain, the change has rendered ridiculous the idea that persuasion expertise can be eradicated by eradicating the persuasion experts. Alongside the art of persuasion has grown a formidable science of the process. For well over 50 years, researchers have been applying a rigorous scientific approach to the question of which messages most successfully lead people to concede, comply, or change. Under controlled conditions, they have documented the sometimes astonishing impact of making a request in one fashion versus making the identical request in a slightly different fashion. Besides the sheer size of the effects these researchers have uncovered, there is another noteworthy aspect of their results—they are repeatable.

Scientists have long employed a set of systematic procedures for discovering *and* replicating findings, including persuasion findings. As a consequence, the study of persuasion no longer exists only as an ethereal art. It is now a science that can reproduce its results. What is more, *whoever* engages in the scientific process can reproduce its results. Brilliant, inspired individuals are no longer necessary to divine the truth about persuasion, for a compelling new reason: The power of discovery doesn't reside, Socrates-style, inside the minds of a few persuasive geniuses anymore but inside the scientific process. As a consequence, knowledge about persuasion can't be eliminated by eliminating, Socrates-style, those who possess it—because somebody else can come along, use the same scientific procedures, and get the knowledge back again. So, (whew) we're all safe from threatened power holders, who should now be more interested in acquiring the information than abolishing it.

We have a right to feel more than just relieved. We are entitled to feel encouraged, even emboldened, by the fact that similar procedures can produce similar persuasion results. If that is indeed the case, it means that persuasion is governed by natural laws. The upshot is a pair of considerable advantages for any prospective persuader. First, if persuasion is lawful, it is learnable. Whether born with an inspired talent for influence or not, whether preternaturally insightful about the process or not, whether a gifted artisan of the language or not, it is possible to learn how to be more influential. By applying a set of principles that govern the persuasion process, communicators can more effectively move acquaintances, neighbors, coworkers, and even superiors (who, I've recently learned, include grandchildren) in desired directions. Second, if persuasion is lawful, it is teachable. Therefore, vital communicators can be trained inside our organizations to apply those same principles to secure crucial commitments, concessions, and consensuses. The impressive contributors to this volume show us an array of persuasion-based lessons that are especially worth learning and teaching.

Scholarly and pragmatic issues aside, I need to acknowledge and convey my personal reactions to the contents and publication of this book. Although there is no English term able to capture those reactions completely, there is a Yiddish word that does the job with remarkable precision. It is *kvelling*, which refers to the process of swelling with pride and delight. Even though this word (rightly) conjoins the two elements of pride and delight into a single experience, they are separable and flow from different sources.[2]

My pride in the book comes from the intense feeling of gratification that so many respected individuals looked at my work and saw fit to honor it in this singularly satisfying way. My delight in the book comes from a recognition of the quality of the product itself. So many times in reading one or another chapter, I'd say to myself, "That's right, that's right! They (the authors) got it exactly right." Even the sequencing of the chapters was impressively wrought—something not easy to do and a credit to the characteristic thoughtfulness with which Doug Kenrick, Noah Goldstein, and Sandy Braver conceived and managed the project.

I recently saw a series of TV commercials for a financial services company in which a 20-something fellow encounters a much older incarnation of himself, who attempts to convince the young man that if he just works hard to do his best, things will go better than he could sensibly predict at that point. If I were to write a version of the ad in which I approached my just-getting-started self with that message, I know I wouldn't have to say anything to persuade him to it: I'd only have to hand him a copy of this book. At that moment in the ad, the camera would register a pair of simultaneously occurring, yet wholly different, facial expressions. The young Cialdini would be displaying absolute astonishment (complete with a tiny run of spittle from the corner of his mouth). The old guy, on the other hand, would be *kvelling*.

Robert B. Cialdini

---

2. Please recognize that, as an academic, I can't help myself in this analytical bent.

CONTENTS

CONTRIBUTORS

Vanessa K. Bohns
Assistant Professor
Department of Management Sciences
University of Waterloo

Sanford L. Braver
Emeritus Professor
Department of Psychology
Arizona State University

Pablo Briñol
Associate Professor
Department of Psychology
Universidad Autónoma de Madrid

Stephanie L. Brown
Associate Professor
Center for Medical Humanities,
    Compassionate Care, and
    Bioethics
Stony Brook University

Jerry M. Burger
Professor
Department of Psychology
Santa Clara University

Abraham P. Buunk
Academy Professor
Royal Netherlands Academy of
    Arts and Sciences, and Dept. of
    Psychology
University of Gröningen

John T. Cacioppo
Professor
Department of Psychology
Director
Center for Cognitive and Social
    Neuroscience
The University of Chicago

Robert B. Cialdini
Emeritus Professor
Department of Psychology
Arizona State University

Stephanie M. Cantu
Graduate Student
Department of Psychology
University of Minnesota

Ap Dijksterhuis
Professor
Department of Social Psychology
Radboud University Nijmegen

Shelli L. Dubbs
Postdoctoral Fellow
School of Psychology
University of Queensland

Kristina M. Durante
Postdoctoral Associate
Carlson School of Management
University of Minnesota

Francis J. Flynn
Associate Professor
Graduate School of Business
Stanford University

Noah J. Goldstein
Assistant Professor
Anderson School of Management
University of California,
    Los Angeles

William G. Graziano
Professor
Department of Psychological
    Sciences
Purdue University

Vladas Griskevicius
Assistant Professor
Carlson School of Management
University of Minnesota

Louise C. Hawkley
Associate Director
Social Neuroscience Laboratory
Senior Research Scientist
Center for Cognitive and Social
    Neuroscience
Department of Psychology
The University of Chicago

Douglas T. Kenrick
Professor
Department of Psychology
Arizona State University

John S. Kim
Graduate Student
Department of Psychology
University of Minnesota

Darwyn E. Linder
Emeritus Professor
Department of Psychology
Arizona State University

Jon K. Maner
Associate Professor
Department of Psychology
Florida State University

Kevin D. Mitnick
Founder
Mitnick Security Consulting, LLC

Chad R. Mortensen
Assistant Professor
Department of Psychology
Metropolitan State College
    of Denver

Steven L. Neuberg
Professor
Department of Psychology
Arizona State University

Richard E. Petty
Professor and Chair
Department of Psychology
The Ohio State University

Petia Petrova
Assistant Professor
Tuck School of Business
Dartmouth College

John W. Reich
Emeritus Professor
Department of Psychology
Arizona State University

Brad J. Sagarin
Professor
Department of Psychology
Northern Illinois University

Mark Schaller
Professor
Department of Psychology
University of British Columbia

Norbert Schwarz
Professor
Department of Psychology
The University of Michigan

Jeffry A. Simpson
Professor
Department of Psychology
University of Minnesota

Hyunjin Song
Postdoctoral Fellow
Department of Psychology
Yale University

Rick van Baaren
Professor
Department of Social Psychology
Radboud University Nijmegen

Jan A.R.A.M. van Hooff
Emeritus Professor
Department of Behavioral Biology
Universiteit Utrecht

Stephen G. West
Professor
Department of Psychology
Arizona State University

INTRODUCTION

FULL CYCLE SOCIAL INFLUENCE

DOUGLAS T. KENRICK, NOAH J. GOLDSTEIN,
AND SANFORD L. BRAVER

A recent headline in the *Times of London* declares that: "social psychology has reached its tipping point." The article goes on to describe an intellectual revolution, in which social psychological ideas are having an increasing influence on politicians and economists. The author discusses the wave of books applying social psychological ideas to other fields, including Gladwell's *Tipping Point,* Ariely's *Predictably Irrational,* Thaler and Sunstein's *Nudge,* and Brafman and Brafman's *Sway.* The author credits "Robert Cialdini's seminal book *Influence*" as one of the key movers of this revolution. Indeed, Cialdini, along with a team of behavioral economists including Ariely, Sunstein, and Daniel Kahneman was called on by Barack Obama to help him win the presidency, and by Al Gore to help him craft his campaign to promote energy conservation. Besides an increasing number of calls to consult with educational, business, and legal organizations on these topics, Cialdini, as the world's foremost expert on social influence, has also been consulted by the British government at 10 Downing Street (who wanted to structure prosocial messages to British citizens), and by NATO in Brussels (who wanted to develop persuasive international negotiation strategies).

From clever titles for persuasion heuristics like *basking in reflected glory, low ball, door-in-the-face, even a penny would help,* to broad theoretical concepts like *full-cycle social psychology,* the *focus theory of normative conduct,* the *negative state relief model of helping,* and *the preference for consistency,* Robert Cialdini has been contributing a steady stream of ideas and eye-catching results for almost four decades. His "influence" has spread well beyond the field of academic social psychology, to business, health, and politics, and beyond the boundaries of North America to many other countries.

With his book *INFLUENCE* having been translated into 26 languages and having sold over two million copies, Dr. Cialdini is one of the most cited living social psychologists in the world today and is considered the foremost expert in the world in the field of influence and persuasion. Indeed, economists Richard Thaler and Cass Sunstein refer to Cialdini as the "great guru of social influence."

This book contains a series of essays written in honor of Cialdini's retirement from Arizona State University (where he has worked his entire career). Rather than seek out personal anecdotes from Cialdini's collaborators, though, we sought to honor Cialdini in a way that would also do what he's done throughout his highly productive career: Explore new facets of human behavior in ways that bridge the best of scientific psychology and application.

Cialdini coined the term "full cycle psychology" to refer to the process of moving back and forth between scientific ideas, laboratory experiments, and applications of those scientific ideas in the real world. To explore the impact of social influence in a full cycle fashion, we not only sought out Bob's former students and collaborators—who as you'll see have achieved renown of their own—we also asked prominent researchers from around the world how they had been influenced by the new developments and ideas that Cialdini has pioneered. As we began to contemplate the revolutionary broadening of the influence of influence research, we realized that there was a profound and important development to be explored. Thus, the book features original essays by leading authors—who span many countries and many disciplines, and who are leaders in both basic theorizing and a diverse range of important applications. These chapters break new ground and promise to be widely influential themselves.

As you'll see, the chapters that follow should not only be of interest to academic scholars from an extraordinary variety of disciplines, but also to the many lay readers who have been enthralled by the umbrella of Cialdini's ideas, a group that continues to expand outside the field of psychology to encompass marketing, economics, political science, and behavioral medicine.

In the first chapter, Mark Schaller from the University of British Columbia joins Arizona State's Douglas Kenrick and Steven Neuberg to discuss scientific influence. They note that connections matter—whether considering Kevin Bacon's position in the network of actors, Paul Erdös's position in the network of mathematicians, or Robert Cialdini's position in the network of psychologists, economists, and politicians. For a research scientist, the most important connections depend on the creativity of his or her ideas, and on how successfully those ideas are marketed to other scientists and practitioners. This chapter derives five broad principles of scientific influence that lurk within Cialdini's body of scientific research.

In chapter two, Stanford Business Professor Francis Flynn joins Vanessa Bohns of the University of Toronto to explore the extent to which people underestimate their influence on others. Their research shows that people can be persuaded to say "yes" if you just give them a chance, and that you don't need a fancy title or massive wealth to have power over others—you just need to know a little bit about the psychology of compliance.

In chapter three, Brad Sagarin (of Northern Illinois University), an expert of resistance to unwanted persuasion, joins Kevin Mitnick, a computer security expert who was once the most-wanted computer hacker in the United States. The chapter describes how Mitnick used "social engineering" to gain access to highly secret computer codes, and goes on to extract some insights about how to defend yourself against such influence-based attacks.

Initial stock offerings on the New York Stock Exchange generate higher prices if the company name is easy to pronounce; ads that rhyme are more persuasive. In chapter four, Dartmouth's Petia Petrova joins Michigan's Norbert Schwarz and Yale's Hyunjin Song to explore the surprising ways in which people's meta-cognitive experiences (how easy it is to create an image linked to a persuasive message, for example) can profoundly influence our decisions.

Can a non-expert sometimes be more influential than an expert? In chapter five, Ohio State's Richard Petty joins Pablo Briñol from the Universidad Autónoma de Madrid to explore some interesting twists in the relationship between thoughtful information processing and the use of simple influence heuristics.

Watch a football game and you're likely to see thousands of fans dressed in the team's colors and holding up banners proclaiming "We're number 1!" More than three decades ago, Robert Cialdini introduced the notion of "basking in reflected glory." In chapter six, Jerry Burger of Santa Clara University looks at some of the research that grew out of the original set of basking studies and some current programs of research that build upon the basking concept.

As one journalist recently put it, popularity is all the rage. In chapter seven, UCLA's Noah Goldstein joins Chad Mortensen (of Metropolitan State College of Denver) to consider the sometimes subtle ways in which we look to other people's decisions to inform our own.

In chapter eight, Vlad Griskevicius, Jeff Simpson, Kristina Durante, John Kim, and Stephanie Cantu (from the University of Minnesota) join forces to examine the fascinating ways in which we are influenced by a simple social ratio–the relative numbers of men and women in our environment. They describe researcher showing how sex ratios influence everything from people's economic decisions to their career choices.

In chapter nine, University of Chicago's John Cacioppo and Louise Hawkley explore the ways in which people are "designed for social influence." They consider the physiological mechanisms that underlie people's motivations to connect with, care for, and seek the approval of, others. They suggest that, although these design features can sometimes make us overly sensitive to social rejection, they helped our ancestors navigate the many obstacles to getting along in human groups.

Those biological dimensions of social influence are explored further in chapter ten by Bram Buunk of the Royal Netherlands Academy of Arts and Sciences, Shelli Dubbs from the University of Brisbane, and Jan van Hooff from the University of Utrecht. As they note, humans are not alone in attempting to influence one another. They explore the many ways in which animals control one another's reproductive behaviors, and then describe some new research demonstrating many of the same phenomena in human beings.

Why is it that, in the wake of Hurricane Katrina, so many flocked to New Orleans to help those in need, while so many others were content to watch from afar? In chapter eleven, SUNY's Stephanie Brown and Florida State's Jon Maner consider the decades of research exploring a question that was central to Bob Cialdini's contribution to psychology: Does true altruism really exist? To this end, their chapter pulls together research and theories from psychology, evolutionary biology, neuroscience, and economics. Their chapter concludes with some recommendations for how research can (and should) inform public policy.

How do you create the next generation of full cycle researchers, with rigorous skills for testing cutting edge scientific ideas in everyday settings? The final three chapters address this question in different ways.

ASU's Stephen West joins Purdue's William Graziano in chapter twelve, to tackle the question of the tension between basic and applied research, and to consider the strengths and weaknesses of some particular research tools. In particular, they consider some alternatives to laboratory experiments that can allow the researchers to draw relatively strong causal inferences about questions that would be impossible to study in the typical experiment.

In chapter thirteen, Rick van Baaren and Ap Dijksterhuis, from the University of Nijmegen, describe a new graduate program in which students are taught how to use and develop scientific knowledge on social influence and apply it to real life problems and challenges, and to translate ideas into solid, creative and catchy experiments in order to affect both academia and the world beyond academia. Their chapter describes two full-cycle interventions their students have conducted.

In the final chapter, Darwyn Linder, John Reich, and Sandy Braver describe how they worked with Bob Cialdini to establish Arizona State's social psychology doctoral training program. They describe how Bob's Full Cycle idea was central to the program, and consider three illustrative lines of research conducted by students and faculty from that program.

These chapters will convince the reader of the remarkable currency and diversity of Bob Cialdini's ideas about the social world. He has stimulated readers and practitioners for decades; he has provoked thoughtful extensions from some of the world's finest researchers; he has probed some of social life's most important and enduring mysteries. And he has approached all this in a clever, lively, accessible and entertaining way. In the course of doing so, he has mentored and trained scores of graduate student protégés (some 70 students have been his coauthors) and honored almost every one of his faculty colleagues by his collaboration. The three of us are proud to have been his students, collaborators, colleagues, and friends, and delighted to be the ones editing this volume not only honoring Bob Cialdini, but collecting for the reading world a grand collection of his influence.

Six Degrees of Social Influence

CHAPTER 1

Six Degrees of Bob Cialdini and Five Principles of Scientific Influence

MARK SCHALLER, DOUGLAS T. KENRICK,
AND STEVEN L. NEUBERG

You know the Kevin Bacon game. If you were in a movie with Kevin Bacon, your Bacon number is one; if you were in a movie with someone else who was in a movie with Kevin Bacon, your Bacon number is 2; and so on. Here's an example: Kevin Bacon was in "A Few Good Men" with Tom Cruise; Cruise was in "The Last Samurai" with Chad Lindberg; Lindberg was in "My Big Break" with Mark Schaller. Ergo: Schaller has a Bacon number of 3. Being egocentric, Schaller prefers to think that Kevin Bacon has a Schaller number of 3.

The Erdös game is the math nerd's version. Paul Erdös co-authored nearly 1,500 articles with over 500 collaborators, who themselves co-authored many articles with many others, and so forth. Just as anyone with a single screen credit can be linked to Kevin Bacon through a series of joint-movie-appearance links, almost any mathematician can be linked to Erdös through a series of co-authorship links. Although he's no mathematician, Schaller has an Erdös number of 6. Or, we could say that Erdös has a Schaller number of 6. So does Albert Einstein. (Kenrick and Neuberg both have Schaller numbers of 1 and so, by this idiotic index, are more successful than either Albert Einstein or Kevin Bacon.)

What do these tenuous connections to Erdös and Bacon have to do with Bob Cialdini and his widespread influence on fields as diverse as psychology, business, political science, and economics? Lurking beneath the silly surface of the Schaller number are some fundamental truths about human nature and the scientific enterprise required to reveal it. These truths are lessons learned from Cialdini himself and uniquely illuminated within his body of work.

LESSON NUMBER ONE: CONNECTIONS MATTER

Among Cialdini's many prominent contributions is a line of research on basking in reflected glory ("BIRGing"). This research illuminates the ways in which people strategically advertise even minimal connections to successful others (Cialdini, Borden, Thorne, Walker, Freeman, & Sloan, 1976; Cialdini & Richardson, 1980). Here's an example: Shortly after Schaller uncovered his Bacon and Erdös numbers, about 30 other people (pretty much everybody he encountered over the next 2 days) found out as well. Cialdini's BIRGing research is typically mentioned to illustrate the subtle ways that people strategically manufacture positive public images. If you dig a little deeper, though, these studies illustrate even more profound truths about the human condition.

Why does Schaller find it gratifying to declare that Kevin Bacon has a Schaller number of 3? If you guessed it has to do with the self-serving consequences of symbolically associating with the winners in the world, you would be partially correct; but there's more to it than that. O.J. Simpson and Charles Manson have Schaller numbers of 3 and 4, respectively, and Schaller was just as quick to tell us about those connections too. Simpson and Manson don't exactly trigger a cascade of warm and friendly feelings. So, why would Schaller publicly announce these unsettling (and hardly self-serving) connections?

Because connections matter, that's why. In the 1970s, psychologists talked a lot about self-serving motives. It's not surprising, then, that self-esteem provided the motivational oomph emphasized in the BIRGing literature. Since then, our motivational horizons have expanded considerably (e.g., Kenrick, Griskevicius, Neuberg, & Schaller, 2010). There is now an enormous body of evidence pointing to a fundamental human need for interpersonal connection, and to its important consequences for human behavior (MacDonald & Leary, 2005; Maner, DeWall, Baumeister, & Schaller, 2007). When folks talk about this need, they don't usually think of Cialdini's BIRGing studies. They should. Long before it was fashionable, Cialdini's studies showed—in a novel and scientifically sexy way—that even tenuous social connections really matter.

Mere interpersonal connection is a powerful force, not just psychologically but sociologically too (Barabási, 2002; Granovetter, 1973; Watts, 2003). Psychologists haven't typically participated in scientific conversations about the sociological implications of interpersonal connections, but there are a few exceptions (e.g., Travers & Milgram, 1969). Of particular note is recent work by Bibb Latané and his colleagues on *dynamic social impact theory* (Latané, 1996, 1997; Nowak, Szamrej, & Latané, 1990; see also Harton & Bourgeois, 2004).

Dynamic social impact theory articulates the mechanisms through which local acts of interpersonal influence shape and reshape the attitudes and opinions of entire populations. This happens only because, within any human population, everyone is connected through a series of interpersonal links to everyone else. Because of these Baconesque links, individual actions reverberate through entire populations to exert global consequences. Because of the power of connection, individual psychology creates human culture.

There are further consequences too. After attending one of Latané's famous Nags Head conferences, Kenrick integrated the dynamic social impact framework with an evolutionary perspective on individual decision-making. The result was a set of novel insights about simple evolved biases that contribute to the emergence of different group geometries and different cultural norms, depending on the specific goals that individuals seek to achieve when interacting with one another (Kenrick, Li, & Butner, 2003). Individuals' decisions—whether focused on self-protection, mating, status, or familial relations—are rarely made with any awareness of the fact that, collectively, these decisions can exert a societal impact. And yet, because of the power of mere interpersonal connection, they do.

The power of connection is on display in the mathematical study of social networks, in the fundamental human need for belongingness, and in Cialdini's BIRGing studies. It's arguably the single most important reason why the psychology of social influence—and the science of social psychology—matters on a global scale.

LESSON NUMBER TWO: REAL LIFE IS SCIENCE'S NATURAL DOMAIN

More than perhaps any contemporary social psychologist, Bob Cialdini has profitably indulged his inner anthropologist. Approximately 95% of published psychological studies are stimulated by previous publications. And probably 95% of those studies have no enduring impact. (OK, We're making up those numbers, but we bet they're not that far off). In contrast, Cialdini's research has often been stimulated by his canny observations of real people doing real things in their real lives; and—no coincidence—this research has been especially influential.

Some of Cialdini's forays into the anthropology of ordinary life were expertly planned. He spent one sabbatical going "undercover" to observe actual influence professionals (waiters, car dealers, pyramid scammers) engaging in acts of professional influence. His observations led to many classic experiments on compliance techniques and the psychological processes that they exploit (Cialdini, 2008). Other lines of research reflect a scientific mind acutely prepared to take advantage of interesting accidents. The BIRGing studies, for example, were inspired by a football game. Cialdini had been poring over some underwhelming results from an experiment on attitude change, frustrated by an insufficiently substantial mean difference on a standard 7-point scale, when he wandered out of his office and into a football stadium at game time:

> The crowd was suddenly up and shouting, and yelling encouragement to their favorites below. Arcs of tissue paper crossed overhead. The university fight song was being sung. A large group of fans repeatedly roared "We're number one!" while thrusting index fingers upward. I recall quite clearly looking up from thoughts of that additional half unit of movement on a 7-point scale and realizing the power of the tumult around me. "Cialdini," I said to myself, "I think you're studying the *wrong* thing." (Cialdini, 1980, p. 22; emphasis in original)

For most of us, that experience would have been a distraction rather than a scientific stimulant. If it was someone else in Cialdini's shoes that day, we might not have the pleasure of talking about BIRGing at all.

Here's the point: Cialdini doesn't just read academic articles or engage in arid exercises in logical deduction to arrive at research hypotheses—he also pays attention to real life.

That seems simple, but it's not. Most of us have had only sporadic success in doing so. When we've been able to, it's paid off. Kenrick was once asked to lecture on attraction to a single's group. Afterwards, several middle-aged women asked if there was any scientific reason why middle-aged men were so interested in younger women. They handed him a pile of singles newspapers, which inspired an intensive study of singles ads from the Netherlands, Germany, and India, and then of marriages from around the world and from different historical periods. One of the resulting publications (which shows that sex differences in age preferences are a human universal; Kenrick & Keefe, 1992) has become Kenrick's most-cited empirical paper ever.

Neuberg too has discovered the value of making an occasional field trip outside of his university office. He once published an article showing that, contrary to popular belief, Valentine's Day tends to be *bad* for most romantic relationships (Morse & Neuberg, 2004). The study was inspired by an out-of-the-blue conversation with a woman upset by her personal Valentine's Day massacre.

And here's one more story: Years ago, stimulated by a brief encounter with a movie star in a Montana health food store, Schaller started a research project on the psychological consequences of fame, which culminated in a weird little one-off article in the *Journal of Personality* (Schaller, 1997). Because that article somehow came to the attention of a filmmaker, Schaller's talking head now occupies about 30 seconds in the documentary film "My Big Break"—enough time for his name to appear in screen credits alongside those of actual actors, like Chad Lindberg. Thus, Schaller owes his Bacon number entirely to the fact that once, in a very modest way, he did what Cialdini does brilliantly all the time: Recognize potentially interesting and understudied psychological phenomena lurking within the great blooming, buzzing confusion of everyday life.

Unlike our own stumbling visits into the real world, Cialdini's thoughtful approach represents an underappreciated form of scientific genius. It's a genius that applies not merely to scientific *inspiration*, but to scientific *explanation* as well. A piece of research inspired merely by previous empirical findings is most likely doomed to do little more than explain those findings in greater detail. A line of research inspired by real human behavior observed in real life is much more likely to apply to, and explain, real human behavior in real life, too.

LESSON NUMBER THREE: ANYTHING GOES

Although Schaller's article on the psychology of fame has had almost no scientific impact, Schaller is unusually fond of it anyway. The reason is not just because of its connection to his Bacon number, but also because the study itself employed methods that are messy and weird and even laughably unrigorous. Schaller's other personal favorites (several of which include things other than individual people as the units of analysis; Schaller, Conway, & Tanchuk, 2002; Schaller & Murray, 2008) don't exactly fit the prototypical profile of rigorous experimental social psychology either.

The same applies to Kenrick. His publications include many whose methods might be characterized as wacky and weird—a species apart from standard laboratory-based experimental social psychology. We've already noted that one of his most cited articles included data obtained not from research participants but from personal ads ("SWF, 34, attractive, seeks . . ."; Kenrick & Keefe, 1992). Another of his favorites is a paper reporting results generated not by actual people, but by computer simulations (Kenrick et al., 2003). And, although Kenrick can't bask in the reflected glory of Kevin Bacon, he did proudly publish a study employing Farrah Fawcett and the rest of "Charlie's Angels" as a methodological device (Kenrick & Gutierres, 1980).

Both Schaller and Kenrick were trained as experimental social psychologists; they received that training from a man—Bob Cialdini—who has received numerous awards for his exceptional abilities to deploy, and teach, the methods of experimental social psychology. So, did they forget the lessons learned from the master of experimental methods? Have their heads gone soft? Were they childishly rebelling against a father figure who they'd have been much wiser to emulate? At the risk of sounding defensive, we think that, rather than reflecting forgetfulness, soft-headedness, or psychoanalytic cliché, both Kenrick and Schaller have been attracted to "alternative" empirical methodologies because they learned to appreciate a deeper methodological and epistemological lesson lurking within Cialdini's approach to social psychological research. The philosopher Paul Feyerabend stated the lesson like this:

> Science is an essentially anarchistic enterprise: theoretical anarchism is more humanitarian and more likely to encourage progress than its law-and-order alternatives.... The only principle that does not inhibit progress is: *anything goes.* (Feyerabend, 1975, p. 23, emphasis in original)

No one would characterize Bob Cialdini as an anarchist exactly. Nevertheless, Cialdini's body of research exemplifies the Feyerabendian philosophy. On the one hand, Cialdini has pursued many empirical investigations employing standard experimental methods within ordinary psychological laboratories. (An example is his influential program of research on helping behavior; Cialdini, Brown, Lewis, Luce, & Neuberg, 1997; Cialdini & Kenrick, 1976; Cialdini, Schaller, Houlihan, Arps, Fultz, & Beaman, 1987). But, on the other hand, many of Cialdini's studies have been conducted on sidewalks, stairwells, parking lots, or in national parks and hotel bathrooms. And the participants were real people going about their real lives, thoughtlessly tossing a bit of trash onto the sidewalk or stealthily pocketing a chunk of petrified wood from a national monument.

Field studies aren't easy to do. They impose considerable constraints on what one can manipulate, measure, and control. They force methodological compromises. Consequently, the conclusions they yield are rarely as inferentially airtight as those emerging from the lab. In a discipline that values variables measured in milliseconds and voxels, most social psychologists don't even consider leaving the lab. But while everyone else is parking their participants in front of computer screens or sliding them into multi-million-dollar fMRI machines, Cialdini is counting dirty towels in hotel bathrooms—and publishing interesting articles about them (Goldstein, Cialdini, & Griskevicius, 2008).

Cialdini's affection for field studies attests not only to his interest in testing hypotheses on real people in their real lives, but also to his deeper commitment to methodological diversity. He has demonstrated the same open-minded attitude to conceptual sources, deriving ideas not only from a variety of social psychological theories, but also from cognitive psychology, sociology, and the human evolutionary sciences (e.g., Cialdini & Kenrick, 1976; Cialdini, Kalgren, & Reno, 1991; Griskevicius, Cialdini, & Kenrick, 2006). In all aspects of his science, Cialdini has masterfully—and influentially—demonstrated the benefits of Feyerabend's motto: Anything goes.

LESSON NUMBER FOUR: BE A FOX

Most researchers apply their talents to very specific areas of inquiry: person perception, say, or attitude change or close interpersonal relationships. Or, they apply a single theoretical perspective to everything. They are like the hedgehog in the classic aphorism (commonly attributed to Archilochus) that "The fox knows many things, but the hedgehog knows one big thing." This hedgehog-like focus is pragmatic at a personal level. (It takes time and effort to develop expertise in any single domain of inquiry; if one pursues research across very different domains, one runs the risk of being a dilettante.) But it limits the scope of one's potential influence.

Happily, being a hedgehog has not been Cialdini's style. He is a fox: He knows many things. The analogy breaks down a bit, perhaps, because Cialdini's foxiness involves knowing many *big* things. Still, Cialdini's foxiness is integral to his considerable scientific impact.

Cialdini's impact results not simply from his seminal contributions to the study of basking in reflected glory, or mood and helping behavior, or the psychology of social norms, or the many other psychological processes affecting behavioral compliance, attitude change, persuasion, and social influence more broadly. Nor does his impact result simply from the many ways in which he has applied fundamental conceptual insights to improve human welfare and resolve social problems (e.g., littering, pollution, and environmental degradation in general; Cialdini, 2003). Nope. In addition to all the things Cialdini has *done*, his impact results from what he has *been*: An example of a highly flourishing fox. He's shown that, even within an academic culture that encourages hedgehoggery, one can still foxily follow one's whims all over the intellectual map—and do so without succumbing to dilettantism and with extraordinary scholarly success.

Whether intentional or not, Cialdini's fox-like approach to scholarship exerts a beneficial influence on his graduate students and collaborators.

Among other adventures, Neuberg has conducted research on impression formation, prejudice, stigma, self-fulfilling prophecies, physical attraction, relationships, prosocial behavior, religion, economic decision-making, and stereotype threat. He has employed cognitive, motivational, anthropological, and evolutionary perspectives in doing so. Kenrick too has employed—and attempted to integrate—a wide range of meta-theoretical perspectives in his studies on personality, kinship, romantic attraction, anticonformity, creativity, contrast effects, religious behaviors, one-night stands, mate preferences, memory, homicidal fantasies, visual attention, and consumer behavior. Schaller has as well. And, in addition to collaborating with Neuberg and Kenrick on some of the projects listed above, Schaller has also conducted research on such diverse topics as the psychological consequences of fame, the popularity of folktales, and the effects of pathogen prevalence on personality. Even within his allegedly more programmatic interest in stereotypes and prejudices, Schaller has flirted with a hard-core information-processing approach, had a love affair with a hotter, wetter approach informed by principles of evolutionary biology, and enjoyed a dalliance with the dynamic consequences of interpersonal communication.

It was that dalliance with dynamical systems that led to a collaboration between Schaller and Bibb Latané (Schaller & Latané, 1996). And because Latané has co-authored articles with actual mathematicians (Lewenstein, Nowak, & Latané, 1990), that dalliance therefore accounts for Schaller's acquisition of a misleadingly low Erdös number. Thus, the fact that Schaller has both a Bacon number and an Erdös number is emblematic of Cialdini's tacit encouragement to avoid any temptation to know just one big thing, and instead to be a fox.

LESSON NUMBER FIVE: MARKETING MATTERS

Schaller's Erdös number, though meaningless, is at least based on some sort of scientific product. The Bacon number, though, has no scientific currency at all. One could argue that the hours Schaller spent being filmed for "My Big Break" would have been more sensibly devoted to actual scholarly work. From this perspective, Schaller's Bacon number isn't just a laughable bit of trivia, it's an index of wasted time.

The same might be said any time any of us chats with a journalist or appears on television. Sometimes these interactions lead to the dissemination of serious scientific information, but often not. Neuberg had the unhappy experience of witnessing carefully articulated conclusions from his evolutionarily informed research on prejudice (Cottrell & Neuberg 2005) become distorted into grossly misleading headlines ("Prejudice Is Hard-Wired into the Human Brain, Says ASU Study"). And Kenrick, whose empirical research on sex and mating is catnip for television talk shows, has seen plenty of potentially productive time disappear when media appearances turned out to focus more on sensationalism than serious science. (He once filmed an interview about evolution and mate choice for a BBC documentary, only to have his answers interspliced with semi-pornographic scenes from a nudist camp called Naked City).

But there's a more positive perspective on media attention. Even if that coverage fails to promote scientific knowledge, it is emblematic of something scientifically good: When newspaper writers and television producers come calling, it suggests that we have produced scientific products that, for whatever reason, people have noticed.

Science is a cumulative enterprise. No scientific theory or empirical finding can hope to have an impact on that cumulative enterprise unless noticed by others. Before it can be noticed, of course, it has to be published; and when top journals have rejection rates of 90%, that's not easy. But publication alone isn't enough. Publication doesn't guarantee attention. Thousands of psychology articles are published every year, and only a tiny percentage of those get noticed in any meaningful way. By one estimate, only 10% of published articles ever get cited even once—a statistic that prompted one philosopher of science to observe that "publishing a paper is roughly equivalent to throwing it away" (Hull, 1988, p. 360).

And so, even in science, marketing matters. Scientists must not only deploy the conceptual and methodological skills to produce novel scientific products, they must also package that product in a way that penetrates the competitive scientific marketplace. Here again, we bow before Bob Cialdini—who has a masterful knack for selling science.

We suspect that Cialdini's considerable scientific influence has been abetted, in part, from his skill in sculpting scientific articles that tell compelling stories. Many scientists fail to do that; they just pile on the results. This is short-sighted. To actually compete successfully in the hypercompetitive scientific marketplace, results need to be packaged and presented so that their story (the specific reason why they make a meaningful contribution to science) is clear, memorable, and sufficiently interesting to demand to be retold to others. Daryl Bem (1987, p. 173) advises psychological scientists to "Think of your data as a jewel. Your task is to cut and polish it, to select the facets to highlight, and to craft the best setting for it." Cialdini is a master jeweler.

It helps to build some "hooks" into the story too. Given the vast number of scientific products that glut the market, readers aren't likely to read an article unless something about it reaches out and demands their attention.

Superficial details matter. For instance, it helps enormously to provide readers with a mnemonic device that captures the essence of the phenomenon (e.g., "door in the face," "social proof," "spyglass self"; Cialdini, 2008; Cialdini, Vincent, Lewis, Catalan, Wheeler, & Darby, 1975; Goldstein & Cialdini, 2007). Imagine if Cialdini had described a subtle strategy of public image management as, say, "a subtle strategy of public image management." Would it have had such an impact? Probably not. Smartly, he called it "basking in reflected glory," which is a lot more memorable.

An article's title also matters a lot. People rarely read an article—or even its abstract—if they don't first find something interesting in its title. Poetic devices and clever wordplay increase the number of readers who read on. "Peacocks, Picasso, and parental investment . . ."; "Going along versus going alone . . ."; "A room with a viewpoint . . .": These and other phrases like them appear in titles above Cialdini's name (Goldstein et al., 2008; Griskevicius, Cialdini, & Kenrick, 2006; Griskevicius, Goldstein, Mortensen, Cialdini, & Kenrick, 2006). None is necessary to describe the findings reported within. But all are linguistically entertaining and help to reel the reader in.

The purist may argue that science should be above this sort of linguistic frivolity and marketing. We disagree. Scientific progress depends on communication and dissemination of scientific findings. To the extent that scientists can—like Cialdini—find ways to make their work more communicable, so that it is noticed and used by others, they are doing their job.

LESSON NUMBER ONE REVISITED: CONNECTIONS MATTER

The Kevin Bacon Game works because movie-making is an intensely collaborative enterprise. So is science. Successful research depends on researchers and research assistants, on research participants, and on rooms full of people behind the scenes (e.g., grant review panels, Institutional Review Boards, etc.). The connections between these people are instrumental to scientific progress.

Some kinds of interpersonal connection matter more than others. Intellectual collaborations indicated by co-authorship are especially important. Sometimes the connections arise almost by chance, such as when Kenrick (who at the time was a first-year graduate student in clinical psychology) took a required course in social psychology from someone he'd never heard of before—a new assistant professor named Cialdini. Sometimes the connections emerge in a more planful way, such as when Schaller applied to graduate school with the specific intention of working with Cialdini, or when Neuberg accepted a job offer with the happy knowledge that Cialdini would be his colleague. These immediate academic connections have stimulated many fruitful collaborations between Cialdini and Kenrick and Schaller and Neuberg (in varying subsets), and between many more of Cialdini's students and colleagues too. The impact of these connections—and thus the impact of Cialdini's scientific influence—doesn't end there. It extends outward to the many hundreds of additional students and collaborators in each of our immediate academic orbits; and it then extends further still to touch many thousands—perhaps even millions—of additional scholars in a complex web of interconnection.

The inescapable point is that interpersonal connections have a pervasive guiding influence on the research projects that shape any scientific field. These connections shape careers, too. It is for that reason that we—Schaller and Kenrick and Neuberg—each feel very glad, and lucky, to have a Cialdini number of 1.

CHAPTER 2

Underestimating One's Influence in Help-Seeking

FRANCIS J. FLYNN AND VANESSA K. BOHNS

Imagine for a moment the anxiety experienced by a prospective groom in the moments leading up to his proposal. Think of the butterflies felt by a Girl Scout knocking on her neighbor's door for a potential cookie sale. Consider the student's apprehension in asking his esteemed professor for a letter of recommendation. The chance that any of these appeals will be accepted is very high. So, what do these individuals have to fear?

Robert Cialdini's book, *Influence* (Cialdini, 1984), has counseled countless readers on the art and science of persuasion. Some have read the book looking for tips on how to become more persuasive, while others have flipped the pages searching for clues on how to protect themselves from persuasive attempts. Whatever they are hoping to find, readers come away with a similar emotional response. Almost without exception, their common reaction is a feeling of surprise. Scan the reviews of *Influence* available online and you will be told in clear detail about a strong sense of shock, awe, and amazement, all centered around how gullible people seem, how transparent effective persuasion tools are, and how willing we all may be to say "yes" to a clever phrasing of a direct request.

The effects described in *Influence* are indeed surprising, but, at the same time, they are also empowering to the casual reader. They verify that tools of persuasion are not possessed exclusively by individuals with unique skills and rare talents; instead, they are simple and subtle approaches to presenting a decision so that others will feel compelled to comply. These tools can be understood, customized, and implemented by anyone—not just used car dealers, door-to-door salesmen, and brand advertisers. In short, what is particularly surprising about Cialdini's book is not his compelling description of how people can be easily influenced, but how easy it may be for each of us to become influential ourselves. If we appreciate the pressure that others face when deciding whether to agree with our requests for help, we may be in a much better position to get help.

This insight has inspired our own research on the topic of help-seeking and compliance. Specifically, we have examined the extent to which people are aware of the most basic weapon of influence—making a direct request for help. Given that we regularly ask people for help or are subject to help requests ourselves, we should be fairly accurate in estimating the likelihood that others will say "yes" to a direct request. However, our research tells a different story—one that suggests people are woefully inaccurate when it comes to predicting others' helpfulness. Rather than give people the benefit of the doubt, most of us wrongly assume that others will say "no" in response to our requests (e.g., to buy a box of cookies or to write a letter of recommendation). In the sections that follow, we describe this systematic bias, highlight its potential utility, and address some of its adverse consequences.

ASK AND YE SHALL RECEIVE

Imagine you are standing in the middle of Columbia University's campus in New York City. You have been searching for a nearby building, but cannot find its precise location. You stop someone walking by and ask that person to provide you with some directions. He or she points you toward the general vicinity of your destination, but you mention that you have been over there before and had no luck. You ask this stranger to escort you over to the exact address, which appears to be about three city blocks (and 5–10 minutes) away. What do you think the stranger will say? More specifically, how many people do you think you will have to approach before you get just one individual to agree to this request?

This scenario is not fictitious. Rather, it describes an exercise we conducted in late 2005 (Flynn & Lake [Bohns], 2008, Study 2). Participants in the study were positioned in the middle of campus and instructed to approach random strangers for an escort to the university gym, which is located at the edge of campus (the Columbia University gym is subterranean and therefore difficult to find). Before completing the task, participants were asked to estimate how many people they would have to approach in order to get one to say "yes." On average, people estimated they would have to ask 7.2 people to get just one to agree. In fact, they needed to approach just 2.3 strangers, on average. While people presumed that about 6 out of 7 of the individuals they approached would refuse to assist them, the reality was that approximately every other person was willing to agree to their request.

This underestimation effect has been replicated in several domains: soliciting charitable donations, asking people for the use of their cell phones, and recruiting people to fill out questionnaires, to name a few. In each case, those seeking help overestimated by as much as 200% the number of people they'd have to ask to get someone to agree with their help request. As it turned out, people were far more likely to say "yes" than participants expected. The participants could get assistance fairly easily, even from strangers, but this potential power—the power of the "ask"—was lost on them.

Why does this happen? We propose that people underestimate givers' willingness to comply in responding to requests for help because they fail to account for the social pressures that accompany help requests. No one wants to reject others, particularly not face-to-face. We all can recognize this fact. Nevertheless, when we consider whether someone will agree to provide help, we pay less attention to the social cost of saying "no" (i.e., the potential embarrassment one might feel for rejecting a request) than potential helpers do. What do we focus on instead? When predicting others' willingness to comply with a request for help, we attend to the costs of saying "yes" (i.e., how much time, effort, and resources are required to comply with the request) rather than the costs of saying "no."

To test this idea, we asked participants in another study (Flynn & Lake [Bohns], 2008, Study 6) to estimate how many people they would need to approach on campus to get one person to fill out a questionnaire. The directness and the magnitude of the request varied across conditions. In one condition, participants were instructed to simply hand passersby a flyer with the request (low social costs of rejection), and in another condition participants asked them directly (high social costs of rejection). The length of the questionnaire also varied, so that half of the participants distributed one-page questionnaires, and the other half distributed 10-page questionnaires. One might expect that people would be far less likely to fill out a lengthy questionnaire than a short one. As it turns out, the passersby were much more susceptible to the directness of the request than its magnitude (they were far more likely to say "yes" in response to a direct request than a flyer, but did not distinguish between a "big" and a "small" request). Participants, however, assumed the opposite was true—their estimates of how many people they would need to ask did not adjust for the manner of the request, just its size.

When we are the ones who need help, we are simply not attuned to the motivation others have to help us. The upshot of this failure in perspective taking is straightforward: People may not take advantage of others' willing-ness to say "yes" because they erroneously assume that their requests for assistance will be rejected. Just think of the opportunities lost. Clients are not called, donors are left unsolicited, and first dates are never proposi-tioned because we simply have a hard time understanding our targets. We cannot appreciate how difficult it is for other people to say "no," even though we have been in that uncomfortable position many times ourselves. As a result, we fail to benefit from cooperation to the fullest extent possible.

WHAT IF PEOPLE WERE MORE WILLING TO ASK?

When we assign Cialdini's text in class, we draw skepticism from some stu-dents who express concern that we are "feeding the sharks." That is, they worry that the only individuals who will make use of effective persuasion tactics are those who wish to satisfy their own Machiavellian interests. In reality, such tactics can be used to accomplish noble deeds as well as evil ones. Thus, the misgivings that people have about who *can* benefit from understanding the principles of influence seem misplaced, perhaps mainly because the terms "influence" and "persuasion" can conjure up images of politicians and snake oil peddlers more readily than images of humanitari-ans and civil rights leaders.

When pushed further, students often reveal a deeper concern that the use of influence tactics will make them appear Machiavellian, even when they are not. This concern is not trivial, given that personal reputation matters in forming, developing, and maintaining social relationships, espe-cially when a personal reputation is negative. Thus, many individuals may balk at the prospect of becoming more persuasive because they worry that using tools of persuasion will elicit enmity from others. Indeed, we often receive the same comment about the underestimation effect—"If people feel more emboldened to ask, won't they just irritate others more with their frequent requests?" Our answer to this question is "no," and we base it on three streams of research that, taken together, suggest people are more likely to walk away with a positive impression of help-seekers than one might assume.

Harshness Bias

Research by Savitsky, Epley, and Gilovich (2001) suggests that people over-estimate how harshly others will judge them. In a series of studies involving social judgment, people anticipated being viewed more negatively for an awkward gaffe, a performance failure, or a personal shortcoming than they actually were. The authors explain this effect by proposing that people tend to be inordinately focused on their own embarrassing circumstances and therefore unable to consider the situational factors that might affect an observer's impressions (e.g., he or she is distracted, overwhelmed by other cues, or attending to a larger set of potential targets). As a result, the anxiety that people experience in violating social norms and anticipating rebuke may be exaggerated.

A similar dynamic may apply to the case of help-seeking. Requesting help can be an awkward experience. Even a request that seems relatively minor, in objective terms, can make the help-seeker feel self-conscious, embarrassed, and guilty, in part because he or she is imposing on the potential helper by asking "for something outside of the addressee's daily routine" (Goldschmidt, 1998, p. 131). One might expect the potential helper to react with displays of annoyance and frustration, but this is rarely the case. People are expected to respond graciously to help requests, even if they do represent a minor imposition (Goffman, 1955; Grice, 1975). Although help-seekers may expect harsh judgment, more often than not they will be pleasantly surprised by others' willingness to satisfy their request.

In our research, we have found that the anxiety help-seekers experience over how their request will come across is surprising to potential helpers who do not know what all the fuss is about (Bohns & Flynn, 2010). In one study, we asked two samples of potential helpers (teaching assistants and peer advisors) to estimate the number of students who would seek their help during a single semester. The peer advisors overestimated by over 60%, and the teaching assistants by 20%, the number of students who would ask them for help. This prediction error emerged even though the peer advisors had been students themselves the prior year, and the majority of teaching assistants had worked as teaching assistants before (often for the same class). Nevertheless, their past experience as help-seekers offered no clues in predicting others' future help-seeking behavior.

Bad Trumps Good

Although help requests tend to be satisfied more often than people expect (Flynn & Lake [Bohns], 2008), there remain times when requests for help are not satisfied, either because the potential helper was unwilling or unable to provide assistance. These episodes are likely to loom large in our minds. In fact, when asked to recall a recent time when they were refused assistance, people are able to recall it more quickly and with greater clarity than a recent time when they were granted assistance. This tendency is reminiscent of work showing that the costs associated with negative outcomes may be weighed more heavily in our minds than the gains associated with positive outcomes (see Baumeister, Bratslavsky, Finkenauer, & Vohs, 2001; Rozin & Royzman, 2001). As time passes, more extensive cognitive processing can even enhance the memory of negative information relative to positive information, which further biases overall impressions (Taylor, 1991).

Negative events tend to be more salient, play a more significant role in forming impressions, and have a larger impact on individual behavior (Amabile, Schatzel, Moneta, & Kramer, 2004; Peeters & Czapinski, 1990; Skowronski & Carlston, 1989). Given this bias toward negative experiences, people might be prone to misjudge the rate at which they have been rejected in the past when attempting to seek help. Because negative outcomes are more salient, episodes of noncompliance may be overrepresented in a help-seeker's mind (relative to episodes of compliance), leading help-seekers to believe that the odds of getting a "yes" in response to an appeal for help is worse than is actually the case. Such a bias may discourage people from asking for help, when in fact their fear of rejection is inflated.

Motivated Reasoning

Ben Franklin once wrote, "He that has once done you a kindness will be more ready to do you another than he whom you yourself have obliged" (Lemay, 1987). The meaning of Franklin's message is that when we perform a favor for another person, we tend to like that person more as a result. The effect is highly counterintuitive, but also highly robust. For example, in a classic experiment by Jecker and Landy (1969), students were asked to participate in a contest in which they had the opportunity to win some cash. In one condition, the researcher asked the contest winner to return the prize money because he had been using personal funds and was now running short. In another condition, this request was posed by an administrative assistant from the psychology department (who claimed that the department was running short on funds). And, of course, there was a third (control) condition in which no request was posed. As it turns out, participants reported liking the experimenter most following the treatment in the first condition—when he asked them to return the money. How can this be? According to the researchers, people are motivated to justify their actions; in this case, the participants convinced themselves that they performed a favor for the experimenter *because they liked him.*

Indeed, help-seeking can be an effective means of reducing interpersonal conflict, although we suspect that it depends on the type of conflict involved.

If the help-seeker was thought to be condescending in the past, asking for assistance may enable that individual to come across as less self-aggrandizing. In a series of studies, Hogan and Flynn (2010) found that people reacted more positively when they were asked for help, rather than being offered help, following a conflict based on perceived condescension. To be clear, this finding is not intuitive. In a separate study, when asked to estimate how effective offering and asking for help would be in resolving a condescension-based conflict, participants expected that offering help would be significantly more effective. So, once again, people may fail to appreciate the potential value of asking for help.

HELP-SEEKING AS A FORM OF INFLUENCE

Research shows many benefits of help-seeking. Not only does asking for help make it likely that we will get what we need (more likely than we think), but we also tend to be judged less harshly than we might imagine—we may even strengthen our relationships by soliciting help. Yet, this is an area in which research findings never seem to find purchase in the "real world." Although there is great value in help-seeking, few seem to appreciate its potential value. Take, for example, a typical employee performance appraisal. Almost every performance appraisal measures whether employees *offer* help to their co-workers. In contrast, performance appraisals rarely measure whether employees *ask* for help when needed. Yet, being willing and able to access the expertise of one's co-workers would seem to be a critical driver of collaboration in organizations.

Why is help-seeking so devalued? Perhaps help-seeking tends to be disregarded because it is often equated with weakness. Many people are all too familiar with the experience of sitting in a car for much longer than necessary because the driver will not stop to ask for directions—doing so may be an admission of incompetence. But, is help-seeking really a position of weakness? At first blush, it seems consistent with a common definition of power: the extent to which an individual can "modify others' states by providing or withholding resources" (Keltner, Gruenfeld, & Anderson, 2003, p. 265). According to this definition, a gas station attendant with first-hand knowledge of local roads and a stockpile of travel maps holds power over the driver—he or she has access to resources that will modify the state of the traveler from lost to found. Thus, the driver is in a position of weakness.

However, there is another, equally important definition of power: power as one individual's "capability of influencing" another (Cartwright, 1965, p. 4). In other words, power is the ability to access someone else's resources and, consequently, to change one's *own* state. Viewed in this light, help-seeking is not a sign of weakness; it is a powerful act. Upon taking a wrong turn, the lost traveler has immediate access to a means by which he or she can rectify the mistake. As our research has shown, he or she needs only to ask for help, and any target will find that he or she is hard-pressed to refuse. In this sense, an individual's power—the ability to access needed resources—often lies in a simple "please," or a willingness to ask.

Conceptualizing help-seeking as a source of influence (rather than a signal of incompetence) can enhance the perceived value of asking for help. Discounting the value of help-seeking not only leads to less asking—and therefore less helping all around—but may serve to stigmatize those who *do* ask. For example, many bullied students do not seek out help because they worry about facing "derision and contempt from others" (Cowie et al., 2002, p. 456). Similarly, in our closest relationships, asking for help can make us feel defeated. According to Niall Bolger and colleagues (Bolger, Zuckerman, & Kessler, 2000), the most effective form of support between couples is invisible support—that which the recipient never has to ask for and is provided covertly. Their research suggests that *even asking for help from one's spouse can make a person feel insecure.* If asking for help were viewed as a sign of strength rather than weakness, perhaps this stigma could be alleviated.

GOAL ALIGNMENT AND INFLUENCE

If we conceptualize help-seeking as a powerful weapon of influence, we must consider how such a weapon can be used wisely. Some people are uncomfortable with influence because they feel that the intent to manipulate others is immoral. According to this view, people should feel free to choose their own course of action rather than feel pressured to make a specific choice. Others counter that many influence attempts are made to persuade people to "do the right thing," or at least do something that would be in the interest of the groups to which they belong. They point to studies of blood donation (Miller & Ratner, 1998), charitable giving (Flynn & Lake [Bohns], 2008), and environmental conservation (Goldstein, Cialdini, & Griskevicius, 2008) as evidence of the social good that can be achieved through carefully designed influence attempts. We suspect that the benefits of using compliance tactics are maximized when the goals of the persuader and the target are in line. That is, the target may have some motivation to agree with a request, but he or she may need additional motivation to take action.

Influence as a "Nudge"

When we ask for help, we often assume that the benefit we obtain necessarily implies a loss for the other party. So, if we ask someone to spend their time helping us on a project and they agree, we assume they are sacrificing time they would have otherwise preferred to spend doing something else. However, this assumption is often incorrect. People are frequently asked or persuaded to do things they would actually *like* to do, but simply had no occasion, justification, or motivation to do. These targets simply need a little nudge to take action. It is likely that they will even feel happy about having been persuaded to act because they feel (perhaps in retrospect) that taking action was in their best interest and aligned with their own preferences.

At Stanford's Graduate School of Business, a high-status executive recently gave an address to the entire first-year MBA class. Impressed by the speech and curious to learn more, one of the students went online, downloaded the executive's e-mail address, and proceeded to send a message to her during the lecture. In his message, the student invited the guest speaker to share a small dinner with him and his classmates in their dorm room. Much to the surprise of the instructor, the student, and his dorm mates, the executive accepted the invitation and showed up for dinner the following week! When others were told of the story, they expressed shock that the executive would agree to attend the dinner, but the executive confided to the instructor that she showed up because she thought it would be fun to meet some bright, young people, particularly those who have enough chutzpah to invite her to dinner during a lecture. Contrary to what the skeptics may have presumed, she was not convinced to do something unpleasant; rather, she was offered an opportunity to participate in an event she considered enjoyable.

Positive Mood as a Side Effect

Even when the task is not especially enjoyable, people often reap emotional benefit from helping others. Sometimes referred to as a "warm glow," helping someone in need can boost our self-esteem ("I'm a caring, helpful person") and has a positive effect on personal mood (e.g., McCullough Emmons & Tsang, 2002). In fact, some research supports a mood regulation model of helping in which people use opportunities to help others either to maintain a positive mood (e.g., Clark & Isen, 1982) or to boost a negative one (Ciladini & Kenrick, 1976). In such situations, in which a help-seeker needs something and a potential helper could use a means of maintaining or boosting his or her mood, both individuals' goals are aligned.

Joint Gain

Finally, there are situations in which two people stand to create joint gain if both are willing and able to exert their influence and push for what they need or want. Imagine a struggling student who approaches a teaching assistant for help with a difficult concept. The TA's first attempt to explain the concept may be muddled and imperfect, leaving the student even more confused. Both individuals now face a choice in this situation. The student, out of embarrassment or to save face for the TA, can either falsely claim that he now understands the concept, or he can continue to ask for the clarification he needs, pushing the TA to explain it more clearly. The TA, on the other hand, can take the student's claim of understanding at face value, or ask the student to demonstrate his or her grasp of the concept. As uncomfortable as it may feel in the moment, both stand to gain from such persistence: The student will get the help he needs, the TA will improve her teaching skills, and both will walk away with a richer understanding of the concept.

In summary, a help-seeker's and a helper's goals are often compatible in many respects. Some potential helpers may be persuaded to do something they would enjoy doing, but could not bring themselves to do without provocation. Others may be persuaded to do something that allows them to feel good about themselves. Still more may be persuaded to do something that is aligned with their own goals. In such cases, "influence" operates more like a gentle "nudge" in the right direction, whereby people feel happy about having been persuaded to act because they recognize that taking action provides mutual benefit.

INFLUENCE WHEN GOALS ARE MISALIGNED

Although goal alignment between helpers and help-seekers can be beneficial, inevitably times occur when a help-seeker's goals conflict with a potential helper's. Politicians, managers, and even parents must often persuade others to take action that contradicts their own inclinations, such as supporting another party's candidate, coming into work on the weekend, or eating their vegetables. In these situations, influence tactics can still be effective in obtaining compliance, but the target may offer their compliance only because they feel "trapped." As one might expect, persuading people to comply with a request that runs counter to their goals can have a significant downside. The target may attribute his or her compliance to the influence of the persuader, interpreting the behavior as externally rather than internally motivated ("I don't really like vegetables, I just eat them because I'm told to do so.") Further, the target may resist the persuasion attempt or resent the persuader, thereby limiting opportunities for future interaction.

To demonstrate this problem, we investigated the tradeoffs of using commitment-inducing scripts (Flynn & Bohns, 2010). In a field study at New York City's Penn Station, targets were approached by an experimenter and asked to fill out a two-page questionnaire. In one condition, they were given a straightforward request, "Would you fill out a questionnaire?" In a second condition, they were asked, "Can you do me a favor?" before hearing the same request (to fill out a questionnaire). Fifty-seven percent of the targets in the former condition complied, whereas 84% of those in the second condition agreed to help. And, for those subjects in the second condition who offered an immediate affirmative response to the "Can you do me a favor" script (e.g., "Yeah sure, what is it?"), the compliance rate was near 100%. In short, targets acted in line with the commitment and consistency principle—they offered some precommitment to comply with the request before hearing the complete details and then found it difficult to go back on their promise.

In this study, use of the commitment-inducing script was effective in increasing compliance. However, we also asked targets, at the end of the questionnaire, to report how much they expected in return for their cooperation (i.e., how large a gift they should be given for their trouble). Targets reported higher expectations of reciprocation when they heard the commitment-inducing script than when they heard only the direct request for help (more than twice as much). In other words, whereas using the script made others more inclined to help immediately, it also made them inclined to request more in return because they felt they had been "trapped" by the experimenter. These results suggest that persuaders' success in using influence tactics can entail tradeoffs—they may get what they want in the short term but perhaps at a higher price in the long term.

Those individuals who are interested in leveraging the power of asking for help may wish to consider the potential risks they incur by doing so. In some cases, targets of help requests could resent an imposition, particularly if they feel they are being coerced into doing something against their will. They may say "yes," but their help may also come at a steep price. At the same time, help requesters may feel encouraged to know that people are more willing to provide help than requesters think. Indeed, many people may respond favorably to the subtle use of pressure to say "yes" to a request for help, so long as they view the helpful act as being consistent with their own preferences and goals. To put it succinctly, people are often willing to help others in need, but may need a small push to move them in the right direction.

NO REGRETS

Despite the risks involved in seeking help, research suggests that, in the long run, we are more likely to regret *not* asking for help than having a request rejected. Consider the findings from a study by Gilovich and Medvec (1994), who asked a random sample of Upstate New Yorkers, "When you look back on your experiences in life and think of those things that you regret, which would you say you regret more, those things that you did but wish you hadn't, or those things that you didn't do but wish you had?" Seventy-five percent of those polled said they experienced greater regret for the things they *didn't* do. Similarly, when another sample of participants were asked what they would do differently if they could live their lives over again, participants of all ages (20 to over 64 years old) were more likely to say they would rectify some regrettable inaction from their past rather than a regrettable action (Kinnier & Metha, 1989). This effect grows even stronger with the passing of time. People asked to report their biggest regrets from the past week more often report things they *did*, but those asked to report their biggest regrets over the course of their lives, report things they *didn't* do (Gilovich & Medvec, 1994).

There may be several explanations for this phenomenon. For one, it is easier to fix regrettable things that one has done, whereas missed opportunities often are fleeting and difficult to recapture (Gilovich & Medvec, 1995). For example, had the student who invited the high-status executive to dinner been met with reproach for making an inappropriate request, he could have apologized and effectively rectified his mistake. But, had he hesitated to ask in the first place, the executive would have left, and with her the opportunity to connect. An alternative explanation for this effect is based on our emotional responses to regrettable actions versus inactions. When we do something we regret, we often experience an immediate "hot" emotional reaction (e.g., embarrassment or anger) that fades over time. However, when an opportunity presents itself and we fail to act, we are likely to experience despair and "wistfulness," emotions that are equally troubling and prone to linger (Gilovich, Medvec, & Kahneman, 1998). In this sense, any embarrassment brought about by the student's bold action would fade more quickly than the wistful despair he might experience by letting the opportunity slip away.

All of this suggests that, although the sting of rejection may hurt, it will also be fleeting. Yet, the anxiety of not knowing what the answer to our request for help *would have been* can stick around to haunt us. In the long run, we are probably better off asking for help than playing it safe. And, in many cases, those we seek help from stand to benefit as well. Just as the book *Influence* has helped many people avoid being talked into things they would rather *not* do, our aim here is to talk people into asking for the things they *do* want. We believe that this can increase the incidence of helping behavior, allowing many people to get the assistance they so desperately need.

CONCLUSION

Cialdini's book, *Influence*, reveals the many ways in which people can be persuaded to agree to almost any request. But perhaps the most significant revelation is the extent to which we are unaware of these influence tactics— not just unaware of their potency, but also their potential. We have the ability to acquire valued resources, obtain critical assistance, or build strong support if we can recognize why people decide to say "yes." As for our own research, we suggest that people can be persuaded to say "yes" if you just give them a chance. In short, what Cialdini's work has taught us, along with a large percentage of the general public, is that you don't need a fancy title or massive wealth to have power over others—you just need to know a little bit about the psychology of compliance. This key insight— a peek at the power that is available to all of us—is why Cialdini's *Influence* endures.

CHAPTER 3

The Path of Least Resistance

BRAD J. SAGARIN AND KEVIN D. MITNICK

Social engineering uses influence and persuasion to deceive people by convincing them that the social engineer is someone he is not, or by manipulation. As a result, the social engineer is able to take advantage of people to obtain information with or without the use of technology.
—Mitnick & Simon, 2002, p. iv

"You can't just make a person up."
"Sure you can, if you know how the system works, and where the cracks are."
—The Shawshank Redemption, 1994

One of the hallmarks of Cialdini's work is his insight that, in the market-place, practitioners live or die by their skill at harnessing the princi-ples of influence. The skilled prosper. The unskilled go out of business.

This chapter explores Cialdini's (2009) principles of influence in a par-ticularly high-stakes domain: The attempt to gain illicit (and, in some cases, illegal) access to privileged information, secured locations, and protected computer systems. Computer hackers attempt to gain such access by exploit-ing technological vulnerabilities in software and hardware. Hackers also use a technique known as *social engineering* to exploit psychological vulnerabili-ties. Social engineering utilizes Cialdini's six principles of influence—the power of reciprocal obligations, small commitments, time pressure, and so on. But, here, the principles are used not to entice the target into buying an unneeded option on a car but to trick the target into disclosing confidential information such as a password or performing an action that leads to a system compromise.

We begin by describing a successful social engineering attack, presented from the perspective of the attacker, carried out against the communications company Motorola (in keeping with the confidentiality norms of psychological research, names of individuals within the company have been changed; for more details about this attack and its aftermath, see *Ghost in the Wires*, Mitnick & Simon, 2011). We then analyze the points of vulnerability exploited by the attack and consider methods by which individuals and organizations can build resistance against such attacks.

THE ATTACK

In 1992, Motorola released its new-generation cell phone. Marketing to an audience raised on Captain Kirk and Mr. Spock, Motorola designed the MicroTac Ultra Lite to be slim, lightweight, and, most importantly, to flip open with a satisfying click just like the Star Trek communicator.

The phone's brain consisted of proprietary software embedded onto a chip, called firmware. This software contained the secrets of Motorola's new technology—secrets of great interest to some hackers. Gaining access to these secrets would require reverse engineering the firmware—a process that could take months or even years—or obtaining access to the original programming instructions or "source code."

My Goal Was the Source Code

In a sense, the motivation for the attack was pure scarcity—the challenge of acquiring the proprietary secrets to the inner workings of the MicroTac Ultra Lite. Adding to the challenge, Motorola's development took place in Schaumburg, Illinois, far enough from my current residence in Denver, Colorado, that I would have to talk the code out of Motorola using just the telephone and the Internet.

I began with a call to directory assistance, which provided Motorola's main number. I called the number and explained to the receptionist that I was looking for the project manager for the MicroTac Ultra Lite. The kind receptionist told me that all cellular phone development is handled out of their Schaumberg facility. She gave me the main number in Schaumburg. I called Schaumburg and asked for the project manager for the MicroTac Ultra Lite. Eight transfers later, I reached the Vice President for the Pan American Cellular Subscriber Group. The VP sent me to Sam, the project manager for the Ultra Lite. The call to Sam went straight to voicemail. Sam's outgoing message explained that she would be out of the office for the next two weeks on vacation and that callers who needed any help should call her assistant, Alice.

"Alice? This is Rick in Arlington Heights." Arlington Heights housed another Motorola research and development facility. "Did Sam leave yet on vacation? Geez! She told me she would send me the source code for the MicroTac Ultra Lite before she left on vacation."

"Which version do you need?" she asked.

A reasonable question, but a tough one to answer. Each company had its own scheme for identifying versions. "How about the latest and greatest?"

After several minutes of typing on her keyboard, she said, "Rick, I found the latest source code, but there're numerous directories with hundreds of files."

"Do you know how to use tar and gzip?" *Tar* was an archival program that took a set of files and combined them into a single large file. *Gzip* was another program that could reduce the size of a large file using a compression algorithm.

"What's that?" she asked.

"It's like winzip in Windows. Would you like to learn?"

"I always like learning new things."

Alice accepted my offer, and I taught her how to use the programs. She proved an adept student, and at the end of that lesson, she assembled the particular version of source code into a 3-megabyte file.

"Do you know what FTP is?" I asked.

"File transfer program?"

"Precisely."

I remembered the IP address for a system that I hacked previously, which I could use as the destination for a file transfer. The IP address, the string of four numbers separated by periods that denoted the address of a computer on the Internet, would raise fewer suspicions than an unknown hostname outside Motorola's domain.

"Can you open an FTP connection to this address?" And I gave her the IP address.

When she tried to open a connection, it kept timing out. After three attempts, she said, "Rick, I'm going to have to talk to my security manager about what you are asking me to do. I'll be right back."

That could be a problem. The security manager might realize that an attack was in progress. "Wait! Wait!" I called, trying to stop her, but she was already gone.

After a while on hold, Alice returned to the phone. "The IP address you gave me is outside of the Motorola campus."

"Uh huh."

"And my manager told me that to send any files outside of Motorola's campus requires the use of a special proxy server."

"Uh huh."

"So, my security manager gave me his personal username and password to our special proxy server so I can send you the file." And with that, she sent the file.

Capitalizing on the rapport I had established with Alice, I later asked her to locate and send some other versions of the source code for the same phone. While archiving one version using tar and gzip, I had Alice include the /etc directory, which, on the Apollo system Motorola used, included a password file with names, phone extensions, and encrypted passwords, and a host file with hostnames and IP addresses of other Motorola computer systems. I thanked Alice and hung up.

With the source code in hand, I decided to see if the extra files I'd acquired would give me access to Motorola's network. I tried the dialup number into the Schaumburg facility I had obtained earlier and found that Motorola was using SecureID, a two-form factor authentication system in which access required a numerical code provided on a physical device called a token given to each user, as well as a PIN known only to the user. The numerical code changed every 60 seconds, so I would need a SecureID token or a person with a token willing to give me the current code over the phone.

Over the next few days, I checked the weather in Schaumburg, waiting for a snowstorm that would provide a plausible reason why a Motorola employee might not be able to drive to work. While waiting for the snowstorm, I tracked down the telephone number of the Schaumburg facility's computer room and extracted the name and working group of an employee from the password file I had tricked Alice into sending me. When the snowstorm hit, I called the computer room.

"Hey, this is Ed Bell in the PACSG group. I need you to do me a big favor. I can't drive in, but I'm working on a critical project, and I need to log in to my workstation. I need my SecureID token that's in my desk—it's in the upper left drawer. Could you please go to my office, get my token out of my desk, and give me the code so I can log in?"

This approach was a risk. I knew Ed Bell worked in the facility, but I had no idea where Ed's office was, let alone whether Ed's SecureID card would be in the upper left desk drawer. I was banking on the fact that the computer operator, Ron, would find it extremely uncomfortable (and inconvenient) to rummage through someone else's desk looking for a SecureID card. The approach also helped build credibility because the request implied that Ed was an authorized employee who had been issued a SecureID token. The problem was just that he didn't have it with him.

Ron explained that he was busy and not allowed to leave operations.

"This is critical. We're up against an announced market date. I've got to get this done! Can you call your supervisor for permission?"

"I can't leave the center."

"Is there anyone else there?"

"No."

With that, I floated the real request. "Do you have a SecureID card in operations?"

"Yes, we have a group one we share from time to time."

"Because you can't go to my desk, could you at least let me use yours?"

"Yes, I think I can, but I'll have to call my supervisor."

Ron called his supervisor on another phone. From the audible half of the conversation, it was clear that the supervisor recognized Ed's name. Ron even vouched for him: "Yeah, I know Ed."

That was convenient. With Ron vouching for me, I knew my identity would not be questioned.

Ron hung up with his supervisor. "My boss wants to talk to you."

So, I called up the supervisor and went through the full story, culminating in the same request: "Can't you authorize Ron to get my SecureID from my desk?" As expected, the supervisor said that Ron was the only person manning the computer room and could not leave. "If you can't do that could you at least let me use the one in operations over the weekend?"

The supervisor relented. "Yeah, that's OK. Here's the PIN code. I'll authorize Ron to give you the token code anytime you need it."

I dialed into the terminal server but could only get to a handful of systems that weren't in the cellular group. I called Ron back. "I have a huge problem. I can't connect to any of my systems in the cellular group. Can you set me up with a temporary account on one of the systems in operations that's accessible via the dialup terminal server?"

"No, but you can use mine temporarily," and Ron changed his password and provided his username and password.

I logged into Ron's account but couldn't connect to any of the systems in the cellular group. I started scanning IP address ranges for systems close to the cellular group, one of which was a NeXT workstation that allowed me to log in as "guest" with no password. I looked at the /etc/password file and found three users who worked in the group. I downloaded the password file and hit it with a dictionary attack. Password files store their passwords in encrypted form. A dictionary attack encrypts each word in the dictionary (supplemented by lists of common names) and checks them against the encrypted passwords. The password for one user, John Cooper, matched. It was "mary."

I tried logging onto the cellular group server using John's username and "mary" as the password. It didn't work. John must be using a different password. But perhaps the old password could convince John to reveal his new one.

I called directory assistance and found a number for John Cooper in a nearby city. I called John at home.

"Hey, is this John Cooper? This is Phillip in ops. We just had a catastrophe. We lost a disk array. We're going through the recovery process, but we're not sure we can recover everything. Just wanted to let you know. I should have your files restored by Thursday."

"What! That's unacceptable!"

"Why?"

"I need my files sooner than that!"

"You're 50th in the queue."

"I need to talk to your boss."

"Listen, I can do you a favor, but it needs to stay between you and I. We're restoring files on a new server. To streamline yours, I need to set up your account. Your username is johnc, and your workstation is lc18, right?" I typed on a keyboard for sound effects. "Oh, is your phone extension still 37765?" Pause. "What password do you want me to use?" Then, after a slight pause, "Oh wait, what is your current password?"

"Who are you again?"

"Phillip in Operations. Of course. You need to verify who I am. Do you have a SecureID token?"

"Yes, why?"

"Let me pull your application." I slammed a couple of filing cabinets and ruffled some paper. "Hmm, the person didn't alphabetize it correctly. Give me a moment." After a pause, "Let me see. Ok, here's yours. You chose the password of: 'mary.'"

After another pause, he hesitantly said, "Yeah. Ok, my password is bebop1."

And I was in.

RESISTING THE ATTACK

As is likely clear to aficionados of the work of Robert Cialdini, Cialdini's principles of influence permeate this social engineering attack. Alice's willingness to archive and send the source code no doubt stemmed, in part, from the reciprocal obligation she felt toward the person who had spent time teaching her how to use archival and compression programs. Later, Ron and his supervisor fell prey to the door-in-the-face technique (Cialdini et al., 1975). The social engineer began by asking Ron to leave the computer center, find another employee's desk, and search through that desk for the employee's SecureID token. When Ron refused, the social engineer retreated to a smaller request: that Ron share the computer center's SecureID token. In contrast to the initial request, which must have seemed both inconvenient and unpalatable, the smaller request was relatively innocuous. Of course, Ron's willingness to comply undermined the very purpose of having the SecureID, a two-form factor authentication system (and Ron might have remembered that, had that been the only request). But the door-in-the-face created a context in which security was not a salient concern.

Cialdini's second principle, commitment and consistency, appeared most prominently as a foot-in-the-door (Freedman & Fraser, 1966), motivating Alice's willingness to archive additional versions of the source code and Ron's willingness to temporarily set a password to one of the systems in operations. In both cases, the targets' prior behavior paved the way for subsequent compliance.

The social engineer's use of Motorola jargon (e.g., PACSG) provided two benefits: It defined him as a member of the ingroup, with all the privileges such membership entails, and it established his credibility, reducing the skepticism his requests might otherwise have elicited. In this case, ingroup membership likely activated Cialdini's principle of liking. Ed Bell was a fellow employee, deserving of the special consideration and affection owed to teammates.

The social engineer leveraged Cialdini's principle of authority in a number of ways. In his initial contact with Alice, he invoked the name and authority of her boss, Sam. Later, he induced Ron's supervisor to authorize the use of the center's SecureID token device. This convinced Ron to provide the SecureID token code, of course, but it may also have indirectly convinced him to temporarily set a new password that Ed could use. Last, the credibility the social engineer established by knowing John Cooper's username, phone extension, and initial password increased John's willingness to disclose his current password.

Cialdini's principle of scarcity manifested most directly in John's reaction to hearing that he was 50th in the queue to get his files restored. The reactance this information likely created (Brehm, 1966) made John quite receptive to the offer to restore his files immediately, despite the necessity to reveal his password. Scarcity also manifested vicariously in Ed's panicked request to Ron, although here it was not Ron's deadline, but Motorola's.

In *Influence: Science and Practice,* Cialdini (2009) offers recommendations for defending against the six principles. These defenses typically rely on detecting when the principles are being employed illegitimately—when they are artificially imported into a situation in which they do not naturally occur (Cialdini, 1996).

With respect to reciprocity, Cialdini (2009) recommends that we accept favors in good faith, but if a favor turns out to be a trick, we should reframe the favor as a sales device and feel no obligation to reciprocate. For commitment and consistency, Cialdini recommends that we attend to the feeling "in the pit of our stomachs when we realize we are trapped into complying with a request we know we don't want to perform" (p. 89). For liking, Cialdini recommends not that we try to fend off the myriad of factors that increase liking, but that we note when we find ourselves feeling undue liking for an influence practitioner. Then, we purposefully separate our feelings for the practitioner from our feelings for the request. For authority, Cialdini recommends that we retain an awareness of the power of authority "coupled with a recognition of how easily authority symbols can be faked" (p. 196). Cialdini's subsequent recommendations focus on situations in which the authority is acting as an expert. In particular, when faced with such an authority, Cialdini recommends that we ask two questions: "Is this authority truly an expert?" (p. 191), and "How truthful can we expect the expert to be?" (p. 192). Finally, for scarcity, Cialdini recommends that we use the heightened arousal that accompanies a scarcity-based appeal as a cue to proceed with caution. Then, we ask ourselves whether we truly want the item for the benefits of possessing something rare or if we simply want it for its utility value, in which case, its limited availability should not factor in.

Will Cialdini's (2009) defenses work against a social engineering attack? Perhaps, in part. In many cases, however, the principles appear legitimate within the context of the social engineer's deception. Alice received some valuable computer training—a favor that carried a legitimate reciprocal obligation. Alice's boss wielded true authority over her (although Alice would have done well to remember that invoking her boss's name does not guarantee that her boss actually authorized the request).

Ron's positive feelings toward fellow Motorola employee Ed Bell probably did not exceed the level of liking appropriate for a coworker. And when Ed retreated from his first request that Ron find Ed's SecureID device, Ron felt a legitimate reciprocal obligation to comply with Ed's second request to use the computer center's SecureID token (although here, Ron and his supervisor might have paid attention to the feeling in the pit of their stomachs that disclosing the center's SecureID token and PIN was not a request they wanted to fulfill).

Last, the panic John felt when he learned that he was 50th in the queue to have his files restored stemmed from true scarcity, just as the gratitude he felt when the social engineer offered to restore his files immediately stemmed from true reciprocity (although as with the computer operator, John's hesitation suggests that he felt uncomfortable about disclosing his password—discomfort that could have cued John to resist).

Thus, although we believe organizations and individuals would profit from learning about Cialdini's principles and his recommendations for their defense, these defenses may prove less effective against a social engineering attack because the skilled social engineer does not provide the cues Cialdini recommends people attend to. Indeed, within the context of the deception weaved by the social engineer, the influence principles are operating quite legitimately.

Nevertheless, we believe effective resistance can be built, based on three factors common to social engineering attacks: (a) a sense of invulnerability, (b) a failure to distinguish innocuous and sensitive information and actions, and (c) a conflict between social norms (particularly politeness norms) and security roles.

As demonstrated by Sagarin, Cialdini, Rice, and Serna (2002), attempts to instill resistance to persuasion will fail if targets are allowed to retain their illusions of invulnerability. Thus, instilling effective resistance requires a demonstration of vulnerability. For an organization hoping to strengthen its defenses against a social engineering attack, a demonstration of vulnerability may be a critical first step. This demonstration can be accomplished at multiple levels.

At the organizational level, companies sometimes engage in penetration (PEN) testing in which they invite a security professional to try to break into the company. To the dismay of these companies, this PEN testing nearly always succeeds. Indeed, past PEN testing has revealed vulnerability at all levels of a company, from the custodial staff (in one PEN testing intrusion, a custodian allowed the social engineer to enter a locked building after hours on the basis of a business suit, a briefcase, and a company business card acquired from the reception area earlier that day) to upper management (one VP lowered his organization's virtual drawbridge by accepting a free printer he had won in a "raffle" concocted by the social engineer and inserting the doctored CD that came with the printer into his computer).

To demonstrate vulnerability at the individual level, some corporate training programs begin with a surreptitious social engineering attack aimed at trainees. Then, the first session of the program opens with the revelation of the attack and the number of people who fell victim. Other training programs include a real-time social engineering attack conducted against a consenting company or a volunteer from the audience (see Littman, 2007, for a description of this type of demonstration using a malware-infected USB flash drive). The volunteer gets a direct demonstration of vulnerability, of course. But more importantly, if the attack is sufficiently compelling, the other trainees are likely to empathize with the volunteer and realize that they would have performed no better. Indeed, anecdotal evidence suggests that readers of texts on social engineering (e.g., *Art of Deception*, Mitnick & Simon, 2002) often adopt the perspective of the target of the social engineering attack, vicariously experiencing the vulnerability of the target.

The second factor common to social engineering attacks is the target's failure to distinguish innocuous information from sensitive information. A social engineer can exploit this informational ambiguity by gathering small bits of information that merit little protection individually, but that provide a façade of credibility when combined. In the Motorola attack, the social engineer swayed Alice by naming her manager and knowing about her manager's vacation plans—information suggestive of legitimacy but, in actuality, publicly available on her manager's voicemail. A company could, of course, instruct its employees to protect all information, to give nothing away without official authorization. But such a policy would be exhausting to maintain and detrimental to work flow. In addition, the task of protecting obviously innocuous information would likely sap the vigilance necessary to protect truly sensitive information. Instead, we recommend that companies analyze the sensitivity of different types of information with a goal of developing a simple classification system that employees will understand, accept, and remember. With such a system in place, employees will know the types of information they must protect (e.g., passwords) and the types of information they can freely share. Furthermore, employees will know that the possession of this latter type of information carries no particular significance and conveys no particular credibility.

The final step in building resistance against social engineering is to provide targets with a method of resolving the conflict between social norms and security roles. Skilled social engineers purposefully create situations that place these factors in conflict. In one social engineering attack, for example, a social engineer gained access to a restricted area by manufacturing a company ID, and then waiting by the access door until a target had swiped his card. Then, before the target had fully walked through the door, he glanced back at the person behind him, saw the company ID card, and held the door open. Although the organization's security protocol required that each person swipe their own access card, politeness norms prohibited the target from slamming the door in the social engineer's face.

Organizations could increase the effectiveness of their security protocols by training their employees to respond to requests that must be denied even when such denials feel impolite. The influence tactic of *altercasting*

(Pratkanis, 2000) could prove useful in such situations by allowing the employee to reframe the denial as a prosocial action that the requestor must support. Such a technique might have enabled Ron to fend off the door-in-the-face: "Surely, as a fellow Motorola employee, you agree that the security of our computer systems is paramount? Great. Then you will understand why we cannot give out our SecureID token code or PIN over the phone."

Although individuals protecting proprietary corporate information or government secrets may be particularly valuable targets for social engineers, potential targets include nearly everyone who uses the Internet. Indeed, a social engineer attempting to manipulate a regular Internet user into executing a malicious piece of software has a variety of options at his or her disposal. For example, the social engineer can configure a USB flash drive to run the malicious software automatically as soon as the drive is plugged into a computer. Then, the social engineer can surreptitiously drop the drive in a location the target is likely to visit. Whether motivated by curiosity, greed, or a prosocial desire to return the drive to its owner, as soon as the target plugs the drive into a USB port, the software is executed and the computer is compromised. Alternatively, the social engineer could emboss the drive with the insignia of an organization with which the target has an affiliation (e.g., the target's alma mater) and then mail the drive to the target. Many people who would be hesitant to plug an unknown USB drive into their computer might readily do so if the drive ostensibly came from a trusted organization.

A somewhat more sophisticated social engineering attack exploits our tendency to trust our friends heuristically, even when the definition of "friends" expands to include people we hardly know. A social engineer targeting a particular person would begin by determining which social networking sites the target uses (e.g., Facebook, Twitter, LinkedIn). Then, the social engineer would attempt to build connections to people the target is already connected with (e.g., on Facebook, the social engineer would attempt to become friends with the target's existing Facebook friends). Once a couple of connections are established, the social engineer would attempt to connect directly to the target (e.g., the social engineer would send a friend request to the target). On many social networking sites, the connection request would include a list of people the target and the social engineer have in common (e.g., the target would see that they have three mutual friends). Often, this will be enough to convince the target to accept the connection request. Then, once the connection is established, the social engineer can post a link to a malicious website on the target's social network page (e.g., on the target's Facebook wall). Because the post comes from a friend, the target might well click on the link without considering the source or the destination.

Fortunately, we believe the three factors critical to building organizational resistance against social engineering can help build resistance in individuals as well. First, individuals must perceive their personal vulnerability to social engineering attacks. We hope the widening discussion of social engineering within the news media will help broaden awareness of this vulnerability.

Second, individuals must understand which actions put them at risk. Some risky actions are obvious. Few people today would e-mail their passwords in response to a poorly written request ostensibly sent from their Internet service provider. Similarly, few people would double click on a EXE file received from an unknown sender. However, other actions may seem innocuous but carry hidden risk. Simply opening a PDF file containing malicious code can compromise a computer running a vulnerable version of Adobe Acrobat Reader (upgrading to the latest version offers some protection against this attack). Similarly, visiting a website and accepting the site's request to install a signed, but forged Java applet can compromise a computer if the applet performs malicious actions—and, unfortunately, a knowledgeable hacker can, within a matter of minutes, clone a web site and place the cloned web site along with the booby-trapped, and forged (e.g., deceptively labeled as being signed by Microsoft) Java applet under a plausible-sounding domain (e.g., "www.harvard-alums.com"). Such a ruse can easily snare targets not paying careful attention. In general, individuals would be wise to be extra cautious when lured to a website or sent an unexpected file. If an individual initiates an action (e.g., requests a file, types in a known web address), it's more likely (although not guaranteed) to be safe.

Third, individuals must develop methods of fending off inappropriate requests. In some cases, this might consist simply of validating seemingly antisocial (but appropriate) action, such as refusing Facebook friend requests from people not known personally. In other cases, it might consist of confirming through a telephone call or personal conversation that a colleague or friend had actually sent a suspicious e-mail, such as a recommendation to visit an odd-sounding website.

Given our increasing reliance on computer systems and the organizations that run them, social engineering represents a substantial and growing danger to our professional and personal lives. We believe, however, that knowledge of Cialdini's (2009) principles of influence, combined with an awareness of the unique factors that characterize a social engineering attack, can help us avoid this path of least resistance.

CHAPTER 4

Fluency and Social Influence

Lessons from Judgment and Decision-Making

PETIA PETROVA, NORBERT SCHWARZ,
AND HYUNJIN SONG

Officials at the National Forest Service were understandably chagrined at the loss of so many irreplaceable artifacts from the Petrified Forest when Cialdini offered them a bit of his typically smart social psychological advice. They had considered using public service messages trying to discourage theft by depicting it as regrettably frequent (e.g., "Your heritage is being vandalized every day by theft losses of petrified wood of 14 tons a year, mostly a small piece at a time"). But Cialdini recognized that by describing the undesirable behavior as common, such messages can actually increase its frequency, rather than reduce it (Cialdini et al., 2006; Cialdini, Reno, & Kallgren, 1990; Goldstin & Mortensen, 2011, Chapter 7, this volume).

To decrease the frequency of undesirable actions, other public service messages ask recipients to imagine potential negative outcomes. Yet, Cialdini's research reveals that because the negative outcomes are often abstract, such messages can make these outcomes seem less likely to occur, in contrast to what the message intended (Cialdini, 2001). For example, Sherman, Cialdini, Schwartzman, and Reynolds (1985) informed students of an illness (Hyposcenia-B) that was becoming increasingly prevalent on campus. When the disease was described with concrete symptoms (low energy level, muscle aches, and frequent severe headaches), students could easily imagine having the disease and saw themselves as highly vulnerable. However, when the symptoms were far less concrete (a vague sense of disorientation, a malfunctioning nervous system, and an inflamed liver), the difficulty of imagining having the disease reduced its perceived likelihood. These findings uncovered an important insight: "It now appears that not only is the content of thoughts generated prior to a judgment or performance important, but the ease or difficulty of generating those thoughts and images also may be a critical determinant of later judgments and behavior" (Sherman et al., 1985).

Over the last couple of decades, numerous studies have indeed shown that the experience of ease or difficulty in generating thoughts (Schwarz et. al., 1991), generating images (Petrova & Cialdini, 2005), processing information (Reber, Schwarz, & Winkielman, 2004), or making a decision (Novemsky, Dhar, Schwarz, & Simonson, 2007; Thompson, Hamilton, & Petrova, 2009) can have a profound influence on judgments and behavior. Here, we examine the implications of these findings for the science and practice of influence and show how failure to take the recipient's fluency experience into account can cause influence attempts to backfire.

FLUENCY AND SOCIAL CONSENSUS: IT SOUNDS FAMILIAR, IT MUST BE POPULAR

One of the most basic forces that influence our behavior are the actions and opinions of others (Cialdini, 2005). Unfortunately, we are poor at tracking how often we've heard or seen something. Instead, we rely on whether it seems familiar—if it does, we've probably heard or seen it before. For example, Weaver, Garcia, Schwarz, and Miller (2007) presented participants with multiple repetitions of the same opinion statement. For some participants, each repetition came from a different communicator, whereas for others, all repetitions came from the same communicator. When later asked to estimate how widely the conveyed opinion is shared, participants estimated higher social consensus the more often they had read the identical statement—even when each repetition came from the same single source. As a result, a single repetitive voice sounded like a chorus.

These findings uncover a valuable lesson for how people construct estimates of group norms. Although considerable research has demonstrated the influence of social norms (for a review see Goldstein & Mortensen, 2011, Chapter 7, this volume), less is known about how people come to identify norms in the first place. Incorporating a fluency perspective reveals a powerful insight: To infer a norm, people draw on the experience of familiarity, but are insensitive to where this fluency experience comes from. Hence, their perceptions may often be faulty and driven by fluency variables that are unrelated to the actual frequency of the relevant opinion or behavior.

Empirical research further demonstrates that variables that facilitate fluent processing (repetition, contrasting background, rhyme) create the impression that a statement is true (McGlone & Tofighbakhsh, 2000; Reber & Schwarz, 1999; Schwarz, Sanna, Skurnik, & Yoon, 2007). This fluency–familiarity–truth link suggests that frequent repetition and design qualities can increase the influence of a message beyond its effect on attention and retention. At the same time, the fluency–familiarity–truth phenomenon presents a problem when we attempt to counter misleading information (e.g., false rumors, myths, misleading ad claims).

Various types of messages try to correct for misleading information by first repeating the false information and then refuting it with counter arguments (e.g., Petrova, Cialdini, Goldstein, & Griskevicius, 2010). Although people may rely on the corrective information when this information is highly accessible, days and weeks later, the corrective facts may not be prominent in the audience's mind. Once memory for substantive details fades and people encounter the misleading statements again, they may increasingly be influenced by the familiarity of the misleading information. This experience of fluency can increase the perceived truth of the misleading statements, rendering the attempt to correct them ineffective (Schwarz et al., 2007).

Given this possibility, organizations may find it safer to refrain from reiterating false information and instead try to make the true information as fluent and familiar as possible. When corrective information is offered, it is important to ensure that the corrective information easily comes to mind when the audience encounters the false information again. An example of how this can be accomplished comes from a set of experiments that tested the effectiveness of a counter message against a misleading ad. To create mnemonic links between the ad and the counter arguments in the message, some of the visual elements that appeared in the ad were incorporated in the counter message as well. Only when the counter arguments were linked to the ad through such retrieval cues did they successfully undermine its impact days and weeks later (Cialdini et al., 2010; Petrova & Cialdini, 2011; Petrova, Cialdini, Barrett, Goldstein, & Maner, 2006).

FLUENCY AND RISK: IT'S HARD TO PRONOUNCE, IT MUST BE DANGEROUS

It is not surprising that familiar options feel safer than unfamiliar ones. In grocery aisles, we often prefer the same familiar vegetables over less familiar exotic ones because we do not want to run the risk of picking one with a strange taste or unknown allergens. Similarly, people perceive technologies, investments, and leisure activities as less risky the more familiar they are with them. But, does this observation really reflect the influence of mere familiarity, or does extended exposure to a potential threat desensitize people to the risks involved? To address this issue, Song and Schwarz (2009) took advantage of the well–established fluency-familiarity link. Given that fluently processed stimuli seem more familiar, they should also be perceived as less threatening and risky.

Empirically, this is the case (Song & Schwarz, 2009; Topolinski & Strack, 2010). In one study (Song & Schwarz, 2009), participants perceived ostensible food additives with hard-to-pronounce names (e.g., Hnegripitrom) as more harmful than food additives with easy-to-pronounce names (e.g., Magnalroxate). In addition, the food additives with difficult names were perceived as more novel than those with easy names, and perceived novelty mediated the influence of ease of pronunciation on perceived risk. Given that none of the participants could know anything about these ostensible food additives (after all, the names were made up), this finding provided first evidence that perceived familiarity, by itself, influences perceptions of risk.

The effects of disfluency are not limited to the perception of negative risks, as in the case of food additives, but can also be observed in the perception of risks that people consider desirable. For instance, people may want to take risky amusement park rides to enjoy the feeling of excitement and adventure. Would their choice be influenced by the ease or difficulty with which the names of the amusement park rides can be pronounced? The answer is a clear "yes" (Song & Schwarz, 2009). Participants perceived rides with difficult-to-pronounce names (e.g., Tsiischili) as more exciting and adventurous than rides with easy-to-pronounce names (e.g., Chunta). Other participants, however, were asked how likely the rides would make them feel sick—and once again, the rides with difficult-to-pronounce names won. Throughout, the ease with which the names of stimuli could be pronounced influenced their perceived familiarity. This perceived familiarity, in turn, influenced how risky the stimuli seemed, no matter if the risk was desirable or undesirable.

Similar observations have been made in a real-world domain with high stakes: people's investments in the stock market. Analysis of the performance of initial public offerings on the New York Stock Exchange revealed that, in the initial weeks after a company goes public, stocks with easy-to-pronounce ticker symbols (e.g., KAR) outperformed stocks with difficult-to-pronounce ticker symbols (e.g., RDO). Investing $1,000 in a basket of stocks with fluent ticker symbols would have yielded an excess profit of

$85.35 over a basket with disfluent ticker symbols on the first day of trading. This advantage dropped to $20.25 by the end of the first year of trading, as more diagnostic information about the companies became available. Presumably, investment opportunities with easy-to-pronounce ticker symbols seemed less risky, giving them a short-term advantage in initial public offerings (Alter & Oppenheimer, 2006).

The link between fluency, familiarity, and risk perception has many practical implications. In certain domains, risk is valued. For instance, in river rafting, bungee jumping, parachuting, or hang gliding, the value of the experience comes from its unpredictable nature (Arnould & Price, 1993). In such cases, disfluency experiences may highlight the promise of adventure and excitement. In other domains, however, such as insurance and food, risk is undesirable. Hence, using novel and interesting but difficult to pronounce names can have a backfire effect. Similarly, policy makers should pay attention to fluency variables to alert consumers to potential hazards and to prevent the erroneous impression that a hazardous product is safe simply because its name is easy to pronounce.

FLUENCY AND FUTURE EXPECTATIONS: IF IT'S HARD TO IMAGINE, IT WON'T HAPPEN

We often think about the future, trying to predict whether a particular outcome will occur. Yet, despite our preoccupation with what comes next, we tend to grossly mispredict the future. Many factors contribute to these mispredictions (Schwarz & Xu, 2011; Ubel, Loewenstein, Schwarz, & Smith, 2005), and our experience of fluency is one of them (Petrova & Cialdini, 2008). For example, we feel less vulnerable to a disease when we find it difficult to recall relevant risk factors or to imagine the disease's symptoms (Rothman & Schwarz, 1998; Sherman et al., 1985). Similarly, finding it difficult to imagine that we may fail to achieve our goals increases our expectations for success (Mandel, Petrova, & Cialdini, 2006).

The experience of fluency in creating mental images also affects how we estimate the likelihood of undertaking specific actions, such as purchasing a product (Petrova & Cialdini, 2005) or helping a victim (Hung & Wyer, 2009). The more difficult it is to imagine the behavior, the less likely we think we are to engage in it. This uncovers an important prospect. Various communicators try to influence individuals' expectations and actions by asking them to imagine a particular outcome. This strategy may be entirely wrongheaded when it is difficult for the audience to generate the suggested images. For example, including imagery appeals in a vacation ad decreased the perceived likelihood of visiting the advertised destination when participants had low imagery abilities or the picture in the ad was too abstract (Petrova & Cialdini, 2005). Even favorable nonexperiential information—such as product comparisons, expert ratings, or statistical information—can make it difficult to imagine the depicted outcome (Petrova & Cialdini, 2005; Thompson & Hamilton, 2006). Thus, in some cases, attempts to engage audience imagination may not only be ineffective, but can backfire and produce the opposite of the intended effect (Petrova, 2006a).

A more subtle implication concerns the effectiveness of hypothetical questions as an influence strategy. A number of studies demonstrate that simply asking people about the likelihood that they will engage in a behavior can make them actually engage in the behavior (Fitzsimons & Morwitz, 1996; Greenwald, Carnot, Beach, & Young, 1987). One reason for the effectiveness of this approach is that, once presented with a hypothetical question about engaging in an activity, people spontaneously try to imagine this activity. Subsequently, they base their perceptions of its likelihood on the ease with which they can imagine it. This process presents an alarming possibility. When it is difficult to imagine the action in question, hypothetical questions will reduce its likelihood (Levav & Fitzsimons, 2006; for a review see Fitzsimons & Moore, 2008).

FLUENCY AND EXPECTED EFFORT: IF IT'S HARD TO READ, IT'S HARD TO DO

High perceived effort is a major impediment of behavior change, from adopting an exercise routine to changing one's diet. But here is what fluency research reveals: The experience of fluency can dramatically change one's perceptions of the amount of effort it would take to complete the task. Even minor irrelevant features can easily bias effort estimates. For example, when exercise instructions were presented in an easy-to-read print font, readers assumed that the exercise would take 8.2 minutes to complete; but when they were presented in a difficult-to-read print font, they assumed it would take nearly twice as long, a full 15.1 minutes (Song & Schwarz, 2008a). They also thought that the exercise would flow quite naturally when the font was easy to read, but feared that it would drag on when it was difficult to read. Given these impressions, they were less willing to incorporate the exercise into their daily routine when it was presented in a difficult-to-read font. Quite clearly, people misread the difficulty of reading the exercise instructions as indicative of the difficulty involved in doing the exercise.

These findings have a valuable implication. If we want people to adopt a new behavior, it is important that our recommendation is not only conceptually clear and easy to follow, but also perceptually easy to process. The goal to present the information in a unique and stylistically interesting way often leads to adopting a unique, but difficult-to-process message. This can have the backfire effect of making the recommended behavior seem unduly demanding.

Of course, disfluency may be advantageous when the goal is to create a perception of effort (Labroo & Kim, 2009). For example, when a recipe for a Japanese lunch roll was presented in the elegant but difficult to read Mistral font, participants assumed that it would require more time and more skill than when it was presented in the easy to read Arial font (Song & Schwarz, 2008a). Hence, there may be advantage for restaurants in describing dishes in a difficult to read font, which conveys that their preparation requires considerable skill and effort. And, the same font may discourage the hobby cook from trying the recipe at home.

An interesting implication also emerges for how we present various requests. To enhance the probability of compliance, one may be tempted to considerably reduce the size of the request. The problem, of course, is that while smaller requests are likely to lead to greater compliance, they are also likely to result in smaller contributions than the requester ideally desires. As a solution to this problem, Cialdini and Schroeder (1976) offered the "even a penny helps," strategy which legitimizes a small contribution without specifically requesting it. The fluency research offers another solution to this problem. By creating an experience of fluency while presenting the request, one can reduce the perceived amount of effort involved in complying without changing the actual request.

FLUENCY AND COMMITMENT: WHEN GIVING PEOPLE CHOICE BACKFIRES

Our motivation to be consistent with previous choices has been well recognized as a profound source of influence in North American cultures (Cialdini, 2008; Cialdini, Wosinska, Barrett, Butner, & Gornik-Durose, 1999; Petrova, Cialdini, & Sills, 2007). From a fluency perspective, however, the experience of difficulty in making a choice can have substantial negative effects.

The detrimental effects of choice difficulty have been well researched (Iyengar & Lepper, 2000; Schwartz, 2004; Sela, Berger, & Liu, 2009). Even when choices are limited to just two options, they frequently involve difficult tradeoffs: quality versus price, benefits versus risks, enjoyment versus effort. The experience of difficulty making these tradeoffs can have various unintended consequences. It can create decision paralysis and choice deferral, lower satisfaction with the decision process, cause people to switch to a different option later, and reduce motivation and commitment to implement the choice. For example, the difficulty of choosing between a digital camera that offered few capabilities but was easy to use or a camera that offered more capabilities but was difficult to use increased the likelihood of switching to a compromise alternative at a later point. Similarly, the difficulty of choosing between writing an essay about an article that was short and dull versus one that was longer and interesting caused participants to write poorer essays in comparison to those who were assigned one of the articles (Thompson et al., 2009).

Inclination to defer choice can occur even when the experience of difficulty arises merely from the print font in which the choice alternatives are described. For example, Novemsky and colleagues (2007) presented participants with the same information about two cordless phones in easy- or difficult-to-read fonts. When asked to choose between the two phones, 17% of the participants postponed choice when the font was easy to read, whereas 41% did so when the font was difficult to read. Apparently, participants misread the difficulty arising from the print font as reflecting the difficulty of making a choice. Supporting this interpretation, the effect was eliminated when the experimenter stated the obvious: "This may be difficult to read because of the print font." In this case, deferral dropped from 41% to 16%, wiping out the difference between the two fonts. These findings highlight that people are sensitive to their feelings of ease or difficulty, but insensitive to where these feelings come from. As a result, they misattribute the experienced ease or difficulty to whatever is in the focus of their attention.

FLUENCY AND LIKING: WE LIKE WHAT'S EASY ON THE MIND

One of the best known fluency effects is the mere exposure effect originally identified by Zajonc (1968): The more often we see an object, the more we like it. From a fluency perspective, repeated exposure is just one of many variables that facilitate fluent processing. If so, any other variable that makes processing easy should also increase liking. Empirically, this is the case, as a growing number of studies shows. For example, we like a stimulus more when a preceding visual or semantic prime facilitates its processing— we even find a picture of a lock more beautiful when it was preceded by the word "key" (e.g., Reber, Winkielman, & Schwarz, 1998; for a review see Reber et al., 2004). This positive response to fluently processed stimuli can also be captured with electromyography, a procedure that measures subtle muscle responses in the face (Winkielman & Cacioppo, 2001), indicating that fluent processing feels good.

Our preference for fluently processed stimuli underlies many of the variables known to influence aesthetic experience, from symmetry and figure–ground contrast to the Gestalt laws—all of these variables facilitate fluent processing (Reber et al., 2004). The same principle is also central to the observation that we prefer prototypical faces over more unusual ones—prototypical faces are easier to process and elicit a more positive affective response (Winkielman, Halberstadt, Fazendeiro, & Catty, 2006). Moreover, this research also sheds light on why scientists and poets alike believe that beauty and truth go hand in hand—intuitive judgments of beauty and truth are based on the same input, namely the experience of fluent processing (Reber, Brun, & Mittendorfer, 2009; Schwarz, 2006).

FLUENCY AND PROCESSING STYLE: DO I NEED TO THINK TWICE?

Fluency experiences can not only directly influence our judgments, but they can also influence how we think. One way in which fluency shapes how we think is by influencing the level of abstractness with which we construe information. Take a study in which participants were asked to describe New York City. When the questionnaire was printed in a difficult-to-read font, participants described New York more abstractly in comparison to participants who received the same questionnaire printed in an easy-to-read font (Alter & Oppenheimer, 2008).

Similar effects have been found outside the laboratory. Consider the online game "Balderdash." Each player fabricates a definition for an obscure English word while other players have to guess which definitions are real and which are false. Examination of the game records revealed that players provided more abstract definitions of words that were difficult to pronounce and more concrete definitions of words that were easy to pronounce. The fluency of pronouncing the word influenced the level of construal with which the word was explained (Alter & Oppenheimer, 2008).

Another way in which fluency shapes thought is by influencing how carefully we consider the information at hand. When presented with the question "How many animals of each kind did Moses take on the Ark?" most people answer "two" despite knowing that the biblical actor was Noah, not Moses. Even when warned that some of the statements may be distorted, most people fail to notice the error because both actors are familiar in the context of biblical stories. However, a change in print fonts is sufficient to attenuate this Moses illusion: When the question was presented in an easy-to-read font, only 7% of the readers noticed the error, whereas 40% did so when it was presented in a difficult-to-read font (Song & Schwarz, 2008b).

In another series of studies participants received a message that contained either strong or weak arguments. Participants were told that the study examined left- versus right-brain thinking and were asked to copy the information in the message using either their dominant hand (fluency condition) or nondominant hand (disfluency condition). Across studies, the results revealed that depending on their focus of attention, participants either directly attributed the disfluency to more negative attitudes or were motivated by the disfluency to engage with the message in a more mindful way. In the latter case, those who wrote with their nondominant hand based their attitudes on the quality of the message arguments to a greater extent than did those who wrote with their dominant hand (Petrova, 2006b; Petrova, Goukens, & Cialdini, 2010).

These findings have some important theoretical and practical implications. On a theoretical level, they suggest that fluency can influence judgment by (a) serving as a source of information and (b) changing how information is represented and processed. From a practical standpoint, the link between fluency and processing style suggests that under some circumstances the experience of disfluency can be a portal for greater engagement and mindfulness.

CONCLUSION

Influence in Fluency

The science of influence, Cialdini reminds us, has always been a collaborative enterprise. Incorporating a fluency perspective to the study of influence brings valuable lessons. People are highly sensitive to their experiences of ease or difficulty. Unfortunately, they are much less sensitive to where these experiences come from. Hence, fluency can influence subsequent judgments and behavior through various routes. First, people may directly attribute the experience of fluency to other aspects of the object or behavior in consideration. Second, people draw on naive theories to infer the meaning of any encountered difficulty. Third, fluency elicits positive affect, which, in turn, can feed into other judgments. Fourth, fluency can influence the way information is processed and increase heuristic thinking. As a result, any variable that facilitates or impairs fluency can profoundly affect the effectiveness of influence attempts.

CHAPTER 5

A Multiprocess Approach
to Social Influence

RICHARD E. PETTY AND PABLO BRIÑOL

People try to persuade others and are also the targets of influence in both professional and personal contexts. Given that persuasion is present in nearly every human interaction, people need to know how persuasion works. Indeed, most people have learned something about persuasion strategies thorough trial and error. Practitioners, like lawyers, politicians, and salespeople, have also devoted an incredible amount of time and effort to understanding persuasion and learning what they can do to be more influential.

Building on this intuitive knowledge and his own systematic observation of persuasion in the real world, Robert Cialdini (2001) has argued that six key factors guide most social influence attempts: scarcity, authority, social proof, liking, commitment, and reciprocity. In his best-selling book, *Influence*, supported by a series of compelling experiments reported in some of psychology's most prestigious journals, Cialdini has pioneered the idea that because of the buzzing world of stimuli and confusion in which we live today, many people respond in an automatic way to influence attempts based on these core principles. For example, people might go along with an authority figure without much thinking because experts are presumed to be correct (e.g., Chaiken, 1980), or they might become more attracted to a restaurant if the parking lot is full rather than empty, taking the apparent popularity of the place as social proof that it must be good. We do not dispute the value of these important heuristics or their operation. Indeed, Cialdini has done a remarkable job of synthesizing the accumulated wisdom on persuasion into just six core principles. We also agree that people often do not have the time or mental resources to think about every persuasive appeal that passes by them each day or every decision they must make. As a result, everybody can fall prey to simple decision rules or triggers that can operate in a fairly automatic manner—just as Cialdini contends.

However, our key point is that the core persuasion variables identified by Cialdini (along with many other ones) do not *always* operate in a mindless way. Thus, influence professionals and laypersons alike should not lose sight of the fact that there is not just one automatic route to influence. As an opening example, consider one of the core Cialdini heuristics—scarcity. At one level, the law of supply and demand—where the scarcity of a commodity makes it more valuable—is the driving force behind virtually all economic behavior (Alchian & Allen, 1967). What core principle could be more basic? In accord with the scarcity principle, social psychological studies on commodity theory (Brock, 1968) have demonstrated that whether people are evaluating cookies (e.g., Worchel, Lee, & Adewole, 1975) or verbal self-disclosures from others (Petty & Mirels, 1981), greater scarcity is often associated with more value (see Lynn, 1991, for a review).

In the absence of much thinking, merely suggesting scarcity likely serves as a simple cue to value that can be invoked without much thinking. However, available research also supports the idea that scarcity does not always serve as a simple positive cue. First, different people can impart different meaning to scarce objects, such as when females value scarce self-disclosures from same sex partners and males do not (Petty & Mirels, 1981). Furthermore, scarcity does not always directly link to perceived value, but can first affect a psychological process that then results in an evaluation. For example, some research has shown that making a persuasive message seem more scarce can increase the extent to which it is processed carefully rather than how favorably it is perceived. Consider a study by Brannon and Brock (2001) in which customers who were ordering at a fast-food drive-through location heard either a strong or a weak appeal to try a new dessert paired with high scarcity ("a special offer for today only") or low scarcity ("available all year") information. When the appeal was a strong one, the scarcity information led to an increase in compliance with the request to try the new product, consistent with the scarcity-leads-to-value hypothesis. However, when scarcity information was paired with a weak appeal, the opposite occurred. Scarcity led to a *reduction* in compliance. This interaction of scarcity and argument quality suggests that scarcity produced enhanced thinking about the content of the appeal, leading to increased acceptance when the appeal was strong but increased rejection when the appeal was weak (see Petty & Cacioppo, 1986).

Our key argument in this chapter is that the six classic influence variables identified by Cialdini do not always operate in a simple heuristic manner.

Rather, in accord with contemporary multiprocess theories of influence, such as the *elaboration likelihood model* (ELM; Petty & Cacioppo, 1986) and the *heuristic-systematic model* (Chaiken, Liberman, & Eagly, 1989), variables such as scarcity affect judgments in different ways depending on how motivated and able people are to think about the appeal or request. When motivation or ability to think are low, the variables identified by Cialdini are most likely to operate as simple heuristics. But other roles are possible as motivation or ability to think are increased. After briefly describing this "multiple roles" notion, we will use it to illustrate how it works for two of the core influence variables identified by Cialdini: authority and social proof. Our review focuses on studies of persuasion—research in which the goal is to change someone's mind. We focus on changes in attitudes (people's general evaluations of people, objects, and issues) because attitudes serve a key mediational role in behavior change (i.e., attitude change often mediates the impact of some influence treatment on behavioral compliance).

MULTIPLE ROLES FOR VARIABLES

A core idea from multiprocess theories of influence, such as the ELM is that how a variable works to produce influence depends on where a person falls along an elaboration continuum (see Petty & Briñol, 2012; Petty & Cacioppo, 1986; Petty & Wegener, 1999, for reviews). That is, how a variable works depends on whether the likelihood of thinking is relatively high, low, or unconstrained (i.e., not predetermined by other variables, such as the presence of distraction). Numerous variables determine where the person falls along this continuum. For example, if a message is high in its personal relevance, the person typically enjoys thinking, few distractions are present, and much time is available for deliberation, then the likelihood of thinking is high. But, if a message is low in personal relevance, the person typically doesn't enjoy thinking, many distractions are present, or little time is available for deliberation, thinking is likely to be low. Of course, in many situations, these variables are at some moderate level (e.g., the relevance might be uncertain, distractions might be present but minimal). In such situations, people would be somewhere in the middle of the elaboration continuum.

The importance of this continuum in the ELM is that it determines, at least in part, how a particular variable, such as scarcity, will produce its influence effect. When the likelihood of thinking is low, the variable is assumed to act as a simple cue, producing an effect on evaluation consistent with its valence (scarcity implies value). This mechanism is the one highlighted by Cialdini. However, when the elaboration likelihood is very high, the same variable can affect influence in a different way. Under high-elaboration conditions, a variable is evaluated as an argument. That is, a person can deliberatively assess whether the scarcity of a product is a good reason to buy it. And, as we describe in more detail shortly, under high thinking conditions, variables can also bias thinking or affect what people think about their own thoughts. Which of these high elaboration processes occurs depends on other factors, such as the relevance of the variable to assessing merit and whether the variable is introduced before or after message processing has been completed. Finally, if thinking is not preset by other variables to be especially high or low, then variables tend to influence how much thinking occurs. For example, as we just noted, people might process information about an item more as its scarcity increases.

The ELM holds that the underlying process by which a variable produces persuasion is important to understand for two reasons. First, the outcome of persuasion can change depending on the mechanism by which the variable operates. Equally important, however, is the finding that there are different long-term outcomes that occur depending on the process. Most importantly, when a variable (e.g., scarcity, liking), produces persuasion by a relatively low-effort heuristic process, that influence is mostly of the moment. That is, the impact occurs only while the heuristic is in mind (e.g., "I'll go along with the likable source right now"), but in the next day or week, the influence is likely to be gone. However, if the same variable produces attitude change because of a higher-effort cognitive process (e.g., liking for the source gets the person to pay attention to and process the strong arguments presented), the influence will likely be more long-lasting, resistant to change, and influential in guiding behavior over an extended period of time. The reason for this is that thoughtfully changed attitudes tend to be more accessible and held with greater certainty (see Petty, Haugtvedt, & Smith, 1995, for a review).

AUTHORITY

Now that we have briefly reviewed the idea that any variable can influence people in multiple ways in different situations, we turn to two of the most studied influence variables—authority and social proof—and describe the multiple processes by which they can work. Although the ability of authorities to influence us can stem from multiple factors, we focus on source credibility because that is where the bulk of research lies.[1]

One determinant of a person's authority is his or her reputation for having extensive knowledge, expertise, and/or honesty, and much research has been devoted to these individual source factors in persuasion. Although there is a tendency to think that credible sources are likely to have just one effect (i.e., increasing persuasion by invoking an automatic heuristic, such as "if an expert says it, it must be true"), in this section, we briefly review research showing that source credibility can produce various effects depending on the circumstances. This means that source credibility can sometimes be associated with increased persuasive impact, but at other times, as was the case for scarcity, credibility can be associated with decreased influence.

According to the ELM, source credibility should serve as a simple cue primarily when people are not engaged in much thinking about the issue. In one study, for example, college students were more persuaded by an expert than a nonexpert source regardless of the quality of the arguments presented, but this simple cue effect only occurred when the issue was presented as very low in personal relevance (Petty, Cacioppo, & Goldman, 1981). When people know the message is irrelevant to them, it is not very adaptive for people to expend their limited cognitive resources to scrutinize the message carefully. Sometimes, however, people are unsure whether the message warrants or needs scrutiny and, in such cases, they can use the credibility of the message source as an indication of whether processing is worthwhile. Research suggests that when the authority of the source is based on expertise, people are more likely to think about the message from a knowledgeable source than from one that lacks knowledge (e.g., Petty, Cacioppo, & Heesacker, 1981). This makes sense as a knowledgeable source provides potentially useful information. Interestingly, if high credibility leads people to think more about weak arguments, then credibility will be associated with reduced persuasion, the opposite of the effect produced when credibility serves as a simple heuristic.[2]

Sometimes, people already know that they want to scrutinize the message, and they are able to do so. In such situations, the credibility of the source can bias the thoughts that come to mind. In particular, if the message is at least somewhat ambiguous rather than clearly strong or weak, the credibility of the source can be used to disambiguate the arguments presented (see also Asch, 1946). This means that people will generate more favorable interpretations of the arguments when the source is highly credible than when the source lacks credibility, leading to an overall increase in persuasion to a credible source but by a thoughtful rather than a heuristic mechanism (see Chaiken & Maheswaran, 1994).[3]

Recently, Briñol, Petty, and Tormala (2004) have argued that source credibility can not only influence how much people think or whether those thoughts are positive or negative (primary cognition), but it can also affect the confidence people have in their thoughts (secondary cognition). *Primary thoughts* are those that occur at a direct level of cognition and involve an initial association of some object with an attribute or feeling (e.g., "this proposal is stupid"). Following a primary thought, people can also generate other thoughts that occur at a second level and that involve reflections on the first-level thoughts ("am I sure that my thought that the proposal is stupid is correct?"). *Meta-cognition* refers to these second-order thoughts, or our thoughts about our thoughts or thought processes (Petty, Briñol, Tormala, & Wegener, 2007). Source credibility can influence attitude change by affecting thought confidence, a process we refer to as the *self-validation* mechanism of persuasion (Petty, Briñol, & Tormala, 2002).

This hypothesis as applied to source credibility relies on the rather obvious assumption that source credibility can influence the perceived validity of the information in a persuasive proposal (e.g., Kaufman, Stasson, & Hart, 1999). More uniquely, the self-validation proposal is that, when a person has already thought about the information in a message and then discovers that it came from a high- or low-credibility source, the person's own thoughts are either validated or invalidated by this news. For example, if, after thinking about a message, a person learns that the source is highly credible, the person could reason, "because the message information is presumably valid, my thoughts in response to this message are presumably valid as well." However, if the source is very low in credibility, because the information in the message might be invalid, one's thoughts about the message should not be trusted either.

In one study examining the self-validation possibility for source credibility, Tormala, Briñol, and Petty (2006) predicted and found that informing people that a message they had already processed came from a high- rather than a low-credibility source led to either more or less persuasion depending on the nature of people's thoughts in response to the message. In two experiments, participants were presented with either a strong or a weak persuasive message promoting *Confrin*, a new pain relief product, and then information about the source was revealed (i.e., the message came either from a federal agency that conducts research on medical products or from a class report written by a 14-year-old student). When the message was strong, revealing that the source was high in credibility led to more favorable attitudes than did the low-credibility source because of greater reliance on the positive thoughts generated. However, when the message was weak and participants generated mostly unfavorable thoughts, the effect of credibility was completely reversed. That is, high source credibility produced less favorable attitudes than did low source credibility because participants exposed to the more credible source had more confidence in their unfavorable thoughts to the weak message and relied on them more.

In a study looking at multiple roles for source credibility, Tormala, Briñol, and Petty (2007) varied the placement of the source information and demonstrated that source credibility affected thought confidence only when the source information followed the persuasive message. When source information preceded the message, it biased the generation of thoughts, consistent with past research (Chaiken & Maheswaran, 1994). This study demonstrates that credibility can have an impact through high thought mechanisms, although the specific mechanism operating was different depending on the placement of the source information. In real life, we can often control when information about the source is revealed. For example, an advertisement can reveal a famous endorser before or after the arguments are presented or we, as individuals, can decide to strategically let people know of our expertise before or after we present our arguments, thereby affecting the process of persuasion.

SOCIAL PROOF OR CONSENSUS

We have discussed the scarcity principle briefly and the authority principle in more detail. And we have argued that each of these can operate in multiple ways in different situations. We now turn to a third principle, often referred to as *social proof* or *consensus*. It is a well-established fact that people frequently use the actions and opinions of others, particularly similar others, as a standard of comparison against which to evaluate the correctness of their own actions (Festinger, 1954). As a consequence of this, groups can exert influence on individuals' attitudes because other people provide an *informational* standard of comparison for evaluating the validity of our own judgments and because they provide *social norms* through which we can gain or maintain group acceptance.

Thus, both informational and normative motives are involved in group influence and can sometime produce a knee-jerk reaction to agree or go along with the group majority (e.g., Cialdini & Trost, 1998; Wood, Lundgren, Quellette, Busceme, & Blackstone, 1994). More surprising, however, is the finding that people sometimes show more agreement when a minority rather than a majority advocates something (e.g., Crano & Chen, 1998; Moscovici, 1980; Mugny & Perez, 1991). To address these different outcomes, we present evidence that an implied consensus can not only influence persuasion by invoking a low-effort heuristic process when people are not motivated or able to think much (as emphasized by Cialdini), but can also operate in other ways when the likelihood of thinking is higher.

As just noted, the available research suggests that endorsement from a numerical majority often produces greater influence than a numerical minority, although sometimes minorities can be more effective. Several of the mechanisms we have already mentioned with respect to scarcity and authority have also been shown to operate for majority versus minority endorsement. Thus, advocacy of a position by a numerical majority (vs. minority) has led to enhanced attitude change by a low-effort acceptance process (majority as a positive cue to validity) when thinking was likely to be low, and by a more thoughtful but positively biased processing mechanism under high thinking conditions (i.e., more favorable thoughts about the message when advocated by a majority).

In one study, for instance, Martin, Hewstone, and Martin (2007) manipulated the extent of thinking and found that when either motivational or cognitive factors encouraged minimal thinking, there was heuristic acceptance of the majority position without detailed message processing. When thinking was high, however, source status biased the thoughts generated. Majority sources tend to produce a positive bias, fostering more favorable thoughts and greater persuasion (see also Mackie, 1987), whereas minority sources tend to foster resistance by negatively biasing message recipients' thoughts (see also Erb, Bohner, Schmalzle, & Rank, 1998). In research in which thinking was not constrained by other variables to be high or low, majority versus minority endorsement has been shown to influence attitude change by influencing the amount of thinking that occurs. When majority versus minority source status affects the extent of processing, it interacts with the quality of the arguments produced to influence attitudes (e.g., Baker & Petty, 1994; for reviews, see Martin & Hewstone, 2008; Tormala, Petty, & DeSensi, 2010).

In addition to these roles, majority versus minority endorsement has also been shown to affect the confidence in which people hold their thoughts in response to a persuasive message. As with source authority, this mechanism has operated when the likelihood of thinking is high, and the extent of endorsement by others is discovered *after* the message processing was completed. In one study (Horcajo, Petty, & Briñol, 2010), participants were presented with a message introducing a new company. The message was composed of either strong or weak arguments about the firm. The gist of one strong argument in favor of the company was that workers report high satisfaction with the company because of the flexibility in the work schedules allowed. In contrast, the gist of one weak argument in favor of the firm was that they used recycled paper in one of the departments during an entire year. After reading and thinking about this information, participants listed their thoughts in response to the company. The strong message led to mostly favorable thoughts, whereas the weak message led to mostly unfavorable thoughts, as intended. Next, it was revealed whether the vast majority (88%) or a mere minority (18%) of the message recipients' fellow students supported the company (see Baker & Petty, 1994).

Consistent with the self-validation hypothesis, Horcajo et al. (2010) predicted and found that the majority or minority status of the endorsement influenced the confidence in which participants held their thoughts about the company. Specifically, participants had higher thought confidence when the company was endorsed by a majority rather than a minority. As a consequence, majority (vs. minority) endorsement increased reliance on thoughts and thus enhanced the argument quality effect on attitudes. This means that when the message arguments were strong, persuasion was enhanced by majority endorsement; but when the arguments were weak, persuasion was reduced by majority endorsement.[4] As is the case with source authority, one can be strategic in when to reveal the extent of endorsement of a proposal.

OTHER HEURISTICS

We have argued that variables such as scarcity, authority, and social consensus can operate in multiple ways in different situations. We also believe that multiple mechanisms could be involved in the remaining persuasion heuristics. For example, consider the principle of liking. As was the case for the other principles we discussed, the dominant understanding of why liking works seems to be as a fairly automatic heuristic. However, our argument, which should be familiar by now, is that, depending on the message recipient's motivation and ability to think, source factors such as liking or attractiveness can influence persuasion in multiple ways: by serving as a simple cue, biasing the thoughts message recipients have, determining the amount of information processing that occurs, serving as a piece of evidence relevant to the central merits of the issue, or affecting thought confidence.

For example, when the issue is an important one, people would be expected to process the attractiveness of the message source as an argument, so it only would have a positive impact when it is relevant to the issue under consideration (e.g., an advertisement for a beauty product, but not for a bank). However, when people are not thinking much, attractiveness has the same positive impact as a simple cue regardless of its relevance (Petty & Cacioppo, 1983). Of course, source attractiveness, like other variables, can influence not only how we think about different requests, but also how we think about our own thoughts. Thus, people would likely be more pleased with their thoughts when they learn that they were presented by a likable rather than an unlikable source (see Briñol & Petty, 2009b).

CONCLUSION

Although we have not reviewed all six of the Cialdini heuristics in detail, we focused on those for which the most relevant research has been conducted. For authority in particular, and for social consensus, scarcity, and liking to a lesser extent, relevant research indicates that a low-effort heuristic process is not the only way in which these variables operate. We believe that similar analyses could be made for the remaining heuristics, commitment and reciprocity.

By examining the psychological processes responsible for attitude change, researchers and practitioners can understand and predict further changes in behavior and maximize the chances of designing effective field interventions. Furthermore, by considering the difference between processes of primary and secondary cognition, our understanding of the principles of influence can be advanced. The self-validation research reviewed has shown that this meta-cognitive mechanism can account for some already established persuasion outcomes (e.g., more persuasion with high- rather than low-authority sources), but by a completely different process than postulated previously. Moreover, we have also been able to obtain findings opposite to those typically observed (e.g., when thoughts are mostly unfavorable, persuasion is reduced when people learn that their thoughts were in response to a high- rather than a low-authority source). We hope that our brief review serves as a reminder of both the complexity and the orderliness of the influence process. Although the influence variables identified by Cialdini are extremely pervasive and important, they do not always operate in the same manner.

ENDNOTES

[1] Authority can also stem from the power of the source. Much prior research has emphasized how source power produces *compliance* rather than internalized attitude change (e.g., Kelman, 1958) by a simple low-effort process, but more recent research documents that power can produce persuasion in more thoughtful ways as well (see Briñol & Petty, 2009a, for a review).

[2] If the knowledge of a source is kept high, but the trustworthiness of the source is varied, then people tend to process a message more if the veracity of the source is in doubt (Priester & Petty, 1995). The advocated position of a source that is highly knowledgeable and trustworthy can easily be accepted without much scrutiny.

[3] Importantly, other research has shown that if people come to believe that their thoughts have been biased by the source, they can adjust their judgments in a direction opposite to the perceived biasing impact (i.e., they engage in correction processes; Petty, Wegener, & White, 1998; Wegener & Petty, 1995).

[4] In virtually all of the prior studies manipulating source status and argument quality, the manipulation of source status has *preceded* presentation of the persuasive message. As explained earlier for source credibility, variables can affect the amount of information processing that takes place, as long as it is not already constrained to be high or low by other variables. In contrast, in the study just described, the status of the source was introduced when processing of the message proposal was already done, and operated through thought confidence. In a study in which the placement of the source status was manipulated, it affected the extent of thinking about the message when it came beforehand but affected thought confidence when it followed the message (Horcajo et al., 2010, Experiment 3).

CHAPTER 6

Basking in Reflected Glory and Compliance with Requests from People Like Us

JERRY M. BURGER

L ook into the stands at any major professional or collegiate sporting event these days, and you most likely will find a sea of team colors. Fans adorn themselves in their team's jackets, tee shirts, sweatshirts, and caps. They wear jerseys bearing the name and number of their favorite player. Faces and even a few bare torsos painted in team colors are not uncommon. Sports merchandising has become a multibillion dollar business and a significant source of revenue for colleges and professional sports franchises. But, nearly four decades ago, when the sports merchandise industry was a small fraction of what it is today, Robert Cialdini and some of his colleagues wondered about the psychological underpinnings of this curious behavior. They dubbed this effort to associate oneself with successful people *basking in reflected glory* (BIRG), and generations of psychology students have been intrigued and delighted by the concept ever since.

This chapter has two goals. First, to look at theory and research on reflected glory basking with special attention to a couple of theoretical loose ends. Second, to examine in depth but one example of current research that ties back to the BIRG concept. Appropriate for a volume devoted to the legacy of Robert Cialdini, that example is the effect of similarity and compliance.

The initial demonstration of reflected glory basking was conducted during the 1973 collegiate football season. Starting with the third week of the season, Cialdini et al. (1976) calculated the percentage of undergraduates in selected classrooms wearing a shirt, jacket, button, etc. with the school's name, insignia, nickname, or mascot on it. The researchers compared the percentage of students who wore school gear on Mondays after the school's team won its weekend game with the percentage who wore their gear on Mondays following a loss or tie. Seven football-crazed campuses were included in the study, and, as expected, the students basked in the reflected glory of their football teams by wearing school-related apparel more often on winning Mondays than on Mondays following a nonvictorious outcome. In follow-up studies, Cialdini et al. looked at the pronouns students used to describe game outcomes. Consistent with the apparel study, students tended to say "we won" when asked about the outcome of a game their football team won and "they lost" when describing a losing effort. This tendency to bask in the reflected glory of successful sports teams has been replicated in several subsequent investigations. Seventy-five percent of the undergraduates in one study used "we" when describing their basketball team's victory the morning after the game, as compared to 52% who used the term when the team lost (Burger, 1985). When one team of researchers asked students to list the sports teams they identified with, the students overwhelmingly named teams that had recently completed a winning season (End, Dietz-Uhler, Harrick, & Jacquemotte, 2002). Another study found highly enthusiastic soccer fans were more likely to use "we" when writing about their team's victory in a fan magazine than when writing about a defeat (Bernache-Assollant, Lacassagne, & Braddock, 2007). And, when researchers asked fans exiting a game how much they associated themselves with the local basketball team, more attendees were willing to align themselves with the team after a victory than after a defeat (Bizman & Yinon, 2002).

But opportunities to bask in reflected glory are not limited to sporting events. We often encounter people who want to highlight their association with successful actors, singers, writers, artists, political leaders, and even historical figures. These individuals want us to know that they come from the same hometown, went to the same school, have the same birthday, etc. as the famous person. In short, experimental evidence and common observations lead to the same conclusion—people like to point out their associations with winners. But why?

At first glance, BIRG seems a bit odd. Unless the students were suited up and on the field Saturday, they should have no reason to flaunt the victory as a personal accomplishment on Monday. To explain this behavior, Cialdini et al. (1976) turned to Fritz Heider's (1958) landmark work. In particular, they pointed to two concepts popularized by Heider—unit relationships and cognitive–perceptual balance. A *unit relationship* is an association people sometimes perceive between themselves and other individuals with whom they share a common attribute. These relationships can be based on important connections like political views or religious beliefs, or they might be formed as a result of relatively trivial and incidental similarities like similar-sounding names or a shared hometown ("You're from Omaha, too?"). Unit relationships are most likely to form when the common attribute between the unit members is not shared by the people around them. Thus, two individuals from Texas are likely to perceive a unit relationship if they run into one another in California, but not if the meeting takes place in Dallas. Important for our purposes here, Heider also maintained that unit relationships have an affective component. That is, we tend to feel at least a little attraction for someone with whom we share this association. Because unit relationships are often quickly formed and quickly dissolved, the liking generated by the association can be fleeting.

The second concept borrowed from Heider is the notion of *cognitive–perceptual balance*. That is, we are motivated to see connections between the elements in our cognitive–perceptual world in a balanced state. Psychologists usually illustrate this concept by drawing relationship triangles. For example, if I like Richard and Richard likes Avril, then I would need to like Avril as well to keep things in balance. Similarly, if I dislike Richard and I learn that Richard likes Avril, then I probably am not going to care much for this Avril, even if I don't know her very well.

Returning to BIRG, Cialdini et al. (1976) argued that the association people see between themselves and successful individuals is a kind of unit relationship. But keep in mind that the unit relationship exists because of an existing shared characteristic (e.g., attending the same school), not because of the success. Baskers are simply trying to make this preexisting association highly visible. Why would they want to highlight this association? According to Cialdini et al., baskers are trying to raise their esteem in other people's eyes. In the football study, undergraduates wore university-related clothing when the team won because the students wanted other people to think more highly of them. In other words, the motivation underlying reflected glory basking is self-presentation. Indeed, in a later article,

Cialdini and Richardson (1980) refer to BIRG as an "impression manage-ment technique." This self-presentation interpretation is perfectly in line with Heider's description of cognitive–perceptual balance. Most people have a positive evaluation of winning teams. If I feel good about the foot-ball team, and I am made keenly aware that Marcus is associated with that team, then, to keep everything in balance, I should also feel good about Marcus. This analysis suggests yet another tactic one may use to bask in reflected glory (Cialdini & Richardson, 1980). We can improve our stat-ure by also pointing out the positive features of someone we are already associated with. Thus, if you know Stephen attends a certain university, and if Stephen points out something positive about that university (e.g., the football team is great), then you should think more highly of Stephen.

Inglorious Baskers

Wearing a team jersey and talking about "our" victory seems harmless enough. But Heider's balance theory suggests two additional—and slightly less admirable—strategies reflected glory baskers can use to elevate their public esteem. First, rather than build up the positive features of people with whom we share a unit relationship, we can also denigrate a person or institution with whom we have a negative connection. That is, if Robert and I are rivals (negative association), and I can persuade you that Robert is not a particularly likeable guy, then, to balance things out, you should feel more positively toward me. Cialdini and Richardson (1980) referred to this strategy as "blasting." Consistent with this analysis, Cialdini and Richardson found that, compared to a control condition, Arizona State University undergraduates gave more negative evaluations of their rival school (the University of Arizona) after the students believed they had just done poorly on a "latent creativity" test.

Another nefarious strategy for improving one's image is to distance your-self from someone with whom you have a unit relationship when that other person is viewed unfavorably. One team of researchers called this tactic "cutting off reflected failure" (Snyder, Lassegard, & Ford, 1986). For exam-ple, you might laugh at a bumbling tennis player who comes in last place in a tournament. If that bumbler turns out to be my brother, balance theory says that—assuming I like my brother—you probably will also think less of me. To avoid this decline in my esteem, I can diminish, deny, or other-wise downplay the association between me and my sibling. He might be my brother, but if I share your laughter at his ineptitude, I may be able to preserve my own standing in your eyes. When we say that "they" lost, we are also saying that we are not one of "them."

This last observation brings us to one of the loose ends in the BIRG literature. Were the undergraduates in the football study trying to bask in the winning team's glory after a success, or were they trying to distance themselves from the losing effort after a defeat (Snyder et al., 1986)? Although Cialdini et al. (1976) focused on the desire to make ourselves look good, it is also possible that the BIRG effect may instead be based on a motivation to keep ourselves from looking bad. Of course, a definitive answer to this question requires additional research. But let me offer for the moment the most likely resolution of this issue. Depending on a number of variables, either or both of these motives can affect our willingness to associate with successful and unsuccessful others. Sometimes we are trying to link ourselves with winners, and other times we are trying to distance ourselves from losers. In the Monday morning attire study, most likely a little bit of both processes was operating.

For Whose Benefit?

From the outset, Cialdini and his colleagues described reflected glory basking as a self-presentation tactic motivated by a concern for what others think. In support of this interpretation, Cialdini et al. (1976) found students were more likely to BIRG when they were in need of an esteem boost; for example, undergraduates were more likely to make the we–they distinction after doing poorly on a quiz. Presumably, the failing participants feared the experimenter (who had administered the quiz and delivered the grade) would think less of them. Associating themselves with the winning team was an effort to offset that negative evaluation.

However, another interpretation is possible. It may be the case that people engage in reflected glory basking out of a concern for personal rather than (or perhaps in addition to) public regard. People might put on team jerseys after a victory simply to feel better about themselves, regardless of what others think of them. The participants who failed the quiz might have been feeling bad about their performance, and they may have associated themselves with the winning team as a way to heal their bruised egos. A quick glance at some of the BIRG studies lends support to this analysis. For example, students in one study said "we won" or "they lost" to an anonymous researcher who phoned to ask about the previous night's basketball game (Burger, 1985). Were these participants really concerned about what this unseen and never-heard-from-again caller would think of them? Or, were they reacting to their own feelings following the game?

Findings from a study by Finch and Cialdini (1989) also lend support to this alternative interpretation. Some participants were led to believe that they shared their date of birth with a dislikable historic figure (Grigori Rasputin, the "Mad Monk of Russia"). These individuals gave kinder evaluations of Rasputin after reading about his exploits than did participants who received no birthday information. Finch and Cialdini argued that the participants were motivated to defuse as much as possible the negativity associated with Rasputin and thereby, consistent with balance theory, reduce the blow they would take for being associated with him. The researchers referred to this process as "boosting." However, the boosting effect was found even though the participant was the only person who knew about the birthday association with Rasputin. In other words, rather than being concerned with what others thought, the participants in this study were simply trying to assuage their own feelings.

So, do people BIRG as a way to make others like them or because they want to feel better about themselves? This is another loose end in the BIRG literature. Again, let me suggest the probable resolution. In all likelihood, it's sometimes one, sometimes the other, and often both. When we tell friends that we went to the same high school as Michelle Obama, it's obviously a ploy to impress others. But it also seems likely that impression management concerns are not necessary for reflected glory basking. Esteem-enhancing strategies often consist of private efforts, such as reminding oneself of personal strengths or reinterpreting information in a self-serving way. In fact, whatever public esteem hike people get from associating themselves with winners most likely comes from their imagined notion of what others think of them. It's unlikely that undergraduates ever hear directly from classmates that their status has risen or fallen as a result of the tee shirt they are wearing that day.

SIMILARITY AND COMPLIANCE: LIKE, YOU LIKE WHO YOU'RE LIKE

One of the first studies to explore how similarity affects compliance provides an entertaining blast from the past along with some interesting results. Participants were undergraduates in the Purdue University Student Union whose appearance identified them as (using the jargon of the day) either "hippies" or "straights" (Emswiller, Deaux, & Willits, 1971). Student researchers altered their own appearance so that half the time they appeared to be a hippie and half the time a straight. The researchers approached participants and asked to borrow some money (a dime) to make a phone call. When the requester and the participant were dressed in a similar manner, participants complied with the request 68% of the time. When their attire and general appearance did not match, the compliance rate dropped to 46%.

There probably are several reasons for the different rates of compliance, including a sense of trust or rapport with the similarly clad requester. But perhaps the most important difference between conditions was the level of attraction. Returning to the earlier analysis, the hippies and straights in the Purdue Student Union most likely felt a unit relationship with the requester who looked like them. If that were the case, then, according to Heider (1958), they also should have felt a bit of liking for this other person.

But would this small dose of fleeting attraction have been sufficient to produce a significant increase in compliance? More recent research suggests that the answer is "yes." Not surprisingly, we are more likely to agree to requests from friends than to requests from people we don't know (Clark, Ouellette, Powell, & Milberg, 1987). Yet, researchers also find that even small and short-lived increases in attraction often lead to significant increases in compliance. Students in one study simply sat quietly across a table from a confederate for a few minutes, a procedure designed to create liking through a mere exposure effect (Burger, Soroka, Gonzago, Murphy, & Somervell, 2001). When later asked by the confederate to read and comment on an eight-page English assignment, 55% of the participants said yes. This rate compares with only 20% who complied when participants had no prior exposure to the requester. Another investigation found an increase in both liking and compliance when participants believed they and the requester had similar personalities (Burger et al., 2001). Other investigators have found an increase in compliance when requesters engaged in a short give-and-take conversation with participants before presenting the request (Dolinski, Nawrat, & Rudak, 2001). When people act like a friend, we tend to respond to them as if they really were a friend.

Trivial Pursuits

In many ways, it's not surprising that we agree to requests from people who are similar to us. We feel more comfortable around folks who come from our part of the country or who share our values or interests. We enjoy being around them and probably trust them more than we trust other people. But what if the similarity we share with this other person provides no useful information about what he or she is like or how well we will get along? Researchers find that we sometimes form unit relationships based on similarities that are purely incidental and often rather trivial. For example, unless you believe in astrology, discovering that you share your birthday with another person should be nothing more than an amusing coincidence. Yet, we've all heard people announce with great pride that they were born on the same day as some famous individual. Moreover, researchers find that these incidental associations often translate into behavior. Participants in one investigation were more inclined to cooperate with their partner in a prisoner's dilemma game when they believed they shared a birthday with that partner (Miller, Downs, & Prentice, 1998). Another set of studies found participants were less threatened by a reactance-inducing essay when they shared either a first name or a birthday with the essay writer (Silva, 2005). And recall how participants altered their perceptions of Rasputin when informed that they were born on the Mad Monk's birthday.

As with fleeting attraction generated through other methods, unit relationships based on incidental similarities also can lead to an increase in compliance. One team of investigators e-mailed requests to students to complete and return a 15- to 20-minute survey about diet habits (Gueguen, Pichot, & Le Dreff, 2002). When the request appeared to come from someone with the same surname as the student, 96% returned the survey. When the e-mail message was from someone with a different name, only 52% complied with the request. Similarly, Garner (2005) found undergraduate students and university professors were nearly twice as likely as a control group to return an unsolicited survey when the person signing the cover letter had a name that was similar—although not identical—to theirs (e.g., Cynthia Johnston and Cindy Johanson).

One team of investigators found significant increases in compliance when participants were led to believe they shared their birthday or their first name with the requester (Burger, Messian, Patel, del Prado, & Anderson, 2004). In another study by these researchers, participants were told they and a confederate both had "type E" fingerprints. In one condition, the experimenter explained that only about 2% of the population has this type of fingerprint. In another condition, participants learned that 80% of the population has type E fingerprints. Later, the confederate presented the participants with the eight-page English assignment request. Participants who thought they shared a rare fingerprint type with the requester agreed 82% of the time, significantly more than the 48% agreement rate in a control group told nothing about their fingerprints. However, when participants believed the fingerprint type they shared with the requester was common, only 55% agreed with the request. Consistent with Heider's analysis, participants appeared to form a unit relationship with the confederate only when the similarity they shared set them apart from most of the people around them.

Can You Fight What You Can't See?

Cialdini (2009) has championed the notion that increased awareness can serve as a defense against con artists and others who exploit our near-automatic tendency to agree to requests under certain circumstances. We can apply this advice to the various techniques people use to create a unit relationship with us just prior to presenting a request. When a salesperson says, "My mother's name was . . ." or "I used to live in . . .," an enlightened consumer should be able to recognize the ploy for what it is.

We should all be on the lookout for these tactics. But what if requesters were able to create a sense of similarity with us in ways we don't even notice? For example, researchers find that we tend to like people who speak approximately the same number of syllables per minute that we do (Buller, LePoire, Aune, & Eloy, 1992). Yet, participants in these studies remain completely unaware that the other person has matched their rate of speech. Other investigations find that we also feel an increase in attraction toward people who simply mimic our body posture and gestures (Chartrand & Bargh, 1999). Again, participants interviewed after their sessions typically express no awareness of the mimicking or their change in liking toward the person mimicking them. Nonetheless, researchers find participants are more likely to agree to a request from someone who has mimicked their physical poses and gestures than from someone who has not (van Baaren, Holland, Kawakami, & van Knippenberg, 2004).

In sum, nearly four decades of research tells us that associations between individuals are common, sometimes trivial, not always recognized, easily exploited, and often powerful.

Caveat emptor.

CHAPTER 7

Social Norms

A How-To (and How-Not-To) Guide

NOAH J. GOLDSTEIN AND CHAD R. MORTENSEN

O f all the loud-talking, high-energy fitness gurus you've seen hawking
crazy exercise contraptions on late-night infomercials, Tony Little
has been one of the most successful in the history of the business. And yet,
his sales techniques have, for the most part, been quite standard, at least
within the infomercial industry: endorsements from D-list celebrities,
before-and-after shots of unhappy blubbery masses magically turned into
smiling underwear models, and an audience displaying enthusiasm that
makes Beatles concerts look tame. However, at the advice of a well-
respected infomercial consultant named Colleen Szot, he made a three-
word change to a standard infomercial line. The result? Sales of his latest
exercise machine product skyrocketed.

Even more astounding than the fact that the change was so small is that
these three words actually implied to potential customers that ordering
the product might be somewhat inconvenient. What were those three
words, and how did they cause sales to climb through the roof?

The change Szot made was to the all-too-familiar call-to-action line.
She modified the traditional line "Operators are waiting, please call now,"
to "If operators are busy, please call again." On the face of it, the change
appears to be rather moronic from a business standpoint. After all, the message seems to convey that potential customers might have to waste their
time dialing and redialing the toll-free number until they finally reach
a sales representative. Yet, looking more deeply, there's more to Ms. Szot's
new call-to-action line than meets the eye. Consider the kind of mental

image likely to be generated when you hear "operators are waiting": dozens of bored phone representatives filing their nails, twiddling their thumbs, or waiting silently for the Grim Reaper to put them out of their listless misery as they wait by their inactive telephones—an image indicative of low demand and poor sales.

Now, consider how your perception of the popularity of the product would change when you hear the phrase "If operators are busy, please call again." Instead of those bored, inactive representatives, you're probably imagining operators going from phone call to phone call without a break. In essence, Colleen Szot was changing the perceived social norm regarding the public's purchasing behavior, knowing that when people are uncertain about a course of action, they tend to look outside of themselves and to other people around them to guide their decisions and actions.

CIALDINI'S FOCUS THEORY OF NORMATIVE CONDUCT

Before we discuss the role norms play in influencing behavior beyond selling somewhat suspect exercise equipment on late-night TV, it's important to understand exactly what we mean when we use the words *social norms*. This term, which is used often by researchers and lay people alike, has been employed to describe everything from the most popular kind of jeans at a given time (ripped, stonewashed, low-rise, skinny, straight leg, boot-cut), to how to eat your soup within a given culture (slurp or no slurp?), to children around the world being taught by their parents that underwear goes *under* their pants, not over (which explains why Superman, an orphan from another planet, doesn't follow one of Earth's most widely accepted norms). Because the meaning of a social norm seems to shape-shift depending on the individual discussing it and the context in which it is being discussed, social norms as a general topic has been the whack-a-mole of social influence—surprisingly difficult to pin down and study reliably—for nearly half a century.

However, looking both to clarify the confusion that had clouded researchers' ability to understand the roles of social norms and to better predict when and which social norms will exert influence, Robert Cialdini and colleagues (Cialdini, Kallgren, & Reno, 1991; Cialdini, Reno, & Kallgren, 1990) developed the *focus theory of normative conduct*. Focus theory has two central propositions. The first is that there are two different types of norms, descriptive and injunctive, which can have considerably different effects on behavior. The second is that any given norm is likely to influence behavior to the extent that it is salient, or currently present in one's mind.

Cialdini et al. (1990) suggested that descriptive and injunctive norms affect behavior through separate sources of motivation. *Descriptive norms* refer to what is commonly done in a given situation, and they tend to motivate behavior by informing individuals of what is likely to be an effective or adaptive course of action in that situation. It was a perceived descriptive norm that Colleen Szot was altering with the changed call-to-action line, knowing that people would think "It must be a good product if everyone else is getting in on it." *Injunctive norms*, on the other hand, refer to what is commonly approved or disapproved within the culture (or within smaller groups), and they tend to motivate behavior through informal social rewards and punishments that are attached to the behavior in question. In brief, descriptive norms refer to perceptions of what *is* done, whereas injunctive norms refer to perceptions of what *ought to be* done.

Descriptive and injunctive norms are often confused as the same thing because what is commonly approved within a culture is also what is commonly done within a culture. For example, injunctive norms dictate that when you hold open a door for someone, he or she should express thanks, which is usually what people do—and how often have you heard someone in this position tell you to go to hell? However, sometimes descriptive and injunctive norms diverge. For instance, although most people probably believe that workers *should not* steal office supplies or pad expense reports (injunctive norm), most workers *actually engage* in this behavior at one point or another (descriptive norm). (Of course, the authors of this chapter are an exception and would never do such a thing, something we've discussed many times over lobster dinners at conferences.) Similarly, although most of society believes that people should come to a full stop at stop signs (injunctive norm), people rarely do (descriptive norm). (Okay, okay, we'll cop to that one.)

Cialdini and colleagues (Cialdini et al., 1990; Kallgren, Reno, & Cialdini, 2000; Reno, Cialdini, & Kallgren, 1993) tested both postulates of focus theory within the context of littering behavior. In one study (Reno et al., 1993, Study 1), library patrons returning to their parked cars passed by a confederate who either littered a piece of trash, picked up a piece of trash, or simply walked by (the control condition). To manipulate the descriptive norm for littering in that setting, the environment was altered to be either completely devoid or completely full of litter. The littering of the rubbish by the confederate was meant to *focus* participants on the descriptive norm of the area (i.e., the presence or absence of other litter in the environment). The researchers found that compared to those in the control conditions, the library-goers in the descriptive norm focus condition littered less only when the environment was litter-free. The picking up of the litter by the confederate, on the other hand, was meant to focus participants on the widely held injunctive norm—that is, people, and society at large, would happily exterminate litterbugs if they could. Accordingly, those in the injunctive norm focus condition littered less than their control counterparts regardless of the state of the surrounding environment, showing that focusing the participants' attention on the injunctive norm overpowered the descriptive norm.

THE CONSTRUCTIVE, DESTRUCTIVE, AND RECONSTRUCTIVE POWER OF SOCIAL NORMS

vaccinations?

When attempting to create a powerful norm-based message, communicators must choose whether to draw people's attention to injunctive norms, descriptive norms, or both. Remember that the two central postulates of focus theory are that norms influence behavior to the extent that they are salient, and that descriptive norms and injunctive norms are capable of eliciting vastly different responses from people, depending on the situation. Unfortunately, communicators often fail to think about the importance of focusing an audience only on norms that are consistent with their objectives. For example, officials attempting to combat detrimental behavior (and raise public awareness of this behavior) often make the mistake of characterizing it as regrettably prevalent, unintentionally focusing their audience on the unfavorable descriptive norm.

One prominent example of a subtle misalignment of injunctive and descriptive norms comes from a commercial created in the early 1970s by the Keep America Beautiful organization (Cialdini et al., 1991). Designed to reduce littering across the nation, the spot begins with a dignified Native American dressed in traditional garb canoeing across a river. As he paddles his way toward the shore, we can see garbage floating atop the waterway and black smoke being belched out by industrial plants. After pulling his craft along a soiled shore, a driver speeding down an adjacent street tosses a bag of trash out of his car, splattering its contents across the Native American's feet. As a lone teardrop slowly works its way down his face, the narrator states authoritatively, "People start pollution. People can stop it."

Several years ago, the Keep American Beautiful organization brought the crying Native American back in another anti-littering commercial that actually amplifies the potentially problematic feature of the original ad. Viewers observe a number of people waiting at a bus stop, engaging in typical activities such as drinking coffee, reading the newspaper, and smoking cigarettes. After the bus arrives and they all hop on, the camera cuts to the empty bus stop, now completely covered with cups, newspapers, and cigarette butts. The camera slowly zooms in to a poster of the same teary-eyed

Native American sadly overlooking the garbage. As the screen fades to black, the following text appears on the screen: "Back by popular neglect."

Think about this line for a moment. Back by *popular neglect*. What kind of message is conveyed by this phrase and by the littered environments featured in both of these ads? Although the injunctive norm against littering is clear and powerful, both of the ads focus viewers on a descriptive norm for littering that suggests that, despite strong disapproval of the behavior, many people do in fact litter. In other words, it's entirely possible that the descriptive norm depicting the prevalence of littering behavior may have actually undermined the power of the anti-littering injunctive norm. As another example, visitors at Arizona's Petrified Forest National Park read signs that say, "Your heritage is being vandalized every day by theft losses of petrified wood of 14 tons a year, mostly a small piece at a time."

Although these statements might be accurate and are obviously motivated by the best of intentions, the people behind these campaigns may fail to recognize that by using a negative descriptive norm as part of a rallying cry, they might be inadvertently focusing their audience on the prevalence, rather than just the undesirability, of that behavior. To test this idea, Cialdini and colleagues (Cialdini, 2003; Cialdini et al., 2006) created two signs designed to deter petrified wood theft at Petrified Forest National Park; one was injunctive in nature and the other was descriptive in nature. The researchers secretly placed marked pieces of petrified wood along visitor pathways, and alternated which of the two signs were posted at the entrance of each pathway. The injunctive normative sign stated, "Please don't remove the petrified wood from the park, in order to preserve the natural state of the Petrified Forest," and was accompanied by a picture of a shady-looking character (in fact, Bob Cialdini in his best cloak-and-dagger costume) pilfering a piece of petrified wood, with a red circle-and-bar (i.e., the universal "No" symbol) superimposed over his hand. The descriptive normative sign, based on messages currently in use by the park at that time, emphasized the prevalence of theft. It informed visitors that "Many past visitors have removed the petrified wood from the park, changing the natural state of the Petrified Forest," and was accompanied by a picture of several park visitors taking pieces of wood.

The results should absolutely petrify the Park's rangers. Compared to a no-sign control condition in which 2.92% of the pieces were stolen, the descriptive norm message resulted in significantly more theft (7.92%). In other words, the types of signs used throughout the park at the time were not only failing to prevent wood theft—they actually appeared to be promoting it! The injunctive norm message, in contrast, resulted in marginally less theft (1.67%) than the control condition. These results suggest that when a descriptive norm for a situation indicates that undesirable behavior is prevalent, communicators might indeed cause unintentional damage by publicizing this information. What are the alternatives then? Think about what the data from the control condition indicate: Over 97% of park visitors leave the park *without* taking a pretty paperweight home to grandma, meaning that millions of visitors over the past decade have left the park just as they found it. In other words, the exact same descriptive norm information can be honestly reframed to communicate quite a different message. However, even in situations in which the cards are stacked against communicators of normative messages and most people are performing an undesirable behavior, this research reveals an ace in the hole: Simply communicating that the behavior is strongly disapproved, without providing any data on what the majority of people are doing, can have a positive effect on reducing these behaviors.

The Petrified Forest research shows that norms can influence behaviors in ways that are constructive or destructive, depending on the type of norm conveyed. But there is one type of norm in which the exact same information can lead to positive or negative behavior depending on who the audience is: the descriptive norm as conveyed by an average. Whether it's the mean number of drinks consumed by college students when they party, the average amount of credit card debt carried by most Americans, or the mean number of hours Americans spend each week finding ways to expand that debt, measures of central tendency such as the mean can potentially result in constructive influence for some and destructive influence for others.

As we have already discussed, descriptive norms provide a standard that people are motivated to follow. Because people tend to measure the appropriateness of their behavior by how far away they are from the norm or average, being deviant is being above *or* below the norm. This means that the average information may serve as a sort of "magnetic middle" that draws people toward the norm regardless of whether they are above or below the norm. For example, if a company memo communicates that employees come late to work 2.7 days per month on average, the worst offenders— those who come late 7 days per month—are likely to start coming in on time more often. However, the norm that might have a constructive influence on perpetually tardy workers might prove to have a destructive influence on perpetually on-time workers, causing even the goodiest of goody-two-shoes employees to go bad.

This raises an important question: If descriptive norms can elicit such an undesirable and inadvertent backfire effect, is there a way to eliminate this problematic effect? As we discussed earlier, according to focus theory, people tend to be most strongly influenced by the norm that is most salient at a given time (for a review, see Cialdini & Goldstein, 2004). What this means is that, in situations in which descriptive normative information might normally produce an undesirable backfire effect, it's possible that adding an explicit and attention-grabbing injunctive element to the message might prevent the occurrence of the backfire effect.

To explore this issue, Schultz, Nolan, Cialdini, Goldstein, and Griskevicius (2007) conducted a field experiment in the context of household residential energy consumption and conservation. In the study, the authors obtained permission from participating residents to read their energy meters at various times. After obtaining initial energy usage measures, households were divided based on whether their energy consumption level was either above or below the average household in the community. Next, all households received feedback about how much energy they had consumed in the prior week. However, half of the households were randomly assigned to receive additional information about the energy consumption of the average household in their neighborhood over the same period (the descriptive norm). The other half of the households received the same descriptive normative information as the first group, but also an injunctive message conveying that their energy consumption level behavior was either approved or disapproved. Specifically, households that were consuming less than the average received a smiley face (☺), whereas those that were consuming more than the average received a frowny face (☹).

The study revealed three important findings. First, for households consuming more energy than their neighborhood average, descriptive normative information alone decreased energy consumption. Second, for households consuming less energy than their neighborhood average, the same descriptive normative information *increased* energy consumption—in other words, it actually produced an undesirable backfire effect. Third, and perhaps most important, for the households consuming less energy than their neighborhood average, providing both descriptive normative information *and* an injunctive message that others approve of their conservation behavior prevented these undesirable backfire effect from occurring; these households continued to consume energy at low rates.

The results of this study demonstrate not only the power of the average to bring people's behaviors toward it like a strong magnet, but also how communicators can reduce the likelihood of their message backfiring for those already performing better than average: whether it's smiley faces, thumbs up, gold stars, or just good old-fashioned thank yous, communicators should convey their approval for, and appreciation of, those already acting in a socially desirable way.

Although progress has been made in exploring the ways in which descriptive and injunctive norms spur people's actions, the underlying psychology has remained relatively unexplored. However, recent research by Jacobson, Mortensen, and Cialdini (2011) has theorized that, because people follow descriptive and injunctive norms for different reasons, each norm is likely to work via a different process. More specifically, they theorized that self-regulation (or willpower) should be differentially required for each, resulting in very different outcomes depending on the willpower possessed by a target. Because descriptive norms serve as simple heuristics indicating what is best for an individual, following them should save effortful thinking and not require much in terms of willpower. Injunctive norms, on the other hand, are about behaving for the approval of others. This often requires more systematic thinking and the resolution of conflicting motives (i.e., setting aside what is easiest or best for an individual in the short term in order to gain social approval), and this does require effortful self-control. So, whereas following a descriptive norm does not necessitate using any willpower, following an injunctive norm requires it, even if the behavior advocated by the norms is identical. For example, if you mow your lawn simply because everyone else in your neighborhood does, it may not seem quite as grueling as if you do it only because you fear the wrath of your neighbors (or at least fear hearing your neighbors say, "So . . . I see your grass is really growing these days").

To test the role of self-regulation in normative influence, the researchers manipulated participants' levels of willpower, which has been shown repeatedly in past research to be a depletable resource (Baumeister & Vohs, 2004). To accomplish this, participants watched a video of an interview either while actively regulating behavior (i.e., avoiding looking at words that appeared conspicuously, and annoyingly, in the corner of the screen) or without regulating their behavior. Participants were then asked if they would volunteer to complete additional surveys after finishing the study and were also provided either a descriptive or injunctive norm for doing so. The descriptive norm informed participants that many past students had chosen to do additional surveys, but the injunctive norm instead provided information about what most past students approved, stating that previous students had reported that they thought students *should* be willing to complete extra surveys. Supporting the theory, students agreed to complete significantly fewer surveys after reading other students believed they should do the surveys (the injunctive norm) if they had first been depleted of willpower than if not. However, this same depletion led those in the descriptive norm condition to volunteer for marginally *more* surveys. In other words, depleting the ability to exert willpower had the opposite effect in this case, making it more difficult to avoid just going along with the crowd.

The researchers also replicated the results in a field study that took place in two identical psychology classes. As in the first experiment, students were asked by researchers to volunteer to complete extra surveys and provided either a descriptive or injunctive norm for doing so. However, in one class, students were asked before the day's class began, whereas students in the other class were asked afterward. Despite the fact that we hold a biased belief that psychology classes are among the most interesting offered at any school, the class's activities scheduled for that day were particularly difficult and depleting of willpower. This served as a natural manipulation; students used a lot of willpower during the activity and therefore had less of it after the class than before the class. Similar to the lab study, this depletion of self-regulatory resources again led the injunctive norm to be significantly less effective, but also led the descriptive norm to be significantly more effective. In fact, the injunctive norm was significantly more influential than the descriptive norm before class, and the exact opposite was true after class, further illustrating the importance of choosing your norms carefully depending on the situation. These results have interesting implications for everyday life—not only for those of us who wish to ask for favors in the classroom before or after class, but also for people in the workplace at the beginning or end of the day, or in a doctor's office after a short or long visit. When willpower becomes scarce, people are less like likely to do what they are told *should* be done and more likely to do what *is* done.

WHOSE NORMS ARE MOST INFLUENTIAL?

At this point, it should be quite clear that social norms exert a powerful influence on people's behaviors. And we know that people will follow the herd regardless of whether the herd is grazing where it should or running roughshod over protected land. But, for any practitioner looking to harness the power of social norms, it's important to acknowledge that there are many different herds out there. So, whose social norms are people most likely to follow? In other words, for any given situation, there are numerous groups out there that individuals might follow. To which groups should communicators point to when conveying social norms?

The social identity literature has shown that individuals are most likely to conform to the norms of a given reference group when they see themselves as similar in identity to the reference group. These literatures examine how personal similarities (e.g., in attitudes, gender, ethnicity, age, values) between a target individual and a group of people influence the target's adherence to the group's social norms (e.g., Terry & Hogg, 1996; Terry, Hogg, & White, 1999). However, comparatively little research exists that examines the role that *contextual* similarities (e.g., similarities in situations, circumstances, and physical locations) play in adherence to reference group norms. Goldstein, Cialdini, and Griskevicius (2008) attempted to fill this gap by examining whether the physical location in which behavior takes place influences conformity to that behavior. They argued that adhering to what they call *provincial descriptive norms*—the descriptive norms of one's local setting and circumstances—tends to lead to more accurate and effective decision-making than does adhering to more global descriptive norms. After all, the old adage tells us that we should do as the Romans do *when we are in Rome*—not Egypt. In contrast, much of the current social norms literature, which focuses on the importance of personal similarities, would emphasize that when in Rome, we should do what people we most identify with would do regardless of surroundings. Consistent with this idea, Goldstein and colleagues found that hotel guests who learned the norm of their immediate surroundings (i.e., the provincial norm for their particular room: most people in their room reused their towels) were more likely to participate in the towel reuse program than were those who learned of the more global norm, which was less immediate to their surroundings (i.e., the norm for the whole hotel: most people in the hotel reused their towels).

The results from this experiment suggest that communicators thinking about using a descriptive norm in their persuasive appeals should ensure that the norms are originating from a group that is as situationally similar to the intended audience's circumstances or environment as possible. For instance, assuming the norms were aligned with the desired behavior, a campaign to reduce littering throughout California should take a localized approach. In other words, instead of advertising the norms for the state of California as a whole, they should advertise the norms of each city, town, or even neighborhood within their respective areas. Similarly, assuming the norms do not differ by location, a manager at a large, multinational corporation would optimize her persuasive prowess by conveying to the employees at her branch the norms of their particular branch, rather than either the norms of another branch or the norms at the organizational level. Finally, it should be noted that the majority of people who have read this book in exactly the spot in which you are currently reading it have immediately wired their life savings into the authors' bank accounts. (It was worth a try.)

CONCLUSION

Prior to the focus theory of normative conduct, the utility of research on normative influence had been questioned for decades, with some stating that the concept was vague and contradictory. People say that a camera is really only as good as its lens; fortunately, the lens through which Robert Cialdini observed the influence of social norms on everyday behavior was one-of-a-kind, bringing this previously fuzzy concept into sharp focus and providing the clearest picture yet of what norms are, how they operate, and how to use them. Still, there is much more to understand about the process of norm-based influence. We are certain that focus theory will continue to have an impact in the decades to come, both within the psychological community and beyond it.

CHAPTER 8

Evolution, Social Influence, and Sex Ratio

VLADAS GRISKEVICIUS, JEFFRY A. SIMPSON,
KRISTINA M. DURANTE, JOHN S. KIM, AND
STEPHANIE M. CANTU

One of Bob Cialdini's lasting contributions to science and practice is his identification of the principles of influence. One of these principles—scarcity—states that opportunities and objects are more desirable when they are scarce or dwindling in availability. From "only one minute remaining!" to "a maximum of four per person!," the scarcity principle has been applied to many products, services, and other wares peddled by merchants.

In this chapter, we examine a different dimension of the scarcity principle by considering how scarcity applies to people. Specifically, we explore how behavior is influenced when there is a "scarcity" of men or women. Although the ratio of men to women in human populations tends to be roughly equal (James, 1987), the question of what happens when one sex becomes scarce is much more than academic. Sex ratio has begun to deviate markedly from equality (50% men and 50% women) in many populous countries (Guilmoto, 2009; Zhu, Li, & Hesketh, 2009). In the most striking case, China will soon have many millions of surplus males, producing an adult sex ratio of over 120 males to 100 females (Hesketh, 2009). In addition to global demographic shifts, sex ratios can also differ within a given region. For example, in the United States, the ratio of men to women is 116 to 100 in Las Vegas, but only 88 to 100 in Birmingham, Alabama (Kruger, 2009).

This chapter addresses how the ratio of males to females within a population—a concept studied extensively in evolutionary biological approaches to animal behavior—impacts *human* behavior. Although the human mind is believed to use sex ratio information as a cue to adjust mating behavior and family life (Guttentag & Secord, 1983; Hesketh & Zhu, 2006), we consider how the ratio of men relative to women might affect assorted human behaviors, ranging from economic decisions to career choices. When aggregated in large populations, these effects could have significant societal and economic consequences. We also consider links between psychology and physiology, discussing possible hormonal mechanisms that might regulate behaviors governed by sex ratio differences.

The scarcity of men and women—an inherently *social* aspect of the environment—also has important implications for social influence. Because sex ratios can differ in workplaces, classrooms, negotiation rooms, juries, and other settings where important decisions are made, a consideration of sex ratio introduces new directions for the study of social influence.

EXISTING RESEARCH ON SEX RATIO

Sex ratio tends to exert the strongest effects on behavior when an imbalance exists in reproductive-aged males and females (James, 1987). This specific sex ratio is called the *operational sex ratio*, which is the ratio of reproductively available males to females in a population (Emlen & Oring, 1977; Fossett & Kiecolt, 1991).

Animal research shows that changes in sex ratio influence mating effort, which includes mate search, courtship, and intrasexual competition (Kvarnemo & Ahnesjö, 1996; Taylor & Bulmer, 1980). For example, as sex ratio shifts from being female-biased (relatively more females) to male-biased (relatively more males), male gray mouse lemurs spend more effort on mate search (Eberle & Kappeler, 2004), and male European bitterlings intensify intrasexual competition over mates (Mills & Reynolds, 2003). Similarly, in the two-spotted goby, male–male competition increases as the sex ratio moves from female-biased to male-biased across the mating season (Forsgren, Amundsen, Borg, & Bjelvenmark, 2004).

Much correlational research also suggests that sex ratio is systematically related to human mating patterns (e.g., Barber, 2001; Licher, Kephart, McLaughlin, & Landry, 1992; Pollet & Nettle, 2008; Schmitt, 2005; Stone, Shackelford, & Buss, 2007). Most of this work has focused on how sex ratio relates to marriage and family outcomes, supporting predictions derived from evolutionary biology, social psychology, and mating economics (Baumeister & Vohs, 2004; Gangestad & Simpson, 2000; Kenrick & Luce, 2000; Pederson, 1991). For example, whereas female-biased sex ratios (relatively more women) are historically associated with lower marriage rates, more out-of-wedlock births, and lower paternal investment, male-biased sex ratios are associated with the reverse patterns (Guttentag & Secord, 1983; South & Trent, 1988). Sex ratio also appears to affect intrasexual competition in humans. As members of one sex become scarce, members of the more abundant sex should become more intrasexually competitive. Indeed, male aggression and violence tend to increase as populations become more male-biased (Barber, 2003).

EMERGING RESEARCH ON SEX RATIO

Given the lack of causal evidence regarding whether sex ratio influences human behavior (Hesketh & Zhu, 2006), we have begun conducting experiments to test whether perceived sex ratio actually changes psychology and behavior. Because sex ratio is most directly relevant to mating concerns, we began by examining whether manipulating perceived sex ratio influences relationships (Kim, Griskevicius, & Simpson, 2010). Individuals in committed relationships first read news articles describing the local population as either male-biased or female-biased. Afterward, people indicated how satisfied they were in their current relationship. We found that, when individuals in relationships perceive that there are fewer opposite-sex individuals in their local environment, both men and women become more satisfied with their relationships and feel psychologically closer to their partners. However, when individuals in relationships perceive that their partners have more romantic alternatives, men and women use different tactics to prevent their partners from leaving the relationship. In particular, when there is a scarcity of women, men in relationships become more vigilant and intrusive, attempting to prevent their partners from engaging in activities that might threaten the relationship. In contrast, when there is a scarcity of men, women in relationships become less intrusive and give their partners greater freedom, overlooking potential transgressions.

These experimental findings have interesting implications for how sex ratio might influence relationships, such as by creating biases in mate perception (Haselton & Nettle, 2006). For example, female-biased ratios might lead women to develop positive illusions of their male partners, perceiving their current mates as being better than they really are. Such positive illusions could, in turn, motivate women to retain their mates. Because sex ratios can differ widely within different regions, these imbalances may have interesting implications for relationships in different geographical regions. For example, given that Las Vegas has one of the most male-biased populations in the United States, professional gamblers living near the Strip might actually be *more* committed husbands.

Sex ratio might also impact many other areas of life. To begin examining this possibility, we tested how perceived sex ratios affect financial decisions, preferences, and expectations regarding saving, borrowing, and spending (Griskevicius, Tybur, Ackerman, Delton, & Robertson, 2010). In one experiment, participants viewed photo arrays indicative of the local population that were either male-biased or female-biased. Participants then made financial choices related to the time-value of money. For example, people chose between actually receiving $37 tomorrow versus receiving $54 in 33 days. Sex ratio had a significant effect on men's (but not women's) financial choices, whereby male-biased sex ratios led men to opt for smaller, more immediate gains. This finding is consistent with the idea that, as sex ratio becomes more male-biased, men invest more in *current* mating effort and intrasexual competition.

Consistent with the notion that a scarcity of women leads men to prefer immediate monetary gains, a second study found that male-biased sex ratios led men to both save less money from a paycheck and be more willing to borrow money for immediate purchases (Griskevicius et al., 2010). Specifically, male-biased sex ratios led men to cut their monthly savings by an average of 44.7%, and to almost double the amount of money they wanted to borrow each month. Supporting the idea that this money should be spent on mating effort, a final study found that male-biased sex ratios led both women and men to expect men to spend more money on mating-related products. When there were relatively more men, men were expected to spend an average of $6.01 more for a Valentine's Day gift, $1.51 more on an entrée for a dinner date, and $278 more for an engagement ring. These male-specific findings are consistent with other research indicating that men's mating success is linked to financial resources in many cultures (Buss, 1989) and that mammalian females become choosier when exposed to male-biased sex ratios (Balshine-Earn, 1996; Kvarnemo & Forsgren, 2000).

Consideration of how sex ratio influences financial decisions suggests that the male-biased demographic shifts currently occurring in many parts of the world (e.g., China) could have large economic consequences. Consider the fate of an aging generation of men who, as younger adults, spent and borrowed money instead of saving it. Caring for such populations will require increasing government expenditures. This problem will be exacerbated if there are fewer younger workers to support this large population of pensioners. But our findings may also have important practical implications. Many contemporary economic and social problems have been caused by excessive financial risk-taking that has prioritized short-term rewards over long-term stability (e.g., investing in subprime mortgages, drilling for oil in delicate environments). When sex ratios become more male-biased, problems associated with financial risk-taking could become even more prevalent. Our studies, however, suggest reasons for optimism. We have found that men's preferences shift toward less impulsive and more prudent financial choices merely by presenting them with visual images or written depictions of purported local female-biased sex ratios. This suggests that managers might be able to use sex ratio cues to create environments that facilitate more judicious financial decision-making. For example, office spaces might be assigned strategically to create a female-biased ratio of employees in a particular location of the office where risk-aversion is desired.

We have also begun examining how sex ratio impacts men's and women's desire to pursue a career. Consider how the number of men and women in the local environment might affect choices between investing in one's career (e.g., climbing the corporate ladder) versus settling down and starting a family. We have found that when sex ratios are female-biased, women prioritize their careers over starting a family (Durante, Griskevicius, Cantu, & Simpson, 2010). This suggests that perceptions of the availability of mates can have dramatic consequences for whether women choose a briefcase over a baby. Indeed, male-biased sex ratios led women to opt out of the workplace and desire to start a family instead. Men's motivations for careers show similar patterns, whereby male-biased sex ratios lead men to invest more heavily in their careers, consistent with the notion that a scarcity of females motivates males to intensify intrasexual competition. These findings have important implications for how the availability of mates might also impact educational attainment, such as whether people spend many years earning a postgraduate degree or forgo college altogether.

Recent research also suggests that the salience of same-sex rivals, one component of sex ratio, can even influence religious beliefs (Li, Cohen, Weeden, & Kenrick, 2010). After individuals viewed dating profiles of attractive same-sex people, they became more religious and more supportive of stricter social mores. These findings are consistent with the premise that religiosity might serve as a strategic component of one's mating strategy (Weeden, Cohen, & Kenrick, 2008). Because greater religiosity is typically associated with enforcing monogamy and relationship commitment, it makes adaptive sense to become more religious (and more enforcing of relationship commitment) when there is an abundance of suitors vying for one's current romantic partner. Religiosity, however, is malleable. When men viewed dating profiles of attractive women, men became less religious.

Implications for Future Research

Sex ratio is likely to have important effects on many areas of life, including person perception, aggression, consumer behavior, and friendship. Consider, for example, whether a scarcity of women should lead men to behave more cooperatively or more competitively toward other men. Although male-biased sex ratios tend to amplify intrasexual competition, this does not necessarily mean that men will blindly act more competitively. One possibility is that a scarcity of women will lead men to tighten coalitional bonds with male allies, similar to the way in which middle-ranking chimpanzees form coalitions to topple troop leaders (de Waal, 2000). If so, male-biased sex ratios might lead men to be more competitive with strangers, but more cooperative with individuals from their own coalition (see Van Vugt, De Cremer, & Janssen, 2007). Women might behave similarly in response to female-biased sex ratios, but future research is needed to clarify the similarities and differences in men's and women's evolved affiliation psychologies.

Sex ratio may also have important consequences in smaller settings, such as when the ratio of men to women differs in an office, classroom, business negotiation, or on a jury. For example, men often vie for status by intentionally disagreeing with other men (Griskevicius, Goldstein, Mortensen, Cialdini, & Kenrick, 2006). To the extent that intrasexual competition intensifies under male-biased sex ratios, courtroom juries, which are composed of twelve strangers, might be less likely to reach consensus when there are more men than women. Sex ratio differences might also have dramatic consequences for businesses. Most consumer products, for example, are first tested extensively in focus groups, which are used by companies to decide whether a product idea should be pushed forward or abandoned. Sex ratio could affect the degree to which focus groups judge products, not on their inherent qualities but on extraneous factors such as the number of same-sex individuals in a focus group. For example, a scarcity of women in a mixed-sex group is likely to make men more competitive, leading them to worry more about their own rather status than the accuracy of their judgments. By understanding how the mere number of men and women in a setting affects attitudes and behavior, real or perceived sex ratios could be arranged strategically to facilitate desired influence outcomes.

INDIVIDUAL DIFFERENCES AND SEX RATIO

Thus far, we have discussed how a skew in sex ratio can produce similar types of responding by most people. However, sex ratio might sometimes exert different effects on different individuals. Recent animal research, for example, shows that male-biased sex ratios lead different males to adopt alternate mating tactics (Magellan & Magurran, 2007; Weir, Grant, & Hutchings, 2010). These findings are consistent with the notion that psychological adaptations, such as those that are sensitive to sex ratio cues, are designed to be sensitive not only to external factors (i.e., situations), but also to internal factors (i.e., individual differences).

Which individual differences are likely to be most important? Consider the mating tactics of scorpionflies (Thornhill, 1980), which use two mating tactics: a chivalrous tactic of providing a prospective mate with a gift (a tasty and nutritious dead insect), or a vulgar tactic that forces copulation without a gift. Although the gift tactic is much more effective at leading to a successful mating, it is difficult and time-consuming to find desirable gifts. In contrast, whereas the forced mating tactic is much less effective at producing a mating, it does not require looking for any gifts. The specific tactic adopted by a male depends on the environment (e.g., the level of intrasexual competition) and the male's *competitive ability*.

In environments that contain many rivals (e.g., those with male-biased sex ratios), male scorpionflies that have high competitive ability use the gift tactic. But the same rival-heavy environment leads males that have low competitive ability to use the forced mating tactic. This divergent pattern makes adaptive sense when one considers that the costs associated with the gift tactic are not identical for all males. When there are many rivals competing for mates, only the most capable males can find and secure scarce gifts. Thus, even though the gift tactic is effective for males who are best able to secure gifts, it is ineffective for less capable males, leaving them with few opportunities to mate. Accordingly, it makes adaptive sense for less capable males to switch to a different tactic, especially when intrasexual competition is high.

Recent Findings Highlighting Individual Differences

We have started to examine whether sex ratio might produce different outcomes depending on an individual's mate value. Mate value reflects a person's general desirability as a mate, as perceived by similar-aged opposite-sex people. Mate value correlates with a person's ability to compete for mates because higher mate-value individuals can attract and retain higher-quality and/or more mates. We predicted that a scarcity of mates should lead those who have higher versus lower mate values to use different tactics to cope with increased competition.

Earlier, we noted that a scarcity of the opposite sex led people to invest more in their careers. But whereas some careers provide excellent job stability (e.g., teacher, government administrator), other careers provide better opportunities for financial rewards (e.g., stock broker, inventor). In our research, we have found that, for higher mate-value men, increased competition due to male-biased sex ratios leads these men to desire careers in which they could become rich; conversely, for lower mate-value men, male-biased sex ratios lead them to want careers that provide more stability (Durante et al., 2010). Because most women value as long-term mates those men who have the ability to acquire resources (Buss, 1989), men who can compete for mates appear to be more motivated to obtain financial status under conditions of increased competition. Conversely, a volatile career path might be too risky for men who have lower mate value, especially when mate competition is steep. Meanwhile, women in our studies showed the reverse pattern. Among higher mate-value women, increased competition (i.e., female-biased sex ratio) led them to desire careers that would provide stability, whereas for lower mate-value women, female-biased sex ratios lead them to want careers that could result in financial wealth. These results suggest that women who can secure a mate more easily might forgo a high-investment career trajectory, whereas women who are less able to compete for mates allocate effort to careers with more financial rewards.

Implications for Future Research

Sex ratio and the moderating effects of certain individual differences have intriguing implications for voting patterns, advertising, and business practices. Each year, for example, many lawsuits are filed against companies for using unfair or discriminatory pricing. "Fairness," however, is a subjective concept. Many businesses use two types of pricing strategies: fixed pricing or variable pricing (Heyman & Mellers, 2008). In fixed pricing, prices remain constant regardless of when a purchase is made, who makes it, or how much of the good is purchased (e.g., grocery store items, television sets). In variable pricing, the price of the product can vary dramatically (e.g., an airplane ticket, a movie ticket, car insurance). Sex ratio may alter perceptions of fairness. Sometimes, fairness might imply that everyone has equal access to a product and pays the same price; at other times, fairness might mean that prices ought to differ (e.g., that people who have more money should pay more, that people who plan ahead should get a discount). This suggests that when ratios are male-biased, men high in competitive ability might perceive variable pricing as fair, whereas men lower in competitive ability might perceive fixed pricing as fair. Future research is poised to examine how sex ratio might influence various behaviors as a function of individual differences relevant to competitive ability, such as mate value, intelligence, health, strength, socioeconomic status, and other differences.

SEX RATIO AND HORMONES

Certain hormones may be pivotal mediators or moderators of links between sex ratio and how individuals behave, especially in situations that evoke concerns about competition (Mehta & Josephs, 2010b). We now discuss the roles that three hormones—testosterone, estradiol, and cortisol—might play in these processes.

Testosterone, Estradiol, and Cortisol

Testosterone (T) is a hormone responsible for producing and maintaining masculine secondary sexual characteristics. In many species, T levels are positively related to social rank and dominance (Sapolsky, 1991), decreasing when an individual's social status declines and increasing when it rises (Mazur & Booth, 1998). In humans, individuals who have higher basal T are more aggressive and dominant, more vigilant to dominance cues, and less aware of others' submission cues (e.g., Archer, 2006; Wirth & Schultheiss, 2006). Moreover, being in a committed relationship, marriage, or parenthood suppresses T in men and women (e.g., Burnham et al., 2003).

Several studies have examined the role of T when an individual's status is experimentally manipulated. When men who have higher T lose status, they pay more attention to status cues, become less happy, and perform more poorly on cognitive tasks (Josephs, Sellers, Newman, & Mehta, 2006). Higher T individuals also experience increases in cortisol (a marker of anxiety) after losing status, but decreases in cortisol after gaining it (Mehta, Jones, & Josephs, 2008). These findings suggest that high T motivates people to increase and maintain their social status. Once status is achieved, high T individuals relax and function well. Low T individuals, by comparison, are less reactive to gains or losses in status, but they become upset when they achieve higher status (Mehta & Josephs, 2010b). Thus, lower T individuals may prefer and feel more comfortable in lower status positions, perhaps because they cannot compete effectively in higher-status roles.

Estrogen (estradiol; E) is a female hormone responsible for female fertility, sexual behavior, and motivation. Basal E correlates positively with basal T, and it has effects for women that parallel those of T in men (Faruzzi, Solomon, Demas, & Huhman, 2005). Women with higher E have stronger implicit power motives, which are highest in single, unmated women (e.g., Stanton & Schultheiss, 2007). Women who have stronger power motivation also experience larger increases in E after gaining status and larger decreases after losing it (Stanton & Schultheiss, 2007). With regard to mating, higher E women are more attracted to masculine traits in men (Roney & Simmons, 2008), and basal E predicts the amount of mating effort that women exhibit (Durante & Li, 2009). E, therefore, plays a significant role in mating, status-seeking, and cooperation in women.

Cortisol (C), a hormone released during physical activity or psychological stress, prepares the body so that challenges or problems that must be resolved immediately can be dealt with. In humans, higher basal C is associated with greater anxiety and defensiveness (Brown et al., 1996), whereas lower C is linked to stronger social approach tendencies and aggression (Shoal, Giancola, & Kirillova, 2003). C, therefore, is believed to serve a behavioral inhibition function. Indeed, lower C is associated with lower harm avoidance, less self-control, and more aggression (Shoal et al., 2003). When presented with a mating opportunity, lower mate-value men experience increases in C (van der Meij, Buunk, & Salvador, in press), reflecting a stress reaction. In sum, higher levels of C are associated with social inhibition/avoidance, whereas lower levels are related to social approach (Mehta & Josephs, 2010).

T × C Interactions and Sex Ratio

Different hormones most likely operate together in guiding social behavior, especially in status-relevant situations. This may be especially true of interactions between T and C in response to social threats (Hermans, Ramsey, & van Honk, 2008). For instance, individuals who have higher T and lower C are most likely to behave aggressively (Dabbs, Jurkovic, & Frady, 1991). In lab tasks, high T/low C men tend to "rechallenge" opponents following a defeat, whereas higher C men avoid rechallenges (Mehta & Josephs, 2010a). C, therefore, may modulate status-seeking behavior. When status is threatened (e.g., following a loss) and C is low, status-seeking motivation fueled by higher T should be expressed as direct behavioral approach (fight). However, when status is threatened and C is higher, status-seeking motivation ought to be curtailed, and individuals should display behavioral avoidance (flight). Mehta and Josephs (2010a) suggest that high T/high C individuals may view social stressors as *threats* (and thus avoid/flee from such situations), whereas high T/low C individuals might view them as *challenges* (and thus fight/compete).

How might sex ratio interface with T/E and C to affect behavior? When sex ratios are male-biased, high T/low C men should be more motivated to directly engage and vigorously compete with other men, viewing them as challenges to be overcome. In contrast, high C men and especially low T/high C men should avoid, withdraw, or compete poorly in this context, viewing "too many men" as daunting threats to be averted. When sex ratios are female-biased, high E/low C women ought to directly engage and compete with other women, perceiving them as challenges that can be dealt with effectively. The opposite pattern should be found for high C women and especially for low E/high C women, who should perceive "too many women" as threats to be sidestepped.

CONCLUSION

The principles of influence identified by Bob Cialdini have powerful effects on behavior. These principles often steer behavior unconsciously, in part because all of them have evolutionary underpinnings (Sundie, Cialdini, Griskevicius, & Kenrick, 2006). In this chapter, we considered the principle of scarcity from an evolutionary perspective. We focused on how people's behavior might be affected by a novel dimension of scarcity—the scarcity of men in relation to women. Bridging a concept studied in evolutionary biological approaches to animal behavior with human outcomes, we showed that sex ratio also has theoretically consistent effects on human behavior. These effects, however, are not limited to mating or parenting outcomes; they extend to other important domains, such as financial decision-making and career choices. Questions of how and why sex ratio influences different types of behavior have myriad implications, especially for social influence—an indispensable area of the social sciences to which Bob Cialdini devoted his illustrious career.

skip

CHAPTER 9

Designed for Social Influence

JOHN T. CACIOPPO AND LOUISE C. HAWKLEY

Charles Dickens wrote *A Christmas Carol* after reading the Second Report of the Children's Employment Commission, an 1843 parliamentary report on the effects of the Industrial Revolution on poor children. He had intended to write a political pamphlet in an attempt to convince British employers of the need for social and educational reform, but, in a Cialdinian moment, Dickens decided that he would have more influence if he were to instead write a Christmas narrative (Dickens & Douglas-Fairhurst, 2006).

By the opening of the story, the protagonist, Ebenezer Scrooge, had already amassed the wealth and power that many still covet today. Semi-reclusive, cold, stingy, and greedy, Scrooge is depicted as living a materially comfortable but unhappy existence, whereas others, including the Cratchits, endured significant hardships but showed compassion and resilience, with the support of family and friends. The Ghost of Christmas Past reminded Scrooge of a forgotten time when he still cared about and connected with others; the Ghost of Christmas Present showed Scrooge the difference between material wealth and social wealth; and the Ghost of Christmas Yet to Come presaged a future in which his memory and grave were treated with the same disregard and neglect he had shown others.

The surprise is not that Scrooge awakened in the morning a transformed man who felt love, generosity, kindness, and compassion for others and represented the embodiment of the spirit of Christmas; or that these changes left Scrooge full of joy and fully embraced by others in return for his kindness and compassion. Nor is the surprise that Dickens succeeded in raising social awareness of the plight of the children and the poor (Glancy, 1985).

What is perhaps surprising is that modern societies seek the counsel of economic advisors whose expertise is the acquisition of material wealth while dismissing the counsel of behavioral advisors whose expertise is the construction of social wealth and resilience.

SOCIAL INFLUENCE

Social influence is defined as the various ways in which people impact one another. Although this definition makes it clear that social influence includes the direct brain and biological effects of feeling the embrace of a supportive social body—of feeling socially connected, in contrast to feeling isolated, for instance—these influences are typically overlooked in favor of influences like conformity, obedience to authority, compliance, and persuasion. When prospective epidemiological studies, summarized in 1988, revealed that social isolation was a major risk factor for broad-based morbidity and mortality, the effect was thought to be attributable to the direct influence of friends and family on a person's health behaviors (e.g., exercise, eating healthy) (House, Landis, & Umberson, 1988). Two bodies of evidence argue against this interpretation as sufficient and in favor of a more direct and subtle form of social influence. First, measurements of health behaviors in epidemiological and field studies fail to explain the health effect of social isolation in humans (e.g., Hawkley, Thisted, Masi, & Cacioppo, 2010; Seeman, 2000). Second, the isolation of a variety of nonhuman social animals is also associated with earlier morbidity and mortality. The story of social influence in this context extends beyond explicit attempts by friends and family to persuade individuals to exercise better health care.

The health, life, and genetic legacy of members of social species are threatened when they find themselves on the social perimeter. For example, social isolation has been found to have deleterious health effects, including decreasing the lifespan in the fruit fly (Ruan & Wu, 2008); promoting obesity and type 2 diabetes in mice (Nonogaki, Nozue, & Oka, 2007); exacerbating infarct size and edema and decreasing post-stroke survival rate following experimentally induced stroke in mice (Karelina et al., 2009); promoting the activation of the sympatho-adrenomedullary response to an acute immobilization or cold stressor in rats (Dronjak, Gavrilovic, Filipovic, & Radojcic, 2004); delaying the effects of exercise on adult neurogenesis in rats (Stranahan, Khalil, & Gould, 2006); decreasing open field activity, increasing basal cortisol concentrations, and decreasing lymphocyte proliferation to mitogens in pigs (Kanitz, Tuchscherer, Puppe, Tuchscherer, & Stabenow, 2004); increasing 24-hour urinary catecholamine levels and evidence of oxidative stress in the aortic arch of rabbits (Nation et al., 2008);

and increasing the morning rises in cortisol in squirrel monkeys (Lyons, Ha, & Levine, 1995).

Humans are born to the longest period of abject dependency of any species, and they depend on conspecifics across the lifespan to survive and prosper. No surprise that members of our species fare even more poorly when isolated—whether because they are actually living solitary lives or because they simply *perceive* they live in relative isolation. Perceived isolation in humans has been associated with the progression of Alzheimer's disease (R. S. Wilson et al., 2007), obesity (Lauder, Mummery, Jones, & Caperchione, 2006), increased vascular resistance (Cacioppo et al., 2002b), elevated blood pressure (Cacioppo et al., 2002b; Hawkley, Masi, Berry, & Cacioppo, 2006), increased hypothalamic-pituitary-adrenocortical activity (Adam, Hawkley, Kudielka, & Cacioppo, 2006; Steptoe, Owen, Kunz-Ebrecht, & Brydon, 2004), less salubrious sleep (Cacioppo et al., 2002a; Pressman et al., 2005), diminished immunity (Kiecolt-Glaser, et al., 1984; Pressman, et al., 2005), reduction in independent living (Russell, Cutrona, de la Mora, & Wallace, 1997; Tilvis, Pitkala, Jolkkonen, & Strandberg, 2000), alcoholism (Akerlind & Hornquist, 1992), depressive symptomatology (Cacioppo et al., 2006; Heikkinen & Kauppinen, 2004), suicidal ideation and behavior (Rudatsikira, Muula, Siziya, & Twa-Twa, 2007), gene expression—specifically, the underexpression of genes bearing anti-inflammatory glucocorticoid response elements (GREs) and overexpression of genes bearing response elements for proinflammatory NF-κB/Rel transcription factors (Cole et al., 2007, 2011), and an increased risk for mortality (Patterson & Veenstra, 2010; Penninx et al., 1997; Seeman, 2000).

SOCIAL BRAIN

Social species by definition form structures that extend beyond the individual. These structures evolved along with underlying genetic, neural, hormonal, and cellular processes because they helped these organisms survive, reproduce, and care for their offspring sufficiently long that they too reproduced. There is certainly evidence for the view that life can be understood in terms of short-term self-interest. Most species are either born with the capacity to find sustenance and avoid predation sufficiently well that some survive long enough to reproduce, or they are born in such large numbers that some survive long enough to reproduce. It is the ability of such organisms to reproduce that determines what genes constitute the gene pool for the future generations of that species. These genes, in turn, shape the structure and function of the organisms that constitute a species. This reasoning led George Williams (1966) to suggest, a half century ago, that traits that benefit the group at the expense of the individual evolve only if the process of group selection is great enough to overcome selection within groups. He further suggested that group selection is nearly always weak, so that group-related adaptations do not exist (D. S. Wilson & Wilson, 2008). Said differently, there was no influence of the emergent structures created by social organisms on the genetic constitution or predispositions of those species beyond individual-level selection processes. These notions also contributed to the view in the neurosciences in the 20th century that social factors were of minimal interest with respect to basic neural structure or processes.

Genes serve their own selfish interests in the sense that whatever the contributions made by a gene, or set of genes, to an organism's structure and function is passed on to the next generation if and only if the gene made its way to the gene pool. Darwin, who predated knowledge of genes, was puzzled by the observation that many individual organisms appeared to make themselves less fit so that the group might survive. Subsequent generations of evolutionary biologists realized that, even though genes might act as if selfish, the vehicle responsible for the transport of these genes to the gene pool occasionally extended beyond the individual or parent to kin and even to unrelated members of groups. More specifically, in some cases, the group structures formed by social organisms represent naturally selected levels of organization above individual organisms, and multilevel selection theory specifically incorporates group-level influences on selection processes (Wilson, 2007). The notion of "social influence" in this context takes on an expanded meaning.

Sociality may have been a relatively late evolutionary development, but its importance to species survival means that social factors can modulate gene expression and affect basic brain structures and processes (Cole et al., 2007; Meaney, 2004). Indeed, according to the social brain hypothesis, the rapid increase in hominid brain mass and connectivity was the result not of ecological demands, but of the demands of life in human social groups (R. Dunbar, 2004). Dunbar and Shultz (2007) noted that deducing better ways to find food, avoid perils, and navigate territories has adaptive value for all large mammals, but the complexities of these ecological demands are no match for the complexities of life in primate social groups, especially in hostile between-group social environments. These social complexities include recognizing ingroup and outgroup members; learning by social observation; recognizing the shifting status of friends and foes; anticipating and coordinating efforts between two or more individuals; using language to communicate, reason, teach, and deceive others; orchestrating relationships, ranging from pair bonds and families to friends, bands, and coalitions; navigating complex social hierarchies, social norms, and cultural developments; subjugating self-interests to the interests of the pair bond or social group in exchange for the possibility of long-term benefits for oneself or one's group; recruiting support to sanction individuals who violate group norms; and doing all this across time frames that stretch from the distant past to multiple possible futures (Dunbar & Shultz, 2007). Consistent with this hypothesis, measures of sociality in troops of baboons have been found to be highly correlated with infant survival, and cross-species comparisons have shown that the evolution of large and metabolically expensive brains is more closely associated with social than ecological complexity (Dunbar & Shultz, 2007). Moreover, humans and apes share many perceptual, behavioral, and cognitive skills (Tomasello & Herrmann, 2010), but although human children at 2 years of age are very similar to apes in their cognitions about the physical world (e.g., space, quantities, and causality), their cognitions about the social world are already much more sophisticated in terms of reading others' intentions, learning from others, and communicating with others (Herrmann, Call, Hernandez-Lloreda, Hare, & Tomasello, 2007).

SOCIAL ADHESION

Our survival and the survival of our genes depend on our connection with others. Human infants must instantly engage their parents in protective behavior, and the parents must care enough about their offspring to nurture and protect them. If infants do not elicit nurturance and protection from caregivers, or if caregivers are not motivated to provide such care over an extended period of time, then the infants will perish along with the genetic legacy of the parents (Cacioppo & Patrick, 2008; Beckerman et al., 2009). Indeed, human infants are not born a blank slate but rather come pre-equipped with numerous capacities to exert social influence on their caregivers to enhance their own survival (Vallotton, 2009)

Our developmental dependency mirrors our evolutionary heritage. Hunter-gatherers did not have the benefit of natural weaponry, armor, strength, flight, stealth, or speed relative to many other species. Human survival depended on collective abilities rather than individual might. Recent anthropological re-evaluation of the significance of *Ardipithecus ramidus* has led to the conclusion that certain adaptations exhibited by this early hominin species (i.e., diminution of male canine size, upright walking, and absence of ovulatory signaling) reduced intrasexual conflict among males and fostered pair-bonding and greater male parental investment (Lovejoy, 2009). In effect, these adaptations fueled an increase in social connection that contributes to our adaptability and resiliency to this day.

It is the gene that is obligatorily selfish, not the human brain. Genes that promote behaviors that increase the odds of the genes surviving are perpetuated. The genetic constitution of *Homo sapiens* in the long run derives not solely from the reproductive success of individuals, but also from their children's success in reproducing. Hunter-gatherers who did not form social connections and who did not feel a compulsion to return to share their food with or defend their offspring may have been more likely to survive to procreate again, but given the long period of dependency of human infants, their offspring may have been less likely to survive to procreate. The result is selection that strongly favors the ability to process information that could contribute to the formation and maintenance of social capacities and adhesion—that is, a social brain. These social capacities evolved hand in hand with genetic, neural, and hormonal mechanisms to support them because the resulting social behaviors helped humans survive, reproduce, and care for offspring sufficiently long that they too survived to reproduce (Cacioppo et al., 2007; Donaldson & Young, 2008; Lovejoy, 2009). Relative to other animals, the striking development of and increased connectivity within the human cerebral cortex, perhaps especially the frontal and temporal regions, but also medial regions ranging from the prefrontal to the intraparietal lobules, are among the key evolutionary developments in this regard. The expansion of the frontal regions in the human brain contributes to the human capacities for imitation, reasoning, planning, performing mental simulations, theory of mind, and thinking about self and others. The temporal regions of the brain, in turn, are involved with aspects of social perception, memory, and communication.

LONELINESS AS A SOCIAL NEUROSCIENCE CONSTRUCT

Perceived social isolation is known more colloquially as *loneliness*, which, in early scientific investigations, was depicted as "a chronic distress without redeeming features" (Weiss, 1973, p. 15). Loneliness may feel like a painfully miserable, hopeless, and worthless state, but we have found it has a specific structure and a valuable adaptive function.

Given that human survival and prosperity depends on inclusion in and participation with a social group, especially in evolutionary times, when food was scarce and dangers were common, there is an adaptive benefit to having the strong and aversive response of loneliness when an individual feels his or her social adhesion might be weakening or broken, just as there is a benefit to having aversive signals for other conditions critical for survival. Hunger, thirst, and pain have evolved as aversive signals to prompt an organism to change its behavior in a way that protects the individual and promotes the likelihood that its genes will make their way into the gene pool. The social pain of loneliness has evolved similarly—to serve as a signal that one's connections to others are weakening and to motivate the repair and maintenance of the adhesion to others that are needed for our health and well-being, as well as for the survival of our genes (Cacioppo et al., 2006). Physical pain is an aversive signal that evolved to motivate one to take action that minimizes damage to one's physical body. Loneliness is an aversive signal that evolved to motivate one to take action that minimizes damage to one's social body. As such, it is a social influence motivated by the felt absence of a connection to others who can be trusted and with whom one can work together to support personal and collective aspirations.

People differ dispositionally in their sensitivity to the pain of social disconnection (i.e., feelings of loneliness; Boomsma, Willemsen, Dolan, Hawkley, & Cacioppo, 2005) just as people differ in sensitivity to physical pain. Ostracism or objective isolation in most species is associated with an early death (Williams, 2001). In humans, the chronic feeling of social isolation, even when the person remains among others, is associated with significant mental and physical disorders (Cacioppo & Patrick, 2008). Chronic hunger, thirst, and pain can also have deleterious effects for, like loneliness, their adaptive value lies in their effects as acute signals, not as chronic conditions. The opposite of feeling hunger, thirst, pain, or loneliness is feeling normal, and this is the state in which most people exist most of the time.

REFLECTION AND RECAPITULATION

Bob Cialdini is the master of social influence, and he expanded the science and the application of social influence in works ranging from verbal attitude conditioning (Insko & Cialdini, 1969) and low-balling (Cialdini, Cacioppo, Basset, & Miller, 1978) to social (Goldstein & Cialdini, 2007) and descriptive norms. Indeed, a perusal of Cialdini's list of publications reveals that the word "influence" appears more than 50 times. Cialdini's book, *Influence*, has been translated into 26 languages and has sold over 2 million copies. Cialdini's six weapons of social influence are: (1) reciprocity—people tend to return favors; (2) commitment and consistency—people who make a commitment are more likely to exhibit the behavior; (3) social proof—people are likely to do things they see others doing; (4) authority—people will tend to do what they are instructed to do by figures of authority; (5) liking—people are more easily influenced by people they like; and (6) scarcity—people value things they perceive to be scarce. Cialdini certainly influenced one of us (JTC) using a combination of these weapons. Why is social influence so ubiquitous, multifarious, and effective?

Early in our history as a species, we survived and prospered only by banding together—in couples, in families, in tribes—to provide mutual protection and assistance. We review evidence that social influence in humans includes top-down processes operating on biological predispositions to connect, care for, and seek the affirmation of others. The aversive state of loneliness operates at an individual level to shape and maintain meaningful social connections, and at the group level by promoting the consideration of and concern for others. For instance, subjecting young individuals to a temporary period of isolation, as in shunning, ostracism, or time-out, is typically sufficiently aversive that these individuals become more considerate members after being reintegrated into the group. As a result, hominid groups developed greater capacities to respond collectively to new challenges and to rebound from stresses. The influence of such a selection process is strengthened when offspring have long periods of abject dependency because simply surviving to reproduce is not sufficient to ensure one's genes make it into the gene pool. Thus, selfish genes led to a sculpting of a social brain and to social influence processes that are far subtler than have been appreciated in experimental social psychology.

ACKNOWLEDGMENTS

This work was supported by National Institute of Aging Program Project Grant No. PO1 AG18911 & RO1 AG034052-01.

CHAPTER 10

Social Influence on Reproductive Behavior in Humans and Other Species

ABRAHAM P. BUUNK, SHELLI L. DUBBS,
AND JAN A.R.A.M. VAN HOOFF

When we think of social influence, we think of Milgram's authority figure instructing a subject to shock a fellow subject; of Asch's groups, in which the subject hears other subjects say a short line is longer than it appears; or of an advertiser loudly touting the advantages of one detergent over others. All these forms of influence are mediated by words, and indeed most tactics of social influence described by Cialdini (2008) would be impossible without language or are more powerful when language is used. According to Pinker and Bloom (1992), humans' unique capacity of language has played an important role in a cognitive arms race in which individuals tried to influence others for their own interests. "In all cultures, human interactions are mediated by attempts at persuasion and argument" (p. 484). Nevertheless, social influence is not at all restricted to the human species, and animals can communicate about their "ideas" without using words. Consider the following example. "I have a pool in mind. Let's meet there at noon?" Using nonverbal cues, that is what a male hamadryas baboon (*Papio hamadryas*) proposed to the other males of his clan during the early morning gathering. Such gatherings take place daily before the different clans set out on divergent foraging journeys. When Alex Stolba, one of the collaborators in a long-term field project of Zürich primatologist Hans Kummer (1992), saw these daily ceremonies, he wondered what this was about. He eventually concluded that he had witnessed "voting sessions" about the daily itinerary. By carefully recording nonverbal gestures used by the baboons, Stolba was able to deduce that a male envisages a pre-ferred drinking destination and can use a series of gestures to invoke a common image in his fellows, who now judge whether this destination is to their liking. Another example of social influence in nonhuman species was observed in blue tits which, after seeing others prick the aluminum capsules of milk bottles and noting that those were drinking, flew to similar bottles only to find out that there is no food . . . until they discovered by trial and error that they could prick the capsules. By such emulation, this nasty habit (at least for those who bought the bottles) spread all over England in the 1950s (Fisher & Hinde, 1949).

Social influence is a necessary and essential part of animal life, consider-ing that conflicts of interests between animals with different goals are inevi-table. In the remaining part of this chapter, we will focus on a less well-known form of influence, but one that has potentially profound significance—that is, how individuals may influence the *reproductive behavior* of other indi-viduals of the same species for their own benefit. We will present evidence that such influence is a common occurrence in the animal kingdom, for instance by trying to prevent others from reproducing, by forcing the other sex into reproducing, or by inducing one's children to assist in raising their siblings. Particularly, we will show that human reproduction is subject to similar influence from kin. However, as we will argue, humans appear to be unique in that parents are often highly influential in determining the mate choice of their children. This type of social influence—so relevant for survival and reproduction—has, remarkably, not received much attention in the social psychological literature (although anthropologists and sociol-ogists have noted this for long).

SOCIAL INFLUENCE ON OTHER INDIVIDUALS' REPRODUCTIVE BEHAVIOR IN THE ANIMAL KINGDOM

In many polygynous species, males actively try to prevent other males from reproducing and attaining exclusive access to females. This is particu-larly likely to occur when either groups of females or territories can be defended by a single male. In such cases, males, either directly or indi-rectly, will influence the reproductive strategies and fitness of other males. For example, in elephants seals (genus *Mirounga*), males compete with each other by trumpeting loudly, rearing up and pushing against each others' chests while simultaneously attempting to bite the neck, head, and flippers of their opponent (Haley, Deutsch, & le Bouef, 1994). The winners of elephant seal bouts, for example, win a big payoff: By becoming socially dominant, they can gain access to a harem of females. Subordinate males, on the other hand, are relegated to attempting to mate with females that are either going out to sea or are on the periphery of another male's harem. Such attempts to mate are usually disrupted by the dominant male. This is especially true if the female protests the attempted mount and draws the attention of the dominant male (Cox & Le Boeuf, 1977). As a result, many males in polygynously mating mammal species, such as elephant seals, are often directly excluded from mating.

Among spotted hyenas (*Crocuta crocuta*), social influence tactics aimed at fostering one's reproductive success are a basic part of life for both male and female clan members. The offspring of higher-ranking females have an advantage in that they grow faster, have higher survival rates, and reproduce at a younger age than do offspring of more subordinate females (Hofer & East, 2003). Therefore, males have developed an arsenal of strategies to try to manipulate the high-ranking female into mating, ranging from affiliative behaviors to aggression, infanticide and baiting (i.e., groupwise harassing of a female). Intriguingly, females have developed their own tactics to counter the various male strategies. For example, in 35% of cases of baiting, the harassed female counterattacks with the assistance of other clan members, and any male attempting to commit infanticide is halted. Even though females typically prefer to mate with males that have tenure within their group (East, Burke, Wilhelm, & Hofer, 2003), they may use strategies that prevent any one male from monopolizing reproduction. For example, females engage in polyandry and mate before they are receptive and while pregnant. These strategies serve to confuse paternity, so that no male within the group can be certain of their genetic relatedness to offspring. It is suggested that females engage in these tactics to reduce the risk of infanticide by males.

A different type of social influence on the reproductive behavior of other individuals to foster one's own reproductive success is found among so-called cooperative breeders. For example, in the sociable weaver (*Philetairus socius*), parents lower the cost of reproduction by retaining offspring that then serve as helpers-at-the-nest. Conversely, helpers benefit by increasing the survival of nondescendant kin (Covas, Doutrelant, & du Plessis, 2004). Sociable weavers are considered cooperative breeders, in which individuals help raise offspring other than their own. Control over other individuals' reproductive behavior is perhaps most well developed in this type of species. Groups of cooperative breeders can take many forms, ranging from groups composed of parents, their adult offspring, and dependent offspring to groups composed of unrelated adults.

Cooperative breeding is found in multiple classes of animals including insects, fish, and birds, as well as mammals (Rusell & Lummaa, 2009), and may occur particularly when the energetic cost of reproduction may be so high that offspring would not survive without help of others (Creel & Creel, 1991). For example, among African wild dogs (*Lycaon pictus*), the energetic demands of reproduction are extremely high, and only the dominant female is guaranteed to give birth to a litter of pups once a year (Creel, Creel, Mils, & Monfort, 1997). The subordinates contribute to the reproductive success of the dominant female by provisioning her with food during lactation, acting as pup guards at the den while the rest of the pack is hunting, and regurgitating food for the pups (Courchamp, Rasmussen, & Macdonald, 2002; McNutt & Silk, 2008). Most packs display a high level of relatedness, thus subordinates that engage in helping behavior gain benefits through inclusive fitness (Girman, Mills, Geffen, & Wayne, 1997). In general, there is a more stable dominance hierarchy among females than among males. However, dominant individuals of both sexes use aggression to deter the more subordinate pack members from mating. Interestingly, the dominant female and the highest ranking males are significantly more aggressive than subordinate pack members during the breeding season. These behavioral differences are underpinned by hormonal changes in males and females. For the duration of the breeding season, it is not unusual for subordinate members to suffer bite wounds on their face and neck from attacks delivered by the alpha and beta individuals (Creel et al., 1997).

There are also cases in which males actively try to induce their son to abandon his own mating behavior and serve as a helper at the nest. For example, among white fronted bee-eaters (*Merops bullockoides*), it is the female that typically disperses, while the male will stay and help at the nest. Offspring will remain with their parental group (clan) until 1 to 2 years of age. Males may attempt to reproduce within their clan, but they may be harassed by other males, which prevents them from breeding. Interestingly, it is the father that harasses the son. The father does this in an attempt to get the son to abandon his mating prospects and to instead serve as a helper at the father's nest. The harassment used by the father is highly successful at manipulating the son; fathers were successful at recruiting their son as a helper 62%–68% of the time (Emlem & Wrege, 1992). Within this species, having a helper at the nest greatly increases the average number of young fledged. The direct benefit gained by the parent outweighs the inclusive benefit if the son would have bred on his own.

In meerkats (*Suricata suricatta*), subordinates of both sexes are induced to help rear the young of the dominant pair, dominants are very effective in influencing others: and this has a positive affect on the dominant pairs' reproductive output (Spong, Hodge, Young, & Clutton-Brock, 2008). Groups of meerkats may consist of up to 50 individuals and are often composed of a dominant breeding pair and their immature offspring, as well as mature individuals that are usually related to the dominant pair. Just as in African wild dogs, reproduction is quite costly for meerkats. Thus, it is important that the dominant pair control the reproduction of the subordinates. One particularly drastic way the dominant female does this is through the use of infanticide. If a dominant female is pregnant, and a subordinate female gives birth, she will kill, and even consume, the subordinate's offspring (Young & Clutton-Brock, 2006). By doing so, the dominant female ensures that the bulk of resources and care will go toward her own offspring, thus maximizing their chances of survival. This is important to the dominant female as there is a high rate of litter failure. In addition, the dominant female is more likely than subordinates to give birth when no other females are pregnant. She accomplishes this by aggressively evicting subordinates from the group when she is in the later stages of her pregnancy. The stress of being evicted can lead to abortion if the subordinate is pregnant herself. Hence, abortion rates are significantly higher among subordinates than among dominants. The evicted females stay on the fringes of the territory and most will eventually return to their group, although some disperse permanently while others fall prey to other carnivores (Clutton-Brock, Hodge, & Flower, 2008). Taking all of these factors together, 80% of the pups that survive to at least 1 month of age belong to the dominant female (Clutton-Brock et al., 2001).

Perhaps one of the most efficient examples in the animal kingdom limiting the reproductive behavior of other individuals occurs in the naked mole-rat (*Heterocephalus glaber*, see Faulkes & Bennett, 2001, for a review). Astonishingly, more than 99% of individuals never breed. Only the dominant female (the queen) engages in reproduction, normally with a single male (although it is not uncommon for her to mate with two or even three males). A female attains the status of queen by fighting with her rivals within the colony. Afterward, she takes great measures to reproductively suppress members of both sexes from breeding. It is interesting to notice in this species how far-reaching the effect of social influence may be. That is, infertility is socially induced—mere social contact with the queen is enough to change the reproductive potential of subordinate group members. Ovulation is blocked in females, and nonbreeding males have a reduced number of sperm that are also reduced in motility. Although individual reproductive suppression seems a high cost to pay for being part of a mole-rat colony, there is a payoff—because the subordinates are closely related to the queen, they have a partial share in her reproductive success.

THE HUMAN CASE

Just as in the animal examples, humans also exert considerable influence on the reproductive behavior of others. For instance, men and women compete using various influential tactics ranging from physical aggression to malicious gossip. Despotic and religious leaders may try to monopolize the females in the group as well as manipulate the reproductive potential of subordinate males (Betzig, 1986). In intergroup warfare, males and children of the enemy group are killed while females are often taken as mates (Wrangham & Peterson, 1996).

In addition to influence from the same and the opposite sex in humans, there is a considerable degree of kin influence on reproduction. Just as in naked mole-rats and other cooperative breeders, kin, especially parents, might try to prevent some of their offspring from reproducing. Under certain conditions, this tactic is beneficial if it guarantees the fitness of the remaining offspring. Parents who pushed a son into the clergy—and a life of celibacy—might be promoting the fitness of their other offspring. This is especially true if parents have landholding and resources that they do not want to divide up among multiple sons. In this situation, it is more beneficial to concentrate the resources into one son, giving him a higher mate value. Indeed, a study on the family background of Irish Catholic priests born between 1867 and 1911 found that priests were more likely to originate from families with more sons than the national average, and from landholding families, especially from families with landholdings greater in size and wealth than the local average (Deady, Smith, Kent, & Dunbar, 2006).

Influencing One's Offspring's Choice of Mates

Unlike other species, humans are unique in that they not only tend to influence the reproductive behavior of their offspring, but also their offspring's actual *mate choice* (e.g., Dubbs & Buunk, 2010a). Data from 190 hunter-gatherer societies reveal that, in the vast majority of these societies, marriage was arranged by parents and other kin; only in 4% of societies was courtship the primary form of marriage (Apostolou, 2007). This is significant because it is thought that hunter-gatherer societies are representative of the conditions in which humans evolved. This suggests that, at some point during human evolution, parents began to feel that their reproductive interests might be better served by intervening in their offspring's mate choice than by leaving choice up to their offspring. This may be especially true for mothers, as they are more highly invested in their children and are more certain of their genetic relatedness to their children than are fathers (Buss & Schmitt, 1993; DeKay, 1995; Euler & Weitzal, 1996). In addition, women undergo menopause and lose their ability to reproduce directly (Timiras & Valcana, 1972), which may have in part resulted from the fact that it might be more fruitful to invest in one's grandchildren than to produce new offspring oneself. This would have resulted in a strong interest in influencing the mate choice of one's offspring. Interestingly, it has been noted that mothers tend to play a larger role in the lives of their children, including meddling in their children's romantic lives (Bates, 1942; Faulkner & Schaller, 2007) as well engaging in grandparenting (Laham et al., 2005; Michalski & Shackelford, 2005). Research has also found that a poor-quality mate choice is perceived by daughters as being overall more unacceptable to the mother relative to the father (Dubbs & Buunk, 2010b).

This is not to say that fathers do not play a significant role in their children's mating decisions. In societies in which parents arrange the marriages of their children, it is often fathers who make the decisons (Apsotolou, 2007). Fathers may seek to establish alliances or boost their own social status via their children's mating relationships. Supporting this notion is research from Dubbs & Buunk (2010b), which found that daughters perceived that their fathers would, relative to their mothers, have a stronger negative reaction to boyfriends with traits related to low social status, such as being poor, coming from a lower social class than self, having a low education, and being of a different ethnicity. As noted by Trivers (1974), "Parents may also use an offspring's marriage to cement an alliance with an unrelated family or group, and insofar as such an alliance is beneficial to kin of the parent in addition to the offspring itself, parents are expected to encourage such marriages more often than the offspring would prefer" (p. 261).

Parental Influence in Collectivist versus Individualist Societies

In line with the foregoing, parental influence on mate choice appears to be the norm in most cultures throughout history, and even within Western society (e.g., Murstein, 1974; Sprecher &Chandak, 1992). Indeed, 50 years ago, Goode (1959) pointed to the many social influence tactics shown by parents in this context when he observed that "parents threaten, cajole, wheedle, bribe, and persuade their children to 'go with the right people' during both the early love play and the later courtship phases" (p. 45). Although parental influence on mate choice seems a part of the human evolutionary legacy, especially collectivist cultures such as China, India, and Japan have historically, and even presently, been characterized by a high degree of parental influence on their children's mate choice (e.g., Applbaum, 1995; Xie & Combs, 1996). In contrast, romantic love—which represents individual interest—is considered more important as a basis for marriage in more individualistic cultures such as the United States (e.g., Reiss, 1980). Throughout the Middle Ages, young men and women in Western Europe had a level of freedom in their mating behavior that surpassed what is found even today in collectivist societies such as China (de Moor & van Zanden, 2006).

In a series of studies, we developed a scale to assess the degree of parental influence on mate choice and administered this to a variety of samples. As expected, norms favoring parental influence were much more strongly endorsed in Kurdistan, Iraq (a highly collectivist culture) than in the Netherlands (a highly individualistic culture). In a similar study, perceived parental influence on mate choice was, as expected, higher among East Asian Canadians (a relatively collectivist group) than among European Canadians (a relatively individualistic group) (Buunk, Park, & Duncan, 2010). In addition, in a study among international students from 30 different European, Asian, and African countries, we found that the more collectivistic the culture they came from (as assessed by Gelfand, Bhawuk, Nishii, & Bechtold, 2004), the more parental control over mate choice they perceived in their culture.

Although parental influence is stronger in collectivistic cultures, parental influence over mate choice still occurs in individualistic cultures, albeit to a lesser degree. As noted by Bates in 1942, "Parents who are really indifferent to courtship activities of their children are rare" (p. 484). In more individualistic societies parents may use indirect ways to influence their children's mating decisions. For example, it is common for parents to monitor their children's behavior and to set restrictions on dating. This may include setting a curfew or not allowing children to engage in certain behaviors with opposite sex peers, such as spending the night at the house of a boyfriend or girlfriend. In some cases, parents may try to shape their children's social circle to ensure that their children are associating with people the parents would consider acceptable (Das Gupta, 1997; Faulkner & Schaller, 2007; Fleishman & Buss, 2008.) Additionally, it is also possible for parents to effectively transmit their own values about mate choice to their children. This often happens over the course of years, through the parents giving advice, having conversations about marriage, and responding either positively or negatively to their children's dates and romantic partners. By subtly molding their children's preferences, parents can trust that their children will make a good mate choice on their own (Baier & Wampler, 2008; Bates, 1942; Riley, 1994).

Parental Influence on Daughters versus Sons

Importantly, when it comes to relationships and reproduction, parents tend to place more limits on female children. Daughters are more closely monitored than sons, and parents tend to set stricter rules concerning dating and relationships for their daughters. For example, Perilloux, Fleischman and Buss (2008) found that daughters rated their parent's approval of behaviors, such as kissing a romantic partner, having sex in one's home, and having sex elsewhere, significantly lower than did sons. Correspondingly, parents were significantly more upset to learn that their daughters were sexually active compared to their sons. In addition, parents tend to set more restrictions concerning dating, and they give daughters less freedom of choice to choose their own partner than they do sons (Faulkner & Schaller, 2007; Perilloux et al., 2008). There are various reasons for this higher degree of control of daughters. Making a poor-quality mate choice is more detrimental for women, who have a lower limit on their number of potential offspring; parents can be certain that they are actually genetically related to grandchildren from a daughter; the costs of the risk of pregnancy can't be avoided for the female's family, but might be for the male's; and the female's family is more likely to make investments in a daughter's children.

Parent–Offspring Conflict over Mate Choice

The fact that parents attempt to influence their children's mating decisions implies that parents and children do not completely agree over what type of person would be an ideal mate. Indeed, if parents' in-law preferences simply mirrored their offspring's mate preferences, there would have been little reason for parents across cultures to go through the trouble of attempting to control their offspring's mating behavior. In fact, there are good reasons to expect differing opinions between offspring and parents, a number of which follow from Trivers' (1974) parent–offspring conflict theory. Essentially, each offspring attempts to maximize parental investment in itself, sometimes to the detriment of their parents or their siblings. Parents, on the other hand, may better serve their reproductive success by distributing resources more evenly across their offspring, at least in the case that offspring do not differ in their fitness potential.

Recently, we reintroduced the notion of parent–offspring conflict over mate choice (Buunk, Parks, & Dubbs, 2008). That is, preferences of parents and offspring may clash because a specific choice of mate may have different consequences for parents and for offspring. It has been noted for quite some time that, in many species, mate choice is based on at least two considerations: first, the genetic quality of the potential mate (e.g., the absence of bad mutations), and, second, the potential of the mate to make parental investments in one's offspring (e.g., Bateson, 1983). When a child opts primarily for a mate with genetic quality (someone who is highly attractive or creative [cf. Miller, 2001; Nettle, 2007]), parents may perceive that this child runs the risk of attracting a low-investing partner. Consequently, parents might expect that they themselves may have to provide many investments in the resulting offspring, which may be reduce the investments in other children and grandchildren. Moreover, they may feel that, when they themselves die, the survival of their grandchildren is at risk. As parents are thus expected to have evolved preferences for offspring's mates that minimize their own investments, their own genetic interests may be relatively better served if their children acquire highly investing mates (who will invest resources in their grandchildren). Children, however, have an interest in trying to maximize the investments from their parents and may perceive that they would be best off with a mate with good genes and with parents who invest in their grandchildren. In addition, parents' conflicting preferences may also reflect a desire for in-laws who promote ingroup and family cohesion, who raise the status of the family, who will help them in their old age, and who will socialize their grandchildren in a culturally appropriate manner. The implication of this reasoning is that any conflict that exists between parents and children in mate choice is likely to revolve around mate characteristics that connote genetic quality versus parental investment and cooperation with the ingroup.

To assess this type of parent–offspring conflict, we developed a methodology to closely track the mating tradeoffs: Individuals of mating age were presented with a list of traits, formulated to represent the undesirable variant of trait variables (e.g., physically unattractive, different religious beliefs) and were asked to indicate whether this would be *more unacceptable* to themselves or to their parents. Factor analyses showed that the characteristics representing parental investment and cooperation with the ingroup and the characteristics signaling genetic quality were indeed independent factors. Data gathered across several samples from divergent cultural backgrounds (Americans, Dutch, Kurdish, Uruguayans, Argentineans, and exchange students from different countries mentioned previously) provided a consistent picture: Most of the undesirable variants of mate characteristics that connote a lack of genetic quality were perceived by the participants as more unacceptable to the participants themselves, and most of the undesirable variants of mate characteristics that connote parental investment and cooperation with the ingroup were perceived by the participants and by parents themselves as more unacceptable to the parents (Buunk et al., 2008; Buunk & Castro Solano, 2010; Dubbs & Buunk, 2010a; Park, Dubbs & Buunk, 2009). Characteristics that recurred as especially unacceptable to children included lacking a sense of humor, being physically unattractive, and having a bad smell. Characteristics that recurred as especially unacceptable to parents included being divorced and having a different ethnic and religious background.

CONCLUSION

We have tried to demonstrate how pervasive social influence is in the animal kingdom when it comes to fostering one's reproductive interests. In a wide variety of ways, individuals in many species try to block the reproductive possibilities of conspecifics to the benefit of their own reproductive potential. Remarkably, humans often seem to do the *reverse* of what we see in other species. Instead of inducing their offspring to forsake reproduction, they would rather induce their offspring to reproduce—albeit only when the right type of mate is chosen.

This emerging line of research may have various implications. For example, parents will often urge their children to get married and have children; parents will usually try to prevent their children, and especially their daughters, from exposure to undesirable mates; parents may spend more money on the wedding of their child with someone from the ingroup; and, possibly, children will be less likely to reproduce when their parents have less opportunities to control them, for instance because they live far away, or when they perceive that their parents have few resources to invest. Our work may also explain the numerous stories—like that of Romeo and Juliet—that can be found in the literature on the passionate love relationships between children that parents forbid and try to terminate. With their elaborate language, humans have many more possibilities to influence others than other species. Language may have evolved to an important extent by enhancing humans' possibilities for social influence. In the large groups in which humans live, being able to influence others would seem crucial for being able to deal with the many potential conflicts that may arise. In general, trying to influence others and resisting as well as accepting influence from others are crucial and necessary features of all social life. Cialdini's seminal work on social influence focused on humans. Although we have focused on some of the ways in which individuals in various species may influence others' reproductive success, it is clear that social influence applies not only to a wide variety of species, but also to a wide variety of social behaviors.

CHAPTER 11

Egoism or Altruism?

Hard-Nosed Experiments and

Deep Philosophical Questions

STEPHANIE L. BROWN AND JON K. MANER

Science is what you know. Philosophy is what you don't know.
—Bertrand Russell

After the 2010 earthquake in Haiti, Sean Penn put aside his acting career and flew down to Haiti to manage a camp providing humanitarian aid. Hundreds of survivors have benefited from his presence. In 2000, Bill Gates and his wife Melinda established the Bill & Melinda Gates Foundation to promote global health and human development. As of 2008, they had given over $28 billion dollars to charity. In 2010, Faron Hall, a homeless man living in Manitoba Canada, nearly died when he jumped into a freezing river to save a struggling teen whom he had never met. Both made it out alive. These examples, in addition to countless others, paint quite a magnanimous portrait of human nature. Human beings are capable of immense acts of kindness, heroism, and generosity.

But do such seemingly selfless actions reflect the existence of true altruism? Do people ever really act out of a purely selfless desire to enhance the welfare of others? Or, instead, is it possible that even extraordinary acts of kindness such as those of Sean Penn, Bill Gates, and Faron Hall are ultimately guided by self-centered motives?

Whether or not true altruism exists is a question that has intrigued philosophers for centuries. The question delves so deep into what it means to be human that it has taken on an almost mythical quality. And, typically, such questions tend not to be tackled by scientists, perhaps because they are so big that they seem unanswerable. But sometimes the division between science and philosophy becomes blurred, particularly when an intrepid scientist endeavors to tackle one of those really big questions, the kind that addresses a central aspect of basic human nature. The question of true altruism is one of those really big questions, and Bob Cialdini is one of those intrepid scientists.

In trying to answer questions about the existence of true altruism, Cialdini inspired in us and many others a desire to ask foundational questions that cut straight to central issues in human social life. Cialdini doesn't bite off small pieces of the pie. He has helped bring answers to some of the most fundamental questions about human nature. In this chapter, we reflect on how social psychologists like Bob Cialdini provide us with a first-hand picture of how rigorous scientific methods can help people tackle some of the most foundational questions about human behavior. After reviewing some of the early research informing the debate about the existence of pure altruism, we discuss more recent work designed to further expand our understanding of the motives that cause people to help others.

A TALE ABOUT CIALDINI, EGOISIM, AND ALTRUISM

During our undergraduate years, both of us were fascinated by big questions about human nature. But, upon graduating and looking toward our future academic careers, we realized that certain treasured pastimes, such as pondering the existence of altruism, free will, and the meaning of life, would be left by the wayside in favor of doing more practical things, like rigorous experiments that would land us publications in empirical journals.

Or, so we thought. . . . As we embarked on our graduate school careers in psychology, we quickly found ourselves in the midst of one of social psychology's great debates. And this debate involved one of life's biggest questions: the existence of true altruism. In one corner, Professor Robert Cialdini, the world famous author of *Social Influence*, suggested that true altruism might be an illusion—that apparently altruistic acts might instead be caused by self-centered motivations. According to Cialdini, most, if not all, prosocial actions are caused ultimately by egoistic motivations such as the desire to avoid guilt or to enhance one's own mood. In the other corner,

Debate

Professor Daniel Batson, of the University of Kansas who, armed with his empathy-altruism hypothesis, proclaimed altruism alive and well in human prosocial behavior. For two aspiring behavioral scientists, the opportunity to play a small part in this debate was an exciting prospect indeed.

According to Batson, altruism exists insofar as prosocial actions are motivated by a genuinely selfless desire to benefit another person (e.g., Batson, 1991). Batson argued that truly selfless acts could arise out of a feeling of empathic concern for another person. Seeing a young child in pain or distress, for example, could elicit a sense of compassion and sympathy that leads the observer to want to help, not for any selfish reason, but instead because he or she truly wants to benefit the child and end her suffering. Across a large number of empirical studies, Batson amassed evidence for the empathy-altruism hypothesis by showing that factors that increase empathy (e.g., perspective-taking, shared group membership, personal similarity) also tend to increase the likelihood of aiding a person in need of help (Batson, 1998). Having research participants imagine what a person in distress is currently feeling, for example, dramatically increases the likelihood of helping (e.g., Batson et al., 1997).

Cialdini, on the other hand, proposed that actions apparently motivated by selfless desires may in fact be motivated by more egoistic factors. Cialdini argued against the existence of pure altruism, initially on the basis that witnessing an individual in need provokes a variety of aversive feelings in potential helpers (such as sadness, guilt, and personal distress). Using rigorous experimental methods, Cialdini demonstrated that sometimes it is this desire to reduce one's own negative feelings, rather than the desire to benefit the other person, that motivates one to help. In one clever experiment, for example, Cialdini asked research participants to take a pill (actually a placebo) that ostensibly would "freeze" their current mood in its current state. Under those circumstances, people were less likely to help a person in need, presumably because they figured that acts of kindness wouldn't enhance their mood. In this sense, when people help others, they are really helping themselves, and thus the act is not truly selfless (Manucia, Baumann, & Cialdini, 1984).

Batson countered that, even if an individual experiences self-rewards such as enhanced mood or relief from guilt from behaving prosocially, the action is altruistic if it is initially motivated by a desire to help the other person; that is, although self-rewards may be the consequence, they are not necessarily the cause of helping behavior. Thus, both camps agreed on the fact that whether or not true altruism exists comes down to what factors motivate the prosocial action; what comes before the action, not after. What the camps disagreed on, however, was what those motivators actually are.

Our own small part in this debate involved a construct called "oneness"—the notion that our sense of self can include overlap with other people. A prerequisite for altruistic motivation is that the self and other be perceived as separate entities (Batson, 1991, 1998). Cialdini et al. (1997) reasoned that aiding someone with whom one feels a sense of merged identity cannot be viewed as truly selfless because, in such a case, helping another would be helping oneself. Not only do mergings of self and other occur at the psychological level (e.g., Aron, Aron, & Smollan, 1992; Aron Aron, Tudor, & Nelson, 1991), but self–other overlap is also real in the genetic sense: Our own genes reside not only within our own skins but also within the skins of related others (e.g., siblings, parents, offspring). Indeed, the notion of Oneness fits with Hamilton's (1964) principle of inclusive fitness, which explains why helping a relative is genetically self-promoting. In terms of both psychological identity and biological substance, then, there are circumstances in which full self–other separation does not hold, making it difficult (if not impossible) to detach altruistic from egoistic motivation.

Cialdini again used rigorous experimental methods to show that many cases of apparent altruism involve people helping that part of themselves that is merged into their representation of the person being helped. He used methods (e.g., perspective-taking, personal similarity) typically used to increase empathy toward a person in need and showed that, indeed, measures of empathy did appear to mediate effects on helping. However, once the helper's degree of oneness with the target was statistically controlled, it was oneness, not empathy, that mediated effects on helping (Cialdini et al., 1997; Maner et al., 2002). Such findings provided a basis for again arguing that seemingly selfless acts were caused by egoistic, not altruistic, motivators.

The use of experimental methods also allowed us to try resolving the Batson–Cialdini debate by focusing on the level of cost involved in the helping act. We demonstrated that empathy might cause helping behavior, but only if the help was without cost to the helper—what we termed "superficial" helping (Neuberg et al., 1997). Our findings confirmed Batson's earlier work demonstrating that empathic concern does not predict helping behavior under conditions of substantial cost (Batson, O'Quin, Fultz, Vanderplas, & Isen, 1983). The issue of cost is a critical one, because it raises important questions about whether true altruism is meaningful if it disappears under conditions of personal cost. As Batson and his colleagues characterized the problem, empathy-based altruism may be "a fragile flower easily crushed by self-concern." (p. 718) Although this qualification to the empathy-altruism hypothesis has been largely ignored by researchers in other disciplines, who credit empathy with motivating high-cost helping (e.g., Preston & de Waal, 2002), it nevertheless puts in bold relief the need to develop an integrative model of prosocial behavior that specifies the types of behaviors for which egoistic versus altruistic motivations may play a causal role.

IS CARE-GIVING A FUNDAMENTAL HUMAN MOTIVE?

As originally applied by Cialdini, the concept of self–other merging reflects a proximate egoistic mechanism that motivates people to help. As students of Cialdini, however, we had learned the importance of questioning our own theoretical assumptions, and this led us to consider some deeper questions about oneness and prosocial behavior. For example, is it correct to presume, as we did (Neuberg et al., 1997), that oneness is a "nonaltruistic motivator" as opposed to an altruistic one (p. 510)? What is the underlying cause of oneness, and what is its function? And beyond questions about oneness, we wondered: Why does helping others seem to have so many benefits for the self? Why does helping behavior create a positive mood and relieve distress? Why does seeing others' pain make us feel distressed in the first place? From an evolutionary perspective, one could argue that we feel distress upon encountering a family member in pain, because our family shares our genes; helping a family member is like helping ourselves, at least in a genetic sense. But many remarkable prosocial acts are aimed at helping people other than family, such as friends and even complete strangers. How are we to reconcile the knowledge that soldiers in the Iraq war left their own families to fight for the United States? Why would someone like Faron Hall risk his life to save a complete stranger? Neither kin selection (helping to pass on common genes) nor reciprocal altruism (helping to receive help in the future) seemed to completely explain these types of sacrifice, for which the costs of helping appear to far outweigh any immediate or long-term benefits to the self.

We began to revisit Cialdini's idea that evolutionary biology could be used to inform the motivational basis for helping behavior. According to Cialdini, a sense of merged identity or oneness reflects a psychological mechanism by which individuals recognize kin and those likely to reciprocate. And, if this is true, the motivation for costly helping would conveniently occur under conditions in which it is adaptive to sacrifice: under circumstances of shared genes (i.e., kin selection theory, Hamilton, 1964) or when others are likely to return favors (Axelrod & Hamilton, 1981).

Yet, our work had already shown that oneness also powerfully predicts helping among friends and even acquaintances or near-strangers (Cialdini et al., 1997). Such findings led us to hypothesize that the concept of oneness might be capturing something fundamental about human relationships— about the importance of underlying social bonds and their implications for human caregiving. We wondered whether the experience of feeling bonded to another person—the glue that binds social relationships together—could be the motivational mechanism for costly helping.

With this new view of social bonds (as reflected in perceptions of oneness) in hand, we asked ourselves, what can we learn about social bonds if we assume they evolved to motivate helping behavior? As evolutionary psychologists, we reasoned that, at a minimum, social bonds must be capable of resolving self–other motivational conflict in favor of helping another person. We reasoned that social bonds were designed by evolution to help individuals inhibit self-centered impulses in ways that favor the motivation to give help to others.

This led us to wonder about the conditions under which costly helping might produce fitness advantages, in the evolutionary sense. The answer became one of the fundamental tenets of selective investment theory (S. Brown, 1999; S. Brown & R. Brown, 2006; R. Brown & S. Brown, 2006). According to the theory, the significant costs of allocating resources to nonrelatives or nonreciprocators means that social bonds—because they motivate sacrifice—must emerge selectively with recipients who are not likely to exploit altruistic tendencies and with recipients who are in a position to enhance the fitness of the helper. These conditions are met under states of fitness interdependence between two or more individuals. Fitness interdependence refers to circumstances in which (a) efforts to contribute to the well-being of an interdependent partner cause increases in the fitness outcomes for both, and (b) a recipient's dependence on the caregiver reduces the likelihood of exploitation, because exploitation by a dependent other compromises the cheater as much as the helper. Fitness interdependence clearly exists in the case of biological kin, who share genes with the helper. Fitness interdependence can also be signaled by the presence of a reciprocal relationship. But, even beyond kinship and reciprocity, fitness interdependence can produce immense acts of caregiving. One example is circumstances in which individuals perceive that they have common fate related to a survival outcome—e.g., soldiers during wartime or neighbors during an earthquake. One implication of selective investment theory is that, because the vulnerability of the person in need implies a low probability of exploitation, genuine signs of need trigger remarkable instances of sacrifice even for strangers (Brown, Brown, & Preston, in press).

Selective investment theory recasts the functional significance of close, bonded relationships as motivational mechanisms that enable individuals to give away their resources to others. It suggests further that the triggers for social bonds include cues for dependence in others, as opposed to the more traditional view that one's own needs are sufficient to cause individuals to become bonded to others. These propositions are controversial (e.g., Batson, 2006) however, they have acquired increasing empirical support (e.g., Brown, Nesse, Vinoku, & Smith, 2003; Poulin et al., 2010; Brown et al., 2009a). Selective investment theory implies that humans have been endowed with an evolved mechanism for directing help to those in need, contingent on cues for underlying states of fitness interdependence (Brown, Brown, & Preston, in press). Thus, selective investment theory suggests that caregiving is indeed a fundamental human motivation.

Selective investment theory challenges traditional beliefs in rational self-interest as the principal cause of prosocial behavior. Hedonic views of human nature are often reinforced by gene-centric evolutionary theorists, who emphasize that people's actions ultimately boil down to promoting the success of their own genes, rather than the welfare of others. Indeed, the heavy reproductive costs of possible exploitation have led many evolutionary psychologists to summarily dismiss the idea that humans can be motivated to behave altruistically in the absence of clear benefits to personal survival or reproduction. However, if, according to selective investment theory, social bonds selectively emerge when the benefit to fitness is high and the threat of exploitation is low, then new, interesting, and testable questions arise, some of which have led to important discoveries about how helping behavior influences physiology.

IMPLICATIONS OF SOCIAL BONDING AND
PROSOCIAL BEHAVIOR FOR PHYSICAL HEALTH

Theoretical work on the evolutionary significance of social bonds led us to examine new ways of thinking about the influence of close relationships on physical health. Selective investment theory suggests that social bonds that motivate high-cost helping are instantiated in the brain, and that the underlying neural and hormonal features of social bonds and their consequent effect on prosocial behavior have implications for physical health. For example, the hormonal basis of social bonds and helping behavior includes the neuropeptide oxytocin, which not only triggers helping behavior, but also has restorative physiological properties. For example, oxytocin down-regulates hypothalamic-pituitary-adrenal (HPA; stress) axis activity (Carter, 1998) and lowers levels of the stress hormone cortisol, which can be harmful to health with prolonged exposure (Sapolsky, Krey, & McEwen, 2000). Oxytocin is also related to immune function as it is involved in cellular repair, storage of cell nutrients, and cellular growth (Heaphy & Dutton, in press). Thus, bonding and helping behaviors triggered by the bond may be good for one's physical health. Indeed, there is a robust association between social relationships and health, such that people in close relationships are healthier and live longer than do those who are socially isolated (House, Landis, & Umberson, 1988).

These mind–body connections between social bonds, helping behavior, and physiology led us to consider the intriguing possibility that the health benefits of being in close relationships might stem primarily from giving social support, rather than from receiving it (Brown et al., 2003). Indeed, recent evidence suggests that individuals who provide help to others live longer and are healthier than those who do not (Brown et al., 2003; W. Brown, Consedine, & Magai, 2005; Brown et al., 2009b; Post, 2007). These discoveries posed a serious challenge to the social support literature, which tended to take for granted that receiving support was more beneficial for physical health than giving it (House et al., 1988). However, when health scientists began to test their assumptions about the presumed health benefits of receiving social support, the tests produced contradictory findings. Some findings even suggested that receiving support could be harmful to one's health. For example, receiving support is sometimes associated with suicidal thinking among people who feel like a burden (e.g., Brown & Vinokur, 2003) or who feel dependent on their relationship partner (Brown et al., 2003). We now know that there are many psychological and physical benefits to giving social support (Post, 2007). These benefits make sense in light of selective investment theory, which highlights the important motivational properties of caregiving.

BEYOND HEALTH PSYCHOLOGY: TRANSFORMING THE SOCIAL AND BEHAVIORAL SCIENCES

Ultimately, selective investment theory—which elaborated on ways in which oneness might motivate high-cost helping—led to the discovery that helping behavior is involved in regulating physiological states and is linked to longevity (Post, 2007). New frameworks for understanding how, and under what circumstances, helping behavior promotes physical health have led to new theories about the biological nature of the caregiving system (Brown, Brown, & Preston, in press). Interestingly, the influence of the Batson–Cialdini debates on other areas of psychology and neuroscience extend well beyond research programs that evolved directly from the Batson and Cialdini camps, as the debate stimulated new ways of thinking about a range of topics in psychology from emotion (positive and other-focused), to motivation (self- and other-focused), to cognition (e.g., self-expansion, perspective-taking, theory of mind). Many of these insights spawned by the debate highlight the fundamentally interconnected nature of human social groups.

Cialdini's challenges to Batson's empathy-altruism hypothesis also drew attention from scientists outside of psychology, as concepts such as empathy and perspective-taking captivated evolutionary biologists, neuroscientists, and animal behaviorists. As Batson and Cialdini struggled to clarify the existence of true altruism, they were watched by many others interested in finding answers to how and why there is so much apparently selfless sacrifice among human and nonhuman primates. As the concept of empathy became a centerpiece for understanding the psychology of other-directed helping, it also spawned new lines of research in areas such as neuroscience. For example, Stephanie Preston and Frans de Waal published an influential paper on the neuroscience of empathy, articulating an action-perception model of perspective-taking that was grounded in studies of empathy and self–other merging (Preston & deWaal, 2002). Similarly, in the book *The Social Neuroscience of Empathy*, Jean Decety (2009) described two competing forces in the empathic experience: empathic *concern* (an other-oriented response generated from imagining another person in distress) and empathic *distress* (a self-oriented response generated from imagining the self in distress).

The debate over the existence of true altruism even went so far as to breathe life into evolutionary theories of group selection (now referred to as multilevel selection; e.g., Wilson & Sober, 1994). Evidence advanced by Batson, honed to meet the challenges posed by Cialdini, allowed advocates of group selection, such as David Sloan Wilson, to argue that evolutionary selection likely operates at the level of the group, in addition to operating at the level of the individual. Wilson and his colleagues proposed that traits such as empathy, which can compromise the fitness of any one individual, may nevertheless operate powerfully in human societies because it promotes advantages to the group. Groups in which individuals care selflessly for one another could plausibly out-compete and therefore out-reproduce other groups comprised of selfish members who put their own needs above those of the group. Consequently, empathy and other prosocial processes could remain active in the population as a result of group-level selection (Wilson, Van Vugt, & O'Gorman, 2008). Thus, the notion of group selection, which had previously been discarded by sociobiologists as unlikely, was revitalized by the Batson–Cialdini debate.

Although there is still debate as to whether or not true altruism exists, there is no doubt that the Batson–Cialdini debate transformed the landscape of psychology, neuroscience, and evolutionary biology. Their work drew attention to new paradigmatic issues in the behavioral sciences that accelerated thinking in areas ranging from positive psychology to social neuroscience, to multilevel (group) selection. Indeed, the seeds for undermining the dominant "self-interest" paradigm for understanding helping behavior were sown by Cialdini and his long-standing debate with Batson. Indeed, Bob Cialdini's work on prosocial behavior helped facilitate an explosion of new research questions, the integration of which is now changing the landscape of behavioral science and medicine. His penchant for asking big questions has advanced our knowledge of human nature in important ways and has provided insights that have already begun to result in major advances in the science of human caregiving.

CHAPTER 12

Basic, Applied, and Full-Cycle Social Psychology

Enhancing Causal Generalization and Impact

STEPHEN G. WEST AND WILLIAM G. GRAZIANO

BASIC AND APPLIED SOCIAL PSYCHOLOGY: TENSIONS AND RISKS

The Arizona State University police spotted an adult walking alone in a parking garage late at night. The person was older than a conventional student, stylishly dressed, and carried a shoulder bag. He moved systematically through the garage, halting periodically. The police stopped the individual and asked him what he was doing. The individual replied "I work in the psychology department. I am Professor Cialdini. I do research on littering." One of the officers who had just taken a social psychology class started to arrest the suspect. No respectable psychology professor would study something as applied as littering. In the case of Robert Cialdini, the officer was mistaken.

This story, possibly apocryphal, highlights an important fact and Robert Cialdini's place in relation to that fact. Basic and applied social psychology have long been uneasy bedfellows. Over a half century ago, one of giants of social psychology, Kurt Lewin, argued strongly for an integration of the two disciplines. His writings capture the tension that continues even today: "There is nothing so practical as a good theory" (1951, p. 169); "Research that produces nothing but books will not suffice" (1948, p. 203). Yet, with the exception of occasional attempts at reconciliation, the two disciplines have slowly drifted apart. Cialdini's *full-cycle model* described below provides an important bridge between the two disciplines.

Basic social psychology is unexcelled at what it does. It addresses interesting phenomena that occur in the social world, developing theoretical hypotheses to explain those social phenomena. It tests those hypotheses using cleverly designed laboratory experiments that probe hypotheses about processes responsible for the observed outcome. Often, there is general consensus on a small set of paradigms used to study the phenomenon, making findings cumulate more quickly. The result is a science that is enormously satisfying intellectually, and one that provides a wonderful causal understanding of the phenomena it studies. Social psychology tells us much about what people may do in social settings and why. The *hope* is that these understandings are general and apply in the real world. However, the current practice of most basic social psychology conducted in the laboratory provides little formal basis for achieving this hope.

Many critics interested in application have been skeptical of the field's findings. Over the years, mainstream social psychology has focused paradoxically on an increasingly broader domain of questions using an increasingly narrower knowledge base (e.g., Sears, 1986). The prototypical article published in leading social psychological journals reports a test of a theoretically driven hypothesis, investigated in a series of randomized experiments, conducted in the laboratory, with undergraduate participants, and evaluated using short-term outcomes (e.g., West, Newsom, & Fenaughty, 1992. This narrow knowledge base serves to purify the phenomenon, often leading to more coherent theory. But, such purification brings a risk—irrelevance.

To ensure applicability of findings in agricultural research, Sir Ronald Fisher (1935), who developed the randomized experiment, emphasized an open systems model. Treatment conditions were carefully controlled and randomly assigned, but the plants that were the units in his experiments were open to the full, uncontrolled vagaries of natural growing conditions. To this foundation, for better *and* worse, basic social psychologists added a second type of control, adapted from the physical sciences. In the physical sciences, the phenomenon of interest is isolated from extraneous potential outside influences (e.g., electromagnetic radiation). Social psychology has taken this approach to control one step further, creating entirely new (artificial) social environments in the laboratory, sometimes replacing natural human interactions with staged performances by trained confederates or even computer displays of social interactions (Wilson, Aronson, & Carlsmith, 2010). The exact outside influences from which the research is isolated are frequently not clear. Potential mismatches between the social situation created in the laboratory and the social situations of interest in the real world are rarely considered. How such research can produce important results generalizable to the real world or provide a strong basis for the design of programs to change important social behaviors then becomes a topic for open debate.

These and other concerns led to what came to be known as the "crisis in social psychology" in the 1970s. Three inter-related problems associated with basic research identified then continue to this day.

1. The determinants of social behavior and the underlying processes studied in the laboratory by basic social psychologists may not be particularly important in real life (e.g., Helmreich, 1975). There are many aspects to this criticism (see also points 2 and 3 below), but one notable problem is a general lack of basic descriptive work on situations (but see Kelley et al., 2003). Personality psychologists have extensively catalogued the full range of personality traits; epidemiologists have extensively catalogued the environmental risks for various diseases. Yet, social psychologists know little about the frequency or the nature of the general situations in which people—even the undergraduates who are the focus of their research—are likely to display fundamental social behaviors such as aggression, prosocial behavior, or attraction to others in their daily lives. Such basic descriptive work can begin to provide a stronger basis both for evaluating claims of the importance of basic work and for determining the generalization of social psychological findings.

2. The unique environment of the laboratory and participants' awareness of serving as a research "subject" may introduce other processes that can potentially obscure understanding of causal relationships. A variety of artifacts can compromise the scientific understanding of the phenomenon that is attained. A partial list includes experimenter bias, subject motivations, and meta-processing of the situation by participants, in which they attempt to please the experimenter or avoid the experimenter's negative evaluation rather than respond to the social situation (Kruglanski, 1975). Methodological solutions have been developed to address these artifacts in the laboratory (Wilson et al., 2010); they are only rarely implemented in current practice. Field research typically eliminates or at least greatly diminishes the import of these problems.

3. Features of the experimental situation may be unrepresentative of the real world and preclude generalization. Following Cronbach (1980, 1982), generalization of findings is now evaluated along several dimensions[1] including Units (participants), Treatments, Observations, and Settings (UTOS). Cronbach distinguished between lower case *utos*– the specific units, treatments, observations, and settings realized in the research, and upper case *UTOS*– the population

represented by each of the four dimensions to which the researcher wishes to generalize. Basic researchers typically have an interest in generalization *across* different exemplars chosen from each of these dimensions. Does my finding that frustration produces aggression hold across different *units*: males and females, young and old, and different cultural groups? Does it hold across different social *settings*: within family interactions, interactions with anonymous strangers, and interactions with one's boss? In contrast, many applied social psychologists are interested in generalization *to* specific UTOS. For example, Evans, Rozelle, Mittelmark, Hansen, Bane, and Havis (1977) developed a program based on social psychological principles that has had considerable success in preventing the initiation of cigarette smoking. For Evans et al., the target of generalization was clear: Could this smoking prevention program (T) conducted in high school classrooms (S) effectively reduce cigarette smoking (O) in high school students (U)? There was little concern about generalization to other UTOS, but much concern that the program would work in the context of the specific UTOS for which it was designed. A program successful in just this milieu would have major societal benefits.

The statistical method of random sampling from a defined population offers the best basis for generalization; in practice, this method has been implemented only rarely in social psychology for the dimension of Units (participants, e.g., Schwarz & Hippler, 1995). Examples in which random sampling has been implemented for the dimensions of Treatments, Settings, or Observations may be nonexistent. Cook (1990) and Shadish, Cook, and Campbell (2002) offered an alternative, extrastatistical set of principles for enhancing generalization that can potentially serve social psychologists well in practice. These five principles are presented in Box 12-1. Social psychologists are currently uneven in their implementation of these principles in basic research. They do an outstanding job of attempting to meet principle 4, expending enormous effort to rule out alternative explanations related to the interpretation of the manipulated treatment conditions (construct validity of the independent variable). This approach permits them to learn how well their preferred theoretical processes can account for the phenomenon in the specific context of their set of investigations. Sometimes they establish discriminant validity (principle 3). The other principles of generalization are mostly ignored. Following their tack of using artificial social environments as a means of control, many basic social psychologists believe that they can delicately craft their laboratory scenarios and experimental materials to capture just the key active features of social contexts of interest, while removing all extraneous influences, thus meeting principle 1.

1. *Proximal similarly.* The treatments, participants, settings, response measures, and times should include most of the features of the population
of interest, particularly those that are judged to be central.
2. *Heterogeneous irrelevancies.* Aspects of treatments, participants, settings,
response measures, and times that are theoretically expected to be irrelevant to the causal relationship should be as heterogeneous as possible.
3. *Discriminant validity.* To the extent that the treatment affects the intended
construct and not other constructs, the likelihood of causal generalization is supported. To the extent that precise types of participants or
settings can be identified for which the treatment effect holds, the likelihood of generalization to the specific subpopulations of persons or settings is increased.
4. *Causal explanation.* To the extent that a theoretical explanation of the
causal effect can be supported, the likelihood of generalization can be
supported.
5. *Empirical interpolation and extrapolation.* Causal effects are far more likely
to generalize within the range of treatments, persons, settings, times,
and response measures that have been studied. Extrapolation can often
involve threshold effects, change in the functional form, or the presence
of new processes that lead to substantial changes in the magnitude and
even the direction of causal effects.

Yet, without careful descriptive work characterizing the situations associated with their central phenomenon, this belief remains an unverified
conjecture, more art and argument than science.

TOWARD A SOLUTION: THE FULL-CYCLE MODEL

One of the giants of the recent history of social psychology, Robert Cialdini
(1980), proposed the full-cycle model. It overcomes many of these criti-
cisms of basic social psychology. The full-cycle model addresses the first
problem described in the previous section through informal, observational
studies of important social phenomena in their natural contexts in the real
world. The approach lies firmly in Pasteur's quadrant, which combines basic
research with application (see Chapter 14). Cialdini applied this approach
most fully in his analysis of compliance strategies—he has observed sales

professionals in a number of diverse settings such as automobile dealer-
ships and door-to-door sales. He argues that successful salespeople will
incorporate the most powerful and robust compliance techniques through
a kind of natural selection process: Less-effective techniques are winnowed
out in the real world. The remaining techniques that appear in multiple
contexts will be the important ones that deserve careful experimental
study. These techniques *may* have been a focus of prior social psychological theorizing, but often important principles have been overlooked. Social
psychological theory offers no method of valuing the real-world importance of basic principles.

The second problem was addressed effectively in Cialdini's research.
Cialdini maintained basic social psychology's preference for randomized experiments. However, he often preferred to conduct experiments
in his program of full-cycle research in less artificial, naturalistic contexts,
in which he has done some of his most distinctive work. Cialdini, Reno,
and Kallgren (1990) studied the effects of making different types of norms
salient on participants' subsequent littering in parking lots, an amusement
park, and dormitory grounds; Goldstein, Cialdini, and Griskevicius (2008)
studied the effects of different normative messages on towel reuse by
hotel guests; and Cialdini and Schroeder (1976) studied the effectiveness
of different types of compliance requests delivered to citizens on the streets
in a local community. This choice of real-world contexts eliminates the
possibility that artifacts associated with the laboratory are responsible for
the results. Importantly, it also makes the results more credible to applied
researchers, policy makers, and the public.

The final problem is generalization *across* UTOS. Cialdini and colleagues
have relied almost exclusively on replication to make claims of the general-
ity of the effect. Good examples of the use of different participant populations, different settings, and different outcomes to enhance generalization
of the findings can be found in Cialdini and colleagues' full-cycle work
(e.g., Cialdini et al., 1990). However, most of this research has not generally
made formal attempts to probe the external validity of the findings. Indeed,
in his original presentation of the full-cycle model, Cialdini (1980) was less
interested in application than in taking the empirical discoveries back
to relevant real-world settings to identify new principles for further empirical study. Cialdini's full-cycle model emphasizes contributions to basic
social psychology, but in contexts in which potential or actual application is
transparent.

In summary, the full-cycle model offers an important integration of
basic and applied social psychology. It helps identify social psychological processes that are potentially important in the real world, it uses randomized experiments to maximize the strength of causal inference, and it

investigates the processes through which the effect takes place. The interventions manipulated within the full-cycle tradition so far have been simple (e.g., a brief message or request), designed to address a single theoretical component to maximize the construct validity of the independent variable. Once the principles are understood, simplicity of implementation facilitates applications in practical programs. Many of its emphases mirror traditional basic social psychology, but the full-cycle model has a much stronger interest in producing findings that are applicable in the real world. No attempts have been made within the full-cycle model to provide basic descriptive work on the types of situations in which behavior of interest might take place, nor to investigate the potential generalization of causal effects. Instead, the full-cycle model has addressed generalization on a less formal basis.

TOWARD ACHIEVING GENERALIZABLE CAUSAL EFFECTS

Basic social psychologists have focused on maximizing the internal validity of their effects. They wish to be sure that the treatment and nothing else is producing the observed results. Applied social psychologists and policy makers seek internal validity, but also place a strong priority on external validity, so that their findings can be generalized to the real-world contexts of interest. Both types of evidence are necessary for credible research that will have impact beyond textbooks and academic journals. Basic social psychologists have often deferred examination of generalization until some later point in their research programs, a point that for many *never* comes. In contrast, applied researchers sought designs that maximized the strength of the causal inferences that may be made in real-world settings and with the people of interest. Significant progress has been made in addressing many of the traditional challenges to causal inference in field settings: participant attrition, participants failing to comply with the assigned treatment, and nonindependence of data (Shadish et al., 2002; West & Thoemmes, 2010). It is now possible to conduct research in field settings that achieves the best of both worlds: Strong causal inferences with clear real-world applicability (Shadish & Cook, 2009). Here are some designs that can achieve both desiderata.

Randomized Experiments in the Field

In the randomized experiment (RE), units (typically human participants) are randomly assigned to treatment and control groups. This process guarantees that, on average, the distributions of the treatment and control groups will not differ at baseline on any measured or unmeasured variable. The RE produces the most credible and transparent evidence in terms of causal inference. Randomized experiments can be conducted in either laboratory or field settings.

Randomization in field settings can present challenges. Field settings often afford less control over the randomization process. In field experiments, there is often no defined sample of participants, so that randomization must often be conducted based on other dimensions like time, settings, or even observations (dependent variables, Riechardt, 2006). Cialdini and his co-workers have cleverly used the time and setting dimensions as the basis of assignment. Cialdini, Reno, and Kallgren (1990) altered environments to be littered and nonlittered at different times, observing the responses of people who entered the environment. Goldstein et al. (2008) randomly assigned different hotel rooms to receive different normative posters about recycling.

Randomization on dimensions other than participants can potentially complicate the randomization scheme and statistical analysis. Shadish, Cook, and Campbell (2002, pp. 294–311) discuss techniques of randomization in field experiments, as well as some issues often overlooked. Randomization can fail to equate participants, even on average, both because of poor initial implementation of randomization and breakdowns in the experiment following randomization, in which participants successfully alter their own treatment assignment. Successful randomization and its maintenance are key elements in the causal interpretation of randomized experiments.

In Cialdini's research, randomization on the time or setting dimension has been heavily confounded with the participant dimension: This is to the good. In his work, different participants tend to show up at different times and in different settings. This simplifies the analysis, reducing, but not fully eliminating, the need to make adjustments to correct for dependency in the data. The central problem is that two participants who show up during a specified time period (e.g., 3:00–3:30 PM) when a treatment condition is being conducted may be more similar in their littering behavior on average than two other participants, one who shows up at 8:00 AM and one who shows up at 3:30 PM. The problem leads to standard errors of statistical tests that are too small.

When Randomization Is Not Possible

In many cases, randomization cannot be implemented for practical or ethical reasons. Alternative methods of assignment to treatment conditions must be sought. Reichardt (2006) suggested that quantitative assignment rules can be used to assign units—participants, times, settings, or even observations—to treatment conditions. Two variants of this approach, the *regression discontinuity design* and the *interrupted time series design*, are commonly viewed as the strongest alternatives to the RE in terms of causal inference (Shadish et al., 2002; West, Biesanz, & Pitts, 2000). Examples of quantitative assignment designs using settings exist, but are less common. Sometimes assignment to treatment conditions cannot be controlled, as when a treatment is given to one community but not another, or participation in the treatment program versus the standard program is voluntary. These so-called *observational studies* (aka, nonequivalent control group designs) present more challenges to causal inference, but improved solutions that rule out threats to internal validity have been developed.

Regression Discontinuity Design

In the regression discontinuity design, participants are assigned to the "treatment condition" on the basis of a single or composite quantitative baseline measure. For example, students with above a 3.5 grade point average (GPA) during the fall semester are given the special recognition of Dean's List (treatment) during the spring semester. Such assignment rules often are justified when the treatment is perceived as valuable and there are not enough resources to provide the treatment for everyone. The allocation principle is the degree of measured merit, need, or risk, a principle that is well understood and often perceived as fair by society. From a methodological point of view, assignment to treatment conditions is biased—the treatment and control groups are not equivalent at the beginning of the study. Nevertheless, the assignment rule is precisely known, so that the source of bias can be modeled effectively. The treatment effect is manifested by a discontinuity at the cut point on the quantitative baseline measure. Figure 12-1 illustrates the application of the regression discontinuity design to assess the effects on the children's health of a school lunch program given to children whose family income is less than $30,000.

Interrupted Time Series Design

In the interrupted time series design, the treatment program is introduced on the basis of another quantitative assignment dimension—time. The treatment—typically a law, policy, or program—does not exist prior to its implementation. On a specified date, the treatment is implemented and its

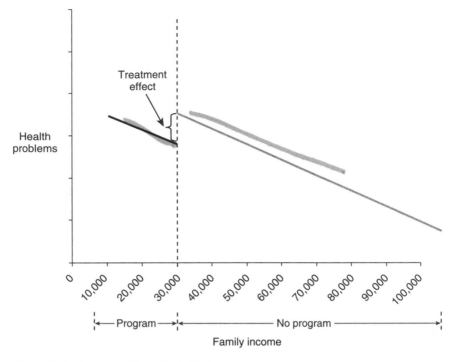

Figure 12-1 Regression Discontinuity Design.
The X-axis is family income; the Y-axis is a measure of health problems. All children whose family income is below the threshold, here $30,000, received the treatment program (school lunch program); all children whose family income is above the threshold do not receive the program. The difference in level between the regression lines for the program and no program groups at the threshold represents the treatment effect. Source: West et al., (2008). Alternatives to the randomized controlled trial. *American Journal of Public Health, 98,* 1359–1366.

effects are observed over time. Hennigan, Del Rosario, Heath, Cook, Wharton, and Calder (1982) investigated the effects of the introduction of television into communities on rates of violent and property crimes. Following the end of World War II, the Federal Communications Commission granted new licenses for television broadcasting to many moderate-sized U.S. cities. New licenses were granted to one set of cities in 1948 and a second set in 1952 (replication). Television broadcasting in the city began on a specific date upon receipt of the license. Violent crimes did not increase following the introduction of television into these communities; however, there was a distinct increase in the rate of burglary. A key challenge of the interrupted time series design is proper modeling of the assignment variable (time) and outcome variables. Additional new issues unique to the design are that some other event (e.g., change in gun laws) or a change in the measurement of the outcome variable (e.g., change in the definition of burglary in police records) could occur at the point of the intervention, confounding the interpretation of the observed results. Inclusion of carefully chosen design features can lead to causal inferences that rival those of the randomized experiment. Shadish et al. (2002) and West et al. (2000) present further discussions.

Observational Studies

Observational studies take advantage of circumstances in which participants receive different treatments. The challenge in observational studies is that the basis of assignment to treatment and control groups is unknown and must be presumed to be nonrandom. Pretest measures on the outcome of interest, as well as other covariates measured at baseline, are necessary to model the process of selection into treatment and control conditions to achieve a valid causal interpretation.

Two different methods have been deployed for improving causal inferences from observational studies. The first is a variant of matching originally developed by Rosenbaum and Rubin (1983). Baseline variables potentially related to both selection into treatment condition and to the outcome are measured. These baseline variables are chosen on an inclusive basis; the goal is to be as comprehensive as possible. The focus then shifts to the prediction of the *propensity score*, the probability that the person is in the treatment group, using these baseline variables. If the participants in the treatment and control groups can be closely matched on the propensity score, then the remarkable result is that, statistically, the treatment and control groups will have the same approximate distribution on all baseline variables that make up the propensity score. This outcome mirrors the outcome of randomization, but only on the variables measured at baseline, not on unobserved baseline variables.

Wu, West, and Hughes (2008; see also Moser, West, & Hughes, 2011) assessed a large sample of first-grade children at high risk of retention on 72 variables believed to be related both to later retention in grade (repeating first grade) and achievement in reading and mathematics. They estimated propensity scores for retention using logistic regression. They used these propensity scores to closely match retained and promoted children on all measured baseline variables. Retained children got a 1-year boost in reading and mathematics achievement during the year they repeated first grade. These initial gains dissipated over time, however, as the retained children encountered new material in subsequent grades. By the end of fifth grade, the retained children did not differ in achievement from their matched controls. Note that retained children were a year behind their promoted controls, achieving only at the same level as the controls did a year earlier. Alternative explanations of the results would need to identify differences between the two groups at baseline that contributed to selection *over and above* the 72 assessed measures.

The second method of improving causal inferences in observational studies involves adding design elements to address each specific threat to internal validity that is plausible in the specific research setting. Reynolds and West (1987) evaluated an intervention designed to increase sales of lottery tickets in convenience stores. Causal inferences were strengthened through the addition of three design elements depicted in Figure 12-2. The intervention and control stores were matched on prior sales of lottery tickets. The treatment stores showed an increase in sales on the outcome measure of lottery tickets targeted by the intervention, but not on other sales categories (e.g., groceries, gasoline) that would be expected to show similar changes if other factors were responsible for the results. The intervention was introduced in the middle of an 8-week lottery ticket sales campaign. The intervention and control stores showed similar sales trends during the 4 weeks prior to the intervention; a jump in sales *only* in treatment stores occurred at the point of the intervention, and this advantage in sales was maintained during the 4 weeks following the intervention. West and Thoemmes (2010) provide an extensive discussion of the strengths and limitations of both the propensity score and design element strategies.

How Well Do the Alternative Designs Work?

A small focused literature has developed that provides an empirical evaluation of the alternative designs. This literature examines intervention studies comparing the results of overlapping REs and nonrandomized alternative designs that share an identical treatment condition. Cook, Shadish, and Wong (2008) found no differences in the treatment effect estimates provided by randomized experiments and either regression discontinuity or interrupted time series designs. A similar comparison of randomized

---

Figure 12-2 Continued

(B) Nonequivalent Dependent Variables. Within the treatment stores, sales of lottery tickets increase substantially following the introduction of treatment. Sales of other major categories (gasoline, cigarettes, groceries (nontaxable), and groceries (taxable) that would be expected to be affected by confounding factors, but not treatment, do not show appreciable change. (C) Repeated Pre- and Post-test Measurements. Treatment and control stores sales show comparable trends in sales during the four weeks prior to and following the introduction of the treatment. The level of sales in the treatment and control scores is similar prior to the introduction of treatment, but differ substantially beginning immediately after treatment is introduced. (Adapted from K. D. Reynolds and S. G. (1987), A multiplist strategy for strengthening nonequivalent control group designs. *Evaluation Review*, 11, 691–714).

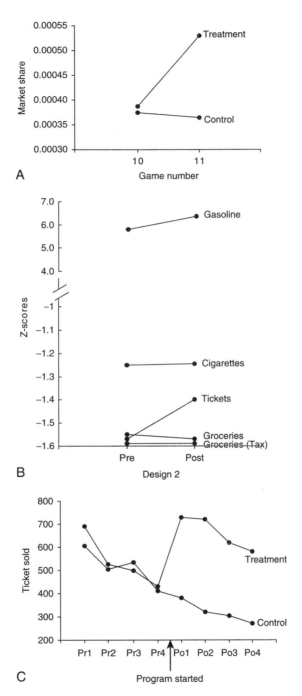

A

B

Design 2

C

Figure 12-2 Some Design Approaches to Strengthening Causal Inferences in Observational Studies.

(A) Matching. Treatment and control stores are selected from the same chain, are in the same geographical location, and are comparable in sales during baseline (lottery game 10). Introduction of the treatment at the beginning of lottery game 11 yields an increase in sales only in the treatment stores.

(Continues on page 130)

experiments and observational studies found differences when the observational study was poorly designed and analyzed. When the selection rule for treatment assignment could be well modeled, or highly similar people participated in the treatment and control groups, no differences in the treatment effect estimates were found between the two designs. Hernán et al. (2008) reanalyzed data from a major randomized trial (Women's Health Initiative) and a large observational study (Nurses Health Study) on the effects of hormone replacement therapy in postmenopausal women on heart disease. Highly disparate results had been reported for the two studies. When the observational study was analyzed using propensity-score methods and the same (intention to treat) causal effect was estimated for similar participants who met the same eligibility criteria, discrepancies were minimal. Shadish, Clark, and Steiner (2008) randomly assigned participants to a randomized laboratory experiment or to an observational laboratory study of the effects of math or vocabulary training, finding little difference in the estimates of the causal effect of training after adjusting for an extensive set of baseline covariates in the observational study. Further studies of this and other similar data sets strongly suggest that comparable results can be achieved with randomized experiments and observational trials if an extensive, carefully chosen set of baseline covariates make adjustments for selection (e.g., Cook & Steiner, 2010).

The alternative designs described previously provide strong causal inferences, admittedly with somewhat less certainty than randomized experiments. They potentially broaden our scientific knowledge base and permit the examination of important applied questions that are not amenable to randomized experiments. These alternative designs can be implemented in the actual targeted settings with the populations, treatments, and measures of interest. These features make the potential usefulness of the results to society transparent.

CONCLUSION

The tension between basic and applied social psychology has played out over more than a half century. Laboratory experimentation permits strong causal inferences and clear understanding of the underlying processes, leading to theoretical advances. Whether the theory and the generated knowledge base has value beyond the laboratory continues to be debated. Issues of relevance, artifacts associated with the laboratory situation, and the lack of formal attention to generalization continue to be raised. Cialdini's full-cycle model has produced a valuable antidote to many of these ills, with its emphasis on identifying truly important social psychological interventions that operate across multiple real-world settings and its emphasis on experiments conducted in field settings. The results clearly contribute to basic social psychological theorizing, overcoming objections of basic researchers that applied research is atheoretical, while making application to real-world issues immediately transparent.

Although laboratory experiments clearly contribute to theory, the underlying causal processes are those that explain behavior in the laboratory. Applied research has an ability to explore realistic limits of social psychological ideas, to show how they are and are not useful, and to help identify gaps in our understanding. Through its focus on simple, single-component interventions, the full-cycle approach has had a unique ability to study the causal processes underlying phenomena within the actual real-world situations in which they occur.

Despite the success of the full-cycle model over three decades, the current hegemony of the basic research perspective has taken its toll. Cialdini (2009) wrote a provocative essay entitled "We have to break up," providing his characterization of the difficulties of making continued contributions to basic social psychology from the full-cycle tradition. Many of his recent publications have appeared in business journals; he found it advantageous to split his academic position, so that much of his recent effort has been allotted to the portion of his position in the business school; and his recent outstanding Ph.D.'s in social psychology have taken positions in business schools. Many basic social psychologists perceived only the well-crafted humor in his essay, interpreting its central message as a joke. Yet, applied social psychologists understood his message all too well. They have drifted into other programs in psychology or other departments that value application. Their students have taken positions in schools of law, health and clinical settings, and schools of education. These losses may potentially diminish the future pool of applied talent in social psychology: Who will be able to devise strong research designs and implement social psychologically based programs in applied settings in the future? If social psychology once again decides to pursue its applied promise, it will face the challenge of relearning earlier, hard-won lessons in designing and implementing research in field and applied settings. The full-cycle model serves as a beacon of one of the best ways to do it.

ENDNOTE

[1] Time is also a potential dimension for generalization, but is rarely considered in most social psychological research. In many cases, failure to generalize over time is accounted for by changes in the units, treatments, observations, or settings that are being considered. For studies of developmental processes and long-term change, consideration of the time dimension is of key importance.

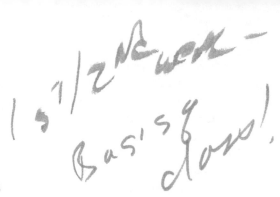

CHAPTER 13

Behavioral Change Cialdini-Style

RICK VAN BAAREN AND AP DIJKSTERHUIS

O n August 31, 2008, 2 PM, Robert Cialdini addressed a congregation of students, researchers, and various professionals at the Radboud University Nijmegen in the Netherlands. It may seem like an ordinary event, but upon closer examination, it provided a perfect illustration of Cialdini's profound influence and ability to inspire. The reason for his visit was the official opening of a brand new master's degree program at the Radboud University in "Cialdini-style": The master's degree in "behavioral change." In this master's degree program, students are taught how to use and develop scientific knowledge on social influence and apply it to real-life problems and challenges.

Having Robert Cialdini there provided the best possible start of this new and exciting master's degree program, because Cialdini spent the lion's share of his academic life working on the three aspects for which this master's degree stands: using practice to understand the theory of influence; using theory to understand the practice of influence; and translating ideas into solid, creative, and catchy experiments that can affect both academia and the world beyond academia.

 After Robert Cialdini was properly introduced, his lecture began with a discussion of some of his famous experiments: The California energy saving studies, the Petrified Forest interventions, and, of course, the hotel towel experiments. After 1 hour and a standing ovation at the end, students, supervisors, and guests were thrilled and ready to start the year, thoroughly inspired by the leading expert they had just listened to. At the time of writing, a year-and-a-half down the road, our students have conducted various "Cialdini-style" experiments, two of which we describe here.

In our master's degree program, the first trimester is packed with theory, mostly consisting of Cialdini's mechanisms (Cialdini, 2009), Knowles' work on resistance to persuasion (Knowles & Linn, 2004), Pratkanis' taxonomy of influence techniques (Pratkanis, 2007), and our own work on automatic influences on behavior (Dijksterhuis, Smith, Van Baaren, & Wigboldus, 2005). In the second and third trimesters, students go out into the "real world," trying to solve real problems. They use the SWITCH (a Dutch abbreviation) intervention model, a staged tool in which students start with a behavioral analysis of the problem, come up with a psychologically founded strategy, design an experimental intervention, and end with a proper effect measure.

The 40 admitted students are free to choose assignments from businesses (consultancy and global advertising agencies), nonprofit organizations (charity, health promotion, safe traffic promotion), government agencies (tax agency, army-air force, local governments), and even a political party. Some examples of the questions they proposed to tackle were: How do you promote the consumption of healthy food in the restaurant of the local zoo? How do you get young drivers to attend a safety program? How do you stimulate taxpayers to pay in time? How do you get more people to donate blood? How do you get (young) people to get involved in politics?

MEAT IN THE ZOO

One example is the Burger's Zoo project.[1] The project was initiated by an organization called the Good Food Alliance, whose primary goal is to promote healthy, sustainable, and "fair" food. Burger's Zoo in Arnhem, The Netherlands, is famous for its beautiful bush, desert, and aquarium displays, and for being the place where Frans de Waal conducted his well-known studies on chimps' social behavior. Burger's Zoo shared the goals of the Good Food Alliance and allowed us to perform experiments in their restaurants. The question was: How can we influence people to eat more healthy food and less "environment unfriendly" proteins during their visit to this Zoo? Our concrete goal was to try to reduce the consumption of meat and to increase the consumption of vegetarian alternatives (which, as an aside, made for an interesting introductory meeting with the people from Burger's Zoo. We met next to the lion's enclosure and, while we all made sincere efforts to think about ways to reduce meat consumption, we saw, from the corners of our eyes, men throwing enormous carcasses over a fence. It was more than a bit distracting). A group of students enthusiastically started on this project. If they succeeded in reducing the unsustainable consumption pattern of thousands of visitors, it would suggest that one could really have a positive effect on the environment and set an example for other big leisure parks.

After an initial analysis, it became clear that this would be quite a challenge. Families visiting the Zoo do this to relax, enjoy themselves, and spend quality time together, to take a break from their busy schedules. Fast food is perceived as the default option for this type of leisure activity. Even families who normally eat very healthy foods allow themselves the "luxury" of unhealthy food during such a day out. Children simply expect they will get French fries with a (meaty) snack, and nobody sees this as a problem. A zoo visit is one of those opportunities in which people do not want to be rigid. When the students interviewed visitors, they almost all said they understood the need for more sustainable food consumption, but . . . not here and not now. How to best approach this problem?

It immediately became clear to us all that we wouldn't get anywhere if we simply tried to consciously persuade or convince people of our goals on their day out. Since a direct approach would most likely only lead to resistance ("Would you mind not spoiling our day out with your political correct blah-blah!? Thank you"). Based on a literature search, we found out that two types of approaches are theoretically most effective in circumstances such as these: Some using mechanisms described by Cialdini and "atmospherical adjustments."

Cialdini's Mechanisms

Of Cialdini's mechanisms of influence, several could be used in the restaurants in Burger's Zoo. Our only constraint was that our interventions would not hinder the normal operations of the restaurants. We decided to use techniques to attract people to certain items on the menu: A suggestion of *scarcity* was elicited by introducing a new kids' menu (the Elephant menu, containing no meat), which was the only menu with which children could get a small, free, toy elephant from the gift shop, and even then there would be limited availability. This was controlled for by an extra condition with the new menu, but without the limited toy.

In another condition, we used *authority* to attract people to the meatless egg-roll. A sign stating "Chef's tip: cheese roll" was placed close to the counter at which egg-rolls and meat alternatives were available. The control condition for this technique was the same counter, but without the sign.

We measured the percentage of products sold (containing vs. not containing meat) to assess the effectiveness of these techniques.

Atmospherical Adjustments

Another approach to attract people to more sustainable alternatives is to use the routines and preferences that people automatically adopt when entering a shop or cafeteria. It is known, for example, that there is, on average, a strong "right-hand bias." People are mostly likely to turn right after entering a store (when there is a choice), and when two or more similar alternatives are presented close to each other, the right-hand one will be valued more and chosen more often than will the left-hand one (for an embodiment explanation, see Casasanto, 2009). We used these insights to promote the sustainable alternative (vegetarian soups) at the soup counter. It turned out that the soup wasn't positioned in a prime spot, given the right-hand preference of most people, so we adjusted part of the routing near the soup counter in such a way that the soup was in the "right" spot. Again we compared this set-up with a control set-up and measured the percentage of soup sold.

The experiments ran for 2 weeks in February 2009. Later, it turned out that the students had been effective in significantly reducing the percentage of meat eaten at the zoo. Whereas the control period showed 29% meat-containing products out of the total products sold (including beverages), the intervention reduced that to 23%. This zoo has about 1.5 million visitors per year; thus, using these simple interventions could lead to 90,000 fewer portions of meat being eaten in a year. Both the Elephant kids' menu intervention (from 0.8% to 2%) and the vegetarian soup intervention (from 3% to 5%) significantly outperformed their respective controls. Unfortunately, the egg-roll (Chef's tip) didn't work, maybe because a cafeteria chef is not perceived as a real authority. Together, these interventions (both the significant and the nonsignificant ones) resulted in the 6% decrease in meat consumption.

Implications

Even when people are out with their family and might not want to be disturbed by intrusive attempts to manipulate their behavior in politically correct ways, there are still subtle ways to promote sustainable food choice. In the end, it is behavior that counts and not people's explicit attitudes. Especially in the domain of sustainability, a seeming paradox exists between what people say they do and what they actually do. When interviewed, most people admit that they think sustainability is important, and they often say that it is one of their worries for their future and their children's future. However, people's actual behavior is often inconsistent with their attitudes; hence, people still too often make the unhealthy, unsustainable choice. In our experience, interventions aimed at promoting sustainability often fail. Such problems can be overcome by *directly* targeting behavior rather than using attitude-focused messages.

Cialdini's "click-zoom" mechanisms—his techniques of influence—that made Cialdini famous and that are often mentioned in this volume, and the related atmospherical interventions, are simple and cost-effective ways to bring about this change. When it concerns food waste, consumer choice, reduction of energy use, and other behaviors susceptible to very large attitude–behavior discrepancies, Cialdini's approach to changing behavior is a very effective one.

ENGAGE TO ENGAGE

The second project we will describe is the Engagement in Politics Study.[2] One of the liberal political parties in the Netherlands approached us with a question: How do we stimulate people who donate to our party to become actual members? Political parties need volunteers to be able to function well—especially while they are campaigning—and it is of crucial importance that enough enthusiastic people put time and effort in volunteering for their party. This specific party we worked with had a database with addresses of about 4,000 people who had donated money in the last 2 years, but weren't members of the party (yet).

Member Inventory and Intervention

Our students first started with a large-scale inventory of both members and former members to see why they had become members or why they had quit. As one may have expected, the better part of the reasons were related to agreement or disagreement with political viewpoints, but another interesting and often mentioned reason for quitting membership emerged: Several members quit because they felt membership was very demanding. One really needed to be very active as a member, and people believed it was impossible to support the party in a more "relaxed" way. Even though it wasn't explicitly communicated to them, people felt that being a member entailed "standing at the barricades" every weekend. In addition to this type of resistance, another type of resistance people expressed concerned skepticism. Because the party is only modest in size and not one of the traditional Dutch "big three," many people believed that it wouldn't help much to join—they would always be too small to be a leading force in the Netherlands.

Based on this analysis, the students developed a strategy and set up a pilot experiment to pre-test several ways to influence potential members (people who donate but are not members). In the pilot test, several different letters were designed, and each version was sent to a separate subgroup of potential members. The first one was the original letter used by the political party in previous attempts. This letter focuses on the party's need for help (e.g., "We need your help in realizing our ideals"). It also expressed the fact that membership is relatively cheap and comes with all sorts of benefits. The *transparency* letter focused on *acknowledging resistance, social proof,* and on the idea that "even one member helps" (the "even a penny helps" technique). In the letter, it was explained that people sometimes think the party is too small to make a difference; but it followed by saying that "the more members we have, the more money and influence will follow." Additionally, people were encouraged to do just as many other new members had done: simply join! Finally, the *support* letter was designed to address the active versus passive membership issue: The letter explained that members are completely free to choose what to do and not to do: "You can get as active or as passive as you want, membership is always appreciated."

In the pilot test, each letter was sent to approximately 250 potential members. The standard letter resulted in eight new members. The transparency and support letters resulted in 11 and 12 new members, respectively. The effect was obviously not significant. However, given the ecological validity of the behavior assessed (the behavior assessed was exactly the behavior the party wanted) and the relatively small sample size, we decided to continue in the same vein. First, the transparency and support letter were integrated into one, leaving us with one experimental letter and one control. In addition, we wanted to test our intervention on a larger scale.

Intervention: Two Letters

Each letter was sent to a group of 2,100 nonmembers (between-subjects design, $N = 4,200$) who had donated money in the past 2 years. The potential members could join by going to the party's website, and the link was given in the letter.

After a few weeks, the control letter had led 30 people to become paying members. The experimental letter resulted in 65 new members, a significant increase. On the one hand, the results are weak in the sense that the "hit-rate" was still only 3%. On the other hand, it is a very cost-effective way to influence behavior, and the behavior is important for many people. Becoming a member of a political party is a bigger deal than merely buying a pack of cookies from the local Girl Scouts. So, 3% is really not bad at all, especially since the letters were sent to people who hadn't responded to various previous attempts.

THE DIFFICULTIES WITH CIALDINI-STYLE BEHAVIORAL CHANGE

The first year of the new master's degree program taught us some valuable lessons and even increased our already significant admiration for Cialdini's achievements. One of the major problems is that there always seems to be a tension between doing the best scientific research and doing the most practical thing. Both in the Burger's Zoo and in our political study, the constraints prevented us from testing separate ingredients of the different interventions. The Elephant menu, for example, had both scarcity *and* an incentive in it, whereas in the political studies, social proof and acknowledging resistance were combined in one letter. In our experience, there are two ways to solve this: One option is to only work on cases in which one has complete freedom to make the interventions and to make sure that one can test each manipulation separately. This requires a very flexible business partner who is capable of accommodating all methodological needs. A second possibility is to separate the final test phase and the pilot test. Lab studies, or small-scale field studies, can be conducted to pre-test the effects of various techniques individually. Subsequently, in the final and grand experiment, the aim is maximum impact rather than testing the unique effect of each individual techniques. In this way, the smaller methodological issues are dealt with in the pre-tests, whereas the practical goals shape the final test.

In line with Cialdini, we try to do both: We work closely with our affiliated companies and agencies and convince them of the need for rigid experimentation. Consequently, the techniques we finally apply are grounded in fundamental research on underlying processes.

It is unbelievably creative and innovative how Cialdini performed the field experiments he did, knowing the constraints he and his team must have faced. When Cialdini officially opened this new master's degree program on behavioral change on August 31, 2008, he also wished us all the luck ... and now we know why.

ACKNOWLEDGMENTS

The authors would like to thank Martijn de Lange, who was internal coordinator of the master's degree in behavioral change from the start, but who will be leading the complete master's degree program in academic year 2010–2011.

ENDNOTES

1 The Meat in the Zoo study was led by Ellen Mvraki, Max Mulders, Kim van der Drift, and Inge Pillon.

2 The Engagement in Politics study was led by Jorn Horstman, Anna Kemmerling, and Marijn van de Vrie.

CHAPTER 14

Collective Full-Cycle Social Psychology

Models, Principles, Experience

DARWYN E. LINDER, JOHN W. REICH, AND
SANFORD L. BRAVER

Forty years ago, a young Bob Cialdini arrived in the Arizona State University (ASU) psychology department. Since then, Bob has worked closely with the three authors of this chapter to develop what we hoped would be a unique program in social psychology. Although a great many social psychologists around the world have joined Bob in developing the collective enterprise of full-cycle social psychology (as evidenced by this book), his vision has influenced most strongly of all the social psychology graduate program we forged together.

The structure of full-cycle social psychology was outlined in a 1980 chapter (Cialdini, 1980). There, Bob argued that research in social psychology should start with observations of human social behavior in natural settings, rather than with the deduction of hypotheses from stated theory. Social psychologists should choose phenomena to study that are important in the course of everyday human social interaction. The second step is to reproduce the phenomenon under controlled circumstances. The next steps (and there could be many) are to propose explanations for the phenomenon based on new or existing theory. These hypotheses are tested in experiments pitting rival hypotheses against one another. When one or more of these accounts receives sufficient empirical support, the final step is for the full-cycle practitioner to move back to the original, natural setting and test the efficacy of interventions based on the experimental results.

Near the end of his full-cycle chapter, Bob wrote, "If one accepts that it is the discipline's social responsibility to identify principles that can be applied to areas of societal concern (Cialdini, Bickman, & Cacioppo, 1979), then it is important to have prior confidence in the strength of those principles to affect behavior in natural settings (Cialdini, 1980)." One clear purpose of this chapter is to make a strong case that the discipline of social psychology should adopt a full-cycle approach focused on human social behavior in natural settings as *the* phenomena to be studied.

The first part of this chapter describes the development of the social psychology graduate training program at ASU, which we designed to support a blend of problem-focused research and theory-testing experiments. Then, we'll describe the broader emergence of a collective effort to employ the tools of full-cycle social psychology to understand the phenomena of human social behavior.

The second part of this chapter uses the lens provided by Stokes' (1997) analysis of scientific research, *Pasteur's Quadrant*, which refers to scientific research conducted with a dual focus: fundamental understanding of the phenomena in question, *and* application to solving practical problems. Social psychology falls entirely within Pasteur's Quadrant, studying phenomena that arise from human social interaction, and requiring both fundamental theory and practical applicability of findings. Full-cycle social psychology results when we try to explain, to predict and, finally, to change human social behavior.

The final section of this chapter argues that the "basic versus applied research" distinction in social psychology has been a mostly false dichotomy. To illustrate, we'll describe three full-cycle research programs conducted by ASU social psychology faculty and students.

HISTORY AND GUIDING PRINCIPLES

Getting Started

Bob Cialdini arrived in the department of psychology at ASU for the fall semester of 1971, joining John Reich, who had been hired in 1965, and Sandy Braver, who had joined the ASU faculty in 1970. This trio was able to gain approval to add one more faculty member and launch a Ph.D. training program in social psychology (the new hire would be the program chair). As a result, Darwyn Linder was hired and arrived for the fall semester of 1972.

The "Founding Four" immediately began planning the structure and content of the ASU Ph.D. training program in social psychology. Training requirements were designed as a functional scholarship to develop in students the skill set and knowledge of the discipline required to become productive scientists. Students were not required to take written comprehensive exams. Instead, courses (proseminar, methods, topic area seminars) were designed and performance was evaluated so that successful completion of a course was sufficient evidence of mastery. A second-year project designed to foster independent research and scholarship was required rather than a formal master's degree. We dropped the requirement that graduate students learn a foreign language and instead required training in a specific research skill (6 semester hours) that added a new dimension to the student's skill set. The doctoral comprehensive exam required a paper showing original scholarship and an oral defense of that paper. The comprehensive exam paper was expected to lead to a dissertation prospectus, dissertation research, and the traditional final oral examination. The goal of training was to produce skilled, knowledgeable scholars without wasting time and effort on requirements that had developed decades ago and did not contribute to the development of the contemporary skills necessary for productive research and publication. We believed that students, rather than undertaking an extended period of academic apprenticeship, would learn most effectively as full collaborators in our research programs and as co-authors of the resulting publications.

Organizational Structures

The Founding Four established several organizational structures and practices that have continued to the present. First, students were required to acquire training experiences from a program-wide array of opportunities, rather than having a mentor's lab serve as the sole training experience. Thus, although a student may have been identified with a specific faculty mentor, virtually all students worked extensively with others of us as well. Breadth of training in other areas of psychology and in related disciplines was fostered by a requirement that at least one member of the doctoral studies committee was to be from outside the social psychology doctoral program faculty.

One singularly important organizational structure, an ongoing research seminar called the Social Psychological Research Institute (SPRI), was inspired by Kurt Lewin's *Quasselstrippe*, which he developed during his tenure at the University of Berlin. The SPRI also includes features from the graduate training programs and faculty experiences of the Founding Four. Some unique features of the SPRI are that it is held off campus, presenters (virtually always student–faculty teams) present work in progress rather than finished research reported in colloquium style, and they are in search of feedback, critique, and advice. The SPRI has a 2-hour time frame, on a regular biweekly schedule. Attendance is expected of all social psychology program faculty and students. Guests from other psychology department programs and other disciplines are welcome. The SPRI is vitally important in fostering the climate of collaborative scholarship that is a hallmark of the program, and in creating awareness and appreciation of all phases of full cycle social psychology.

These structures facilitated the development of collaborations across labs and with other programs and departments while developing norms of openness to other theoretical and methodological perspectives, and they have also led to the development of a collective application of the principles of full-cycle social psychology. No single investigator or single team had to conduct all phases of full-cycle research, but we did so collectively, as a program. This collective endeavor is evident in the kind of grant proposals and internal research proposals generated as the social psychology doctoral program matured.

Accommodating Growth

Starting from the hiring of Linder as program director in 1972, the next faculty hired was Nancy Eisenberg in 1976, followed by Doug Kenrick in 1980, and Steve West in 1981. Nancy Russo joined in 1985, as did Leona Aiken (as ASU associate dean, moving full-time to the program in 1990); Steve Neuberg joined in 1988, Craig Nagoshi and Delia Saenz in 1989, and Dave MacKinnon in 1990. George Knight was an intradepartmental transfer to social in 1997. The faculty remained fully staffed until retirements started, and the current faculty now lists Lani Shiota and Adam Cohen joining in 2006, and Virginia Kwan in 2009.

The new faculty as well as the Founding Four expanded the conceptual and methodological range of the program, shown by the dual membership of a number of faculty in both the social psychology and quantitative methods graduate programs. In addition, strong ties were developed to other departments and programs: the developmental psychology program, the community emphasis within clinical psychology, and the preventive intervention research center, all within in the department of psychology; the Hispanic research center; the women's studies program; the department of Chicana and Chicano studies; the resilience solutions group; the business college; and the college of engineering.

The social psychology program became self-labeled as having a dual emphasis on theoretical and applied work, and purposefully nurtured that emphasis: "We endorse the view that these two arenas represent the respective sides of a single coin—each complementing and enriching the other" (Arizona State

University, 2000). However, Cialdini's full-cycle social psychology model helps us view the two facets of our work in an even more integrative way than the "two sides of a single coin." Rather, the phases of the full cycle stand in a *necessary* relationship, each to the others. The phenomena of human social behavior must be observed in naturally occurring situations, so that hypotheses can be generated and tested in controlled experiments against existing as well as newly proposed theory. In turn, practical solutions can be designed and tested for efficacy in the settings in which the phenomena were initially observed. Kurt Lewin's oft-quoted assertion that, "There is nothing so practical as a good theory," expresses one aspect of the full-cycle model, but does not include the complementary notion that to be "good," a theory must be supported by data collected in the environment in which the target phenomena naturally occur. This necessary complementarity between laboratory experimentation and research in the natural environment is a defining characteristic of full-cycle social psychology.

IS SOCIAL PSYCHOLOGY IN PASTEUR'S QUADRANT?

In retrospect, we can see that having at least a professed interest in "applications" has been a recurring theme in social psychology since its early days. Of course, Lewin is generally credited with fostering such an approach, and he himself engaged in a considerable number of field-based projects (Bickman, 1980). However, before Lewin, in the mid-1930s, Muzafer Sherif was explicitly concerned with real-world relevance of theory and method. His collaboration with Gardner Murphy at Columbia confirmed for both of them the necessity of basing hypotheses on the "actualities" of careful observation of real-world phenomenon, only after which one could formulate a hypothesis for rigorous testing. His oft-repeated phrase, "Experimentation is the crowning touch of analysis," put laboratory research at the end of an extensive period of observation and analysis of a phenomenon in its natural setting. The Robbers Cave study is a classic example of how theory and reality, laboratory and field, can be integrated from the beginning

The "Linear Model" from Basic to Applied Research

Some important distinctions are to be made in how a science approaches real-world phenomena. One way to "do applications" is to follow the path that Donald Stokes has described as the "linear model" in his insightful treatment of the issue in *Pasteur's Quadrant: Basic Science and Technological Innovation* (Stokes, 1997). In this model, any real-world use of a theory or concept to diagnose or perhaps intervene in any natural setting is to follow only *after* it has been carefully defined and rigorously tested in controlled laboratory experimentation. The structure of the linear model is deeply imbedded in American science and American policy. After World War II, President Roosevelt enlisted a leading science policy maker at the time, Vannevar Bush, to develop a postwar policy for the American government to implement in supporting the projected growth of American science. Bush's policy statement, *Science: The Endless Frontier* (Bush, 1945), articulated quite clearly that applied science was *not* to be part of the funding picture. He proposed a clearly stated and very deliberate policy of funding only basic science. His statement, "Applied research drives out pure" set the policy for the government at the time. Psychology's scientific leaders, coming back from their wartime duties, took the same tack as the Bush proposal, and the laboratory-based experimental method came to dominate the field in the immediate postwar period and for a long time afterward. By the late 1960s, the dominant view of social psychology was to think of it as a pure science enterprise. Although the Society for the Psychological Study of Social Issues (SPSSI) had been established in 1936, applied research and practice played only a small role in our discipline after the founding in 1965 of both the Society for Experimental Social Psychology and the *Journal of Experimental Social Psychology*. To the extent that applied concerns had any import in the enterprise of social psychological science, it was through the linear model, the application of existing social psychological theory to social behavior in natural settings (Stokes, 1997; Reich, 2008). Zimbardo (2004) has argued that the application of social psychology has been an outstanding success, but many if not most of the successes he lists are examples of the linear model. Breckler (2007), with the National Science Foundation (NSF) at the time, has argued that the promise of successful applications in the entire field of psychology has yet to be fulfilled, a sentiment shared by many others (Reich, 2008).

Pasteur's Quadrant

Stokes (1997) has challenged the accuracy of assuming the historical dominance of the pure-science, linear model approach from another perspective. As he makes abundantly clear in his analysis, science has been much more than just linear, spectacularly so. He places the linear model in a broader context of a four-fold typology of models of pure and applied science. A brief description here will provide a context to understand how it is that Cialdini's contributions with his full-cycle approach do *not* meet the criteria of the classical linear model but at the same time *do* represent outstanding examples of integrated theory building and application (Reich, 2008).

Stokes categorizes scientific approaches by asking two Yes–No questions: "Is the science focused on a quest for fundamental understanding?" And, the cross-cutting distinction is: "Does it involve considerations of use and applications to solving practical problems?" Four quadrants are generated by this approach. The Bush "pure science" approach would fall into the category of High Basic Science, Low Use Oriented. The classic case is Niels Bohr, whose work on fundamental atomic particles was done for purely knowledge-acquisition purposes, with no consideration of solving any real-world problems. Stokes labels this the Bohrian Quadrant. We have presented it here as the traditionally required first step in the linear model.

The High Basic Science, High Use Oriented approach characterizes the science of Louis Pasteur, the main topic of Stokes' analysis. His early work on crystallography led him to consult with the French wine industry, which in turn led to the discovery of contamination in French wine-making, solved by heating (pasteurization). Stokes labels this the "Pasteurian Quadrant," and it represents the complete integration of pure science and applications arising and developing *simultaneously*, not in a temporal sequence, as in the linear model.

The next Stokes category, the Low Basic Science, High Use Oriented Quadrant, characterizes the work of Thomas Edison. He garnered over 1,000 patents in his life-long career of inventing things to make living better, but he had no interest in basic science and said so ("I am not a scientist, I'm an inventor"). Accordingly, he left no legacy of basic science contributions. Stokes labels this the "Edisonian Quadrant." The fourth quadrant, Low Basic Science and Low Use Oriented, while providing some amusing examples of how humans can waste time, needs no discussion here.

Cialdini's full-cycle approach is probably the closest social psychology has come to matching the principles of Pasteur's Quadrant. We leave it to other chapters in this volume to explore the many ways in which the full-cycle model has been implemented. In the remainder of this chapter, we explore the ways in which the ASU social psychology program provided a supportive environment for Bob's work and, at the same time, gained strength from doing so.

PASTEURIAN SCIENCE IN THE ASU SOCIAL PSYCHOLOGY PROGRAM

Community Collaborations

The program's growth in the size of its doctoral-level training in the early 1970s quickly outstripped state-funded stipends, so funding had to be sought outside the usual sources. ASU is situated in a major metropolitan area, where a considerable number of community mental health centers, social action agencies, and even government programs had on-the-ground ties to significant social problems. The social psychology faculty realized early on that social psychology provided a rich source of highly relevant concepts, which could be applied to those settings in both a diagnostic and experimental framework. We developed a series of half-time placements for our students, paid for by those agencies. The students were able to apply their classroom knowledge and techniques in real-world settings while the supporting agencies were able to greatly enhance their level of conceptual and empirical sophistication. This model has characterized the social program's training functioning for many years.

Applied Research Methodology

Developments external to the program also had a major impact on its adoption of the Pasteurian model. Donald Campbell's work with Julian Stanley (Campbell & Stanley, 1966) and Tom Cook (Cook & Campbell, 1979) was a revolution in thinking about research outside the confines of the standard laboratory methodology. Program evaluation developed into a professional career in many areas of the social sciences, and our social psychology students added it on as one more tool in their set of skills. Thus, while the social program continued to place a strong emphasis on laboratory-based, theory-testing experimental social psychology, many of our students were at the same time working in real-world settings with social agency administrators and faculty researchers as dual mentors.

Examples of Full-Cycle/Pasteur's Quadrant Research at Arizona State University

Numerous examples of the melding of laboratory experimentation and analysis of social phenomena in natural settings characterized much of the research conducted by members of the ASU social psychology program. Below are brief accounts of one example each from the current authors' work and collaborations to provide a sense of the full-cycle/Pasteur's Quadrant process.

Personal Control and Well-being

Having beliefs that one can control the events of one's life has highly beneficial effects, whereas loss of control is harmful. Reich and his close collaborator Alex Zautra, from the ASU clinical psychology program, conducted a series of studies applying control concepts in daily living for samples of college-aged, middle-aged, and older adults. An initial study (Reich & Zautra, 1981) induced participants to engage in low versus high levels of self-chosen (controllable) positive events (vs. no contact controls) over a 2-week period. At follow-up, both intervention groups reported greater pleasantness of their daily experiences and better mental health compared to the controls. Interestingly, they did not differ from each other; even relatively small increases in controllable activities resulted in improvement in well-being. However, covariance analyses showed an interaction with the participants' prior experiences with stressful daily life events. Of those participants reporting higher levels of stressful life events, only the group engaging in higher levels of controllable positive experiences reported significantly reduced psychological distress post-intervention, but distress was not reduced in the lower induced control group. So, our testing of control concepts in a real-world setting revealed a limitation on the effectiveness of the variable; life context matters.

Reich and Zautra (1989) then developed an expanded test of the effectiveness of enhanced personal control, this time for separate samples of community-residing adults experiencing high levels of two distinctly different negative life experiences: physical disability and spousal bereavement (vs. matched controls). Such stressful experiences are risk factors for loss of control and provide a strong test of the effectiveness of a control intervention.

Four biweekly in-home sessions with counselors trained in control concepts were focused on helping the participants become more mindful of the nature and frequency of their naturally occurring controllable daily events ("started a conversation,") and uncontrollable events ("car broke down"). They were then guided in self-chosen ways to enhance the frequency and pleasantness of their controllable events, and to strengthen their coping and acceptance skills to deal with uncontrollable events.

The results showed the control enhancement intervention resulted in significant increases in personal mastery and improved mental health for the disabled group, although it was relatively ineffective for the bereavement group. The disabled group also reported the highest level of pre-experimental distress, confirming the results of the prior experiment. This result signifies the value of considering the relevant characteristics of the population for whom an experimental intervention is to be implemented. As Pasteur showed, the key is to match the theory and concepts with the realities of the problem.

Divorced Dads

Why do many fathers disconnect from their children after divorce? While married, almost all fathers feel concern and love for their children, take pride in their provider role, and make continual sacrifices for them, as mothers do. Why do so many of these dedicated fathers abruptly turn away from their responsibilities when they divorce? To solve this puzzle, Braver worked with Irwin Sandler and Sharlene Wolchik (both were members of the ASU community psychology emphasis within clinical psychology, and of the Preventive Intervention Research Center). One key concept from standard social psychological toolkits they chose to draw upon was *social exchange theory* (Thibaut & Kelley, 1959; Kelley & Thibaut, 1978). According to this notion, all relationships are judged by their participants on the basis of rewards versus costs, and relationships may be abandoned when the latter exceeds the former. This is precisely, they reasoned, what might happen to some divorced fathers when circumstances interfere with the normal benefits of parenthood.

A second core social psychological construct rose to the surface as a key explanatory device in preliminary empirical explorations with this population: perceptions of control. Many divorced fathers, it was found, feel that their children have been wrenched from them by their ex-wives and by the system, and there is nothing they can do about it—they are powerless. It was overwhelmingly these "parentally disenfranchised" fathers, those bereft of any semblance of control of their lives, who became the dropouts and deadbeat dads. Those who remained empowered, those made to feel that carrying out all the obligations of fatherhood was necessary to their children, were generally responsible, involved, and caring.

Joining these two ideas, Braver et al. (1993a) proposed a comprehensive model of father involvement after divorce, then empirically tested it in a three-wave, 4-year longitudinal study funded by the National Institute of Child Health and Human Development (NICHD; Braver et al., 1993b). Strong support for the theory was found (Braver & O'Connell, 1998).

Of course, the full-cycle approach recognizes that, even if well conducted, a longitudinal study cannot fully unravel cause and effect; a convincing experimental test was necessary. Accordingly, an intervention called Dads For Life was developed (Braver & Griffin, 2000), for which social exchange notions and perceptions of control provided the theoretical underpinning. For example, to enhance perceptions of control, flashback videos were created and specific role-plays were devised to impress how much control of their child's upbringing and outcomes fathers actually retained. Then (funded by another grant from NICHD and the National Institute for Mental Health; NIMH), either this intervention or a placebo control intervention was provided at random to a sample of 214 recently divorced fathers (Braver, Griffin, & Cookston, 2005; Braver et al., 2005; Cookston et al., 2007). Results showed that fathers given the Dads For Life intervention ended up behaving in ways that benefitted their child's behavioral health and lowered conflict with the mother.

We see in Dads For Life another example of working in Pasteur's Quadrant, adapting social psychological theoretical constructs to enhance the real-world outcomes for real people, and using applied social science tools to evaluate both the theory and the intervention's ability to improve people's lives.

Behavior in Social Traps

Hunting to extinction or near extinction of the American passenger pigeon, the American bison, and the great whales; the run on banks after the crash of 1929; the jamming of the AM radio band in the early 20th century; and the depletion of fisheries in the world's oceans are all vivid examples in which humans have sought short-term individual gains and triggered long-term collective loss. Historical accounts and observations of behavior in commons dilemmas have been available in abundance, as have economic analyses of decision-making by participants (Hardin, 1968; Platt, 1973). Platt's conceptual analysis relied heavily on behavioral concepts, especially the combination of short-term rewards and delayed negative consequences. Kevin Brechner, one of the first doctoral students to enter the social psychology program, had extensive experience with building electrical circuits and mechanical devices to deliver stimuli and reinforcements to rats and pigeons. For his dissertation experiments, Kevin built an electromechanical social trap analog (Brechner, 1974, 1977). Kevin demonstrated that groups of three participants starting with a small pool and being unable to communicate harvested significantly fewer points than groups starting with a larger pool or being allowed to communicate within the group.

Using a computer-based social trap analog, Greg Neidert, a later doctoral student in the program, conducted dissertation research and follow-up experiments (Neidert, 1986; Neidert & Linder, 1990) that demonstrated the efficacy of having a sense of participation in developing a strategy for managing the commons, and a public commitment to use that strategy. The high-participation, high-commitment groups performed almost flawlessly for 100 trials, the maximum allowed. No participation/no commitment groups exhausted the pool almost as fast as was possible. These laboratory analog results could be tested in field settings, but the issues that arise when trying to intervene in a naturally occurring commons dilemma are daunting. However, Linder was able to use these analyses and results in assisting the U. S. Bureau of Land Management to develop training programs for personnel from both public and private agencies who would be involved in resource-use negotiations between competing user groups in the American mountain west.

Recently, researchers at ASU outside the department of psychology have independently designed a computer-based laboratory analog for commons dilemmas. Janssen et al. (2010) manipulated two independent variables, the availability of communication among participants prior to each harvesting period, and the availability of costly punishment to greedy over-harvesters. Their results replicated Brechner's finding that communication enhanced cooperation in managing the resource and led to increased harvests. Janssen et al. (2010) manipulated communication availability by allowing participants to exchange text messages in a "chat room" prior to the harvesting sessions. This ad lib communication process appears to have resulted in establishing harvesting strategies, as well as promises to use them, similar to the high-participation, high-commitment conditions in Neidert's experiments, and yielding similar results on rates of harvesting and total rewards obtained.

It is striking that this new work was done by researchers with roots primarily in political science and economics. The hypotheses they tested are grounded in the traditions of their home disciplines, especially the economic analyses of behavior in commons dilemmas. There are at least two implications of this partial parallelism. First, there may be examples of full-cycle research in other disciplines in the social and behavioral sciences in which observation and description in field settings are complemented by laboratory experiments. The relationship between classical economic theory and the emergent field of behavioral economics may be an example. Thus, the architecture of full-cycle social psychology may have applications well beyond the range of topics explored in this book. Second, it is possible that a *multidisciplinary* full-cycle research program could be developed in which the various aspects of important social problems could be addressed, collaboratively and collectively, by the several disciplines relevant to the problem. Reform of the U.S. health care system might be addressed as a complex of interlocking problems, rather than being perceived only from the separate perspectives of individual disciplines. Taking such an approach requires laying aside reductionism, as well as the artificial distinction between basic and applied research.

CONCLUSION

The social psychology graduate training program at ASU has been both unique and successful. From a humble beginning in 1972, when four young professors assembled and planned the program, we eventually grew to

17 faculty members. We have trained doctoral students for nearly four decades. We have a record of publication and grant acquisition that compares favorably with the most illustrious social psychology programs, both nationally and internationally. After their studies with us have been completed, our students compete effectively for top faculty and research positions, and many of them go on to illustrious careers.

We believe that this success was no accident. Certainly, we were able to make excellent appointments in our faculty hiring, and excellent choices in our graduate admissions. We were fortunate that our university and the community environment supported this unique program, even when times were difficult. But more than this, we deliberately adopted a program structure that . . . well . . . *worked.* And this structure, we believe, could and should be exported elsewhere, where we believe it could work just as well.

We have written this chapter to make the case that social psychology should be located in Pasteur's Quadrant. This means basic social psychology and applied social psychology should be inextricably bound together into full-cycle social psychology, providing an epistemic framework in which we reach agreement on important phenomena to study and, in a mindful way, apply that framework collectively. This book is filled with examples of that kind of work. That process requires respect for the skills and tools employed by the different researchers who work in each phase of collective full-cycle social psychology efforts, a perspective that we began to develop when we hired Robert Cialdini. The rest is history . . . and possibly a blueprint for a more fully realized social psychology everywhere.

REFERENCES

CHAPTER 1

Barabási, A.-L. (2002). *Linked: The new science of networks.* Cambridge, MA: Perseus.

Bem, D. J. (1987). Writing the empirical journal article. In M. P. Zanna, & J. M. Darley (Eds.), *The compleat academic* (pp. 171–201). Mahwah, NJ: Lawrence Erlbaum Associates.

Cialdini, R. B. (1980). Full-cycle social psychology. In L. Bickman (Ed.), *Applied social psychology annual* (Vol. 1, pp. 21–47). Beverly Hills, CA: Sage.

Cialdini, R. B. (2003). Crafting normative messages to protect the environment. *Current Directions in Psychological Science, 12,* 105–109.

Cialdini, R. B. (2009). *Influence: Science and practice* (5th ed.). Boston: Allyn & Bacon.

Cialdini, R. B., Borden, R. J., Thorne, A., Walker, M., Freeman, S., & Sloan, L. (1976). Basking in reflected glory: Three (football) field studies. *Journal of Personality and Social Psychology, 34,* 366–375.

Cialdini, R. B., Brown, S. L., Lewis, B. P., Luce, C., & Neuberg, S. L. (1997). Reinterpreting the empathy-altruism relationship: When one into one equals oneness. *Journal of Personality and Social Psychology, 73,* 481–494.

Cialdini, R. B., Kallgren, C. A., & Reno, R. R. (1991). A focus theory of normative conduct: A theoretical refinement and reevaluation of the role of norms in human behavior. In M. Zanna (Eds.), *Advances in experimental social psychology* (Vol. 24, pp. 201–234). New York: Academic Press.

Cialdini, R. B., & Kenrick, D. T. (1976). Altruism as hedonism: A social development perspective on the relationship of negative mood and helping. *Journal of Personality and Social Psychology, 34,* 907–914.

Cialdini, R. B., & Richardson, K. D. (1980). Two indirect tactics of image management: Basking and blasting. *Journal of Personality and Social Psychology, 89,* 406–415.

Cialdini, R. B., Schaller, M., Houlihan, D., Arps, K., Fultz, J., & Beaman, A. L. (1987). Empathy-based helping: Is it selflessly or selfishly motivated? *Journal of Personality and Social Psychology, 52,* 749–758.

Cialdini, R. B., Vincent, J. E., Lewis, S. K., Catalan, J., Wheeler, D., & Darby, B. L. (1975). A reciprocal concessions procedure for inducing compliance: The door-in-the-face technique. *Journal of Personality and Social Psychology, 31,* 206–215.

Cottrell, C. A., & Neuberg, S. L. (2005). Different emotional reactions to different groups: A sociofunctional threat-based approach to 'prejudice.' *Journal of Personality and Social Psychology, 88,* 770–789.

Feyerabend, P. (1975). *Against method.* London: New Left.

Goldstein, N. J., & Cialdini, R. B. (2007). The spyglass self: A model of vicarious self-perception. *Journal of Personality and Social Psychology, 92,* 402–417.

Goldstein, N. J., Cialdini, R. B., & Griskevicius, V. (2008). A room with a viewpoint: Using normative appeals to motivate environmental conservation in a hotel setting. *Journal of Consumer Research, 35*, 472–482.

Granovetter, M. S. (1973). The strength of weak ties. *American Journal of Sociology, 78*, 1360–1380.

Griskevicius, V., Cialdini, R. B., & Kenrick, D. T. (2006). Peacocks, Picasso, and parental investment: The effects of romantic motives on creativity. *Journal of Personality and Social Psychology, 91*, 63–76.

Griskevicius, V., Goldstein, N. J., Mortensen C. R., Cialdini, R. B., & Kenrick, D. T. (2006). Going along versus going alone: When fundamental motives facilitate strategic (non) conformity. *Journal of Personality and Social Psychology, 91*, 281–294.

Harton, H. C., & Bourgeois, M. J. (2004). Cultural elements emerge from dynamic social impact. In M. Schaller, & C. S. Crandall (Eds.), *The psychological foundations of culture* (pp. 41–76). Mahwah, NJ: Lawrence Erlbaum Associates.

Hull, D. L. (1988). *Science as a process.* Chicago: University of Chicago Press.

Kenrick, D. T., Griskevicius, V., Neuberg, S. L., & Schaller, M. (2010). Renovating the pyramid of needs: Contemporary extensions built upon ancient foundations. *Perspectives on Psychological Science, 5*, 292–314.

Kenrick, D. T., & Gutierres, S. E. (1980). Contrast effects and judgments of physical attractiveness: When beauty becomes a social problem. *Journal of Personality and Social Psychology, 38*, 131–140.

Kenrick, D. T., & Keefe, R. C. (1992). Age preferences in mates reflect sex differences in mating strategies. *Behavioral and Brain Sciences, 15*, 75–91.

Kenrick, D. T., Li, N. P., & Butner, J. (2003). Dynamical evolutionary psychology: Individual decision-rules and emergent social norms. *Psychological Review, 110*, 3–28.

Latané, B. (1996). Dynamic social impact: The creation of culture by communication. *Journal of Communication, 46*(4), 13–25.

Latané, B. (1997). Dynamic social impact: The societal consequences of human interaction. In C. McGarty, & S. A. Haslam (Eds.), *The message of social psychology* (pp. 200–220). Malden, MA: Blackwell.

Lewenstein, M., Nowak, A., & Latané, B. (1990). Statistical mechanics of social impact. *Physical Review. A, 45*, 763–776.

MacDonald, G., & Leary, M. R. (2005). Why does social exclusion hurt? The relationship between social and physical pain. *Psychological Bulletin, 131*, 202–223.

Maner, J. K., DeWall, C. N., Baumeister, R. F., & Schaller, M. (2007). Does social exclusion motivate interpersonal reconnection? Resolving the 'porcupine problem.' *Journal of Personality and Social Psychology, 92*, 42–55.

Morse, K. A., & Neuberg, S. L. (2004). How do holidays influence relationship processes and outcomes?: Examining the instigating and catalytic effects of Valentine's Day. *Personal Relationships, 11*, 509–527.

Nowak, A., Szamrej, J., & Latané, B. (1990). From private attitude to public opinion: A dynamic theory of social impact. *Psychological Review, 97*, 362–376.

Schaller, M. (1997). The psychological consequences of fame: Three tests of the self-consciousness hypothesis. *Journal of Personality, 65*, 291–309.

Schaller, M., Conway, L. G., III, & Tanchuk, T. L. (2002). Selective pressures on the once and future contents of ethnic stereotypes: Effects of the communicability of traits. *Journal of Personality and Social Psychology, 82*, 861–877.

Schaller, M., & Latané, B. (1996). Dynamic social impact and the evolution of social representations: A natural history of stereotypes. *Journal of Communication, 46*(4), 64–71.

Schaller, M., & Murray, D. R. (2008). Pathogens, personality, and culture: Disease prevalence predicts worldwide variability in sociosexuality, extraversion, and openness to experience. *Journal of Personality and Social Psychology, 95*, 212–221.

Travers, J., & Milgram, S. (1969). An experimental study of the small world problem. *Sociometry, 32,* 425–443.

Watts, D. J. (2003). *Six degrees: The science of a connected age.* New York: Norton.

CHAPTER 2

Amabile, T. M., Schatzel, E. A., Moneta, G. B., & Kramer, S. J. (2004). Leader behaviors and the work environment for creativity: Perceived leader support. *Leadership Quarterly, 15,* 5–32.

Baumeister, R. F., Bratslavsky, E., Finkenauer, C., & Vohs, K. D. (2001). Bad is stronger than good. *Review of General Psychology, 5,* 323–370.

Bohns, V. K., & Flynn, F. J. (2010). Why didn't you just ask? Underestimating the discomfort of help-seeking. *Journal of Experimental Social Psychology, 46,* 402–409.

Bolger, N., Zuckerman, A., & Kessler, R. C. (2000). Invisible support and adjustment to stress. *Journal of Personality and Social Psychology, 79,* 953–961.

Cartwright, D. (1965). Influence, leadership, control. In J. G. March (Ed.) *Handbook of organizations* (pp. 1–47). Chicago: Rand McNally.

Cialdini, R. B. (1984). *Influence: The psychology of persuasion.* New York: HarperCollins.

Cialdini, R. B., & Kenrick, D. T. (1976). Altruism as hedonism: A social development perspective on the relationship of negative mood and helping. *Journal of Personality and Social Psychology, 34,* 907–914.

Clark, M. S., & Isen, A. M. (1982). Toward understanding the relationship between feeling states and social behavior. In A. H. Hastrof, & A. M. Isen (Eds.), *Cognitive social psychology* (pp. 73–108). New York: Elsevier.

Cowie, H., Naylor, P., Chauhan, L. T. P., & Smith, P. K. (2002). Knowledge, use of, and attitudes towards peer support: A 2-year follow-up to the Prince's Trust survey. *Journal of Adolescence, 25,* 453–468.

Flynn, F. J., & Bohns, V. (2010). *Can you do me a favor? Limitations of the commitment and consistency principle in soliciting help.* Unpublished manuscript.

Flynn, F. J., & Lake(Bohns), V. K. B. (2008). If you need help, just ask: Underestimating compliance with direct requests for help. *Journal of Personality and Social Psychology, 95,* 128–143.

Gilovich, T., & Medvec, V. H. (1994). The temporal profile to the experience of regret. *Journal of Personality and Social Psychology, 67,* 357–365.

Gilovich, T., & Medvec, V. H. (1995). The experience of regret: What, when, and why. *Psychological Review, 102,* 379–395.

Gilovich, T., Medvec, V. H., & Kahneman, D. (1998). Varieties of regret: A debate and partial resolution. *Psychological Review, 105,* 602–605.

Goffman, E. (1955). On face-work. *Psychiatry, 18,* 213–231.

Goldschmidt, M. M. (1998). Do me a favor: A descriptive analysis of favor asking sequences in American English. *Journal of Pragmatics, 29,* 129–153.

Goldstein, N. J., Cialdini, R. B., & Griskevicius, V. (2008). A room with a viewpoint: Using social norms to motivate environmental conservation in hotels. *Journal of Consumer Research, 35,* 472–482.

Grice, H. P. (1975). Logic and conversation. In P. Cole, & J. Morgan (Eds.), *Syntax and semantics* (Vol. 3, pp. 41–58). New York: Academic Press.

Hogan, C., & Flynn, F. (2010). *Asking for forgiveness: The impact of giving and seeking help on relationship repair.* Manuscript under review.

Jecker, J., & Landy, D. (1969). Liking a person as a function of doing him a favor. *Human Relations, 22,* 371–378.

Keltner, D., Gruenfeld, D. H., & Anderson, C. (2003). Power, approach, and inhibition. *Psychological Review, 110,* 265–284.

Kinnier, R. T., & Metha, A. T. (1989). Regrets and priorities at three stages of life. *Counseling and Values, 33*, 182–193.

Lemay, J. (Ed.). (1987). *The autobiography of Benjamin Franklin as given in Benjamin Franklin: Writings.* New York: Library of America.

McCullough, M. E., Emmons, R. A., & Tsang, J. (2002). The grateful disposition: A conceptual and empirical topography. *Journal of Personality and Social Psychology, 82*, 112–127.

Miller, D., & Ratner, R. K. (1998). The disparity between the actual and assumed power of self-interest. *Journal of Personality and Social Psychology, 74*, 53–62.

Peeters, G., & Czapinski, J. (1990). Positive-negative asymmetry in evaluations: The distinction between affective and informational negativity effects. *European Review of Social Psychology, 1*, 33–60.

Rozin, P., & Royzman, E. B. (2001). Negativity bias, negativity dominance, and contagion. *Personality and Social Psychology Review, 5*, 296–320.

Savitsky, K., Epley, N., & Gilovich, T. (2001). Is it as bad as we fear?: Overestimating the extremity of others' judgments. *Journal of Personality and Social Psychology, 81*, 44–56.

Skowronski, J. J., & Carlston, D. E. (1989). Negativity and extremity biases in impression formation: A review of explanations. *Psychological Bulletin, 105*, 131–142.

Taylor, S. E. (1991). Asymmetrical effects of positive and negative events: The mobilization-minimization hypothesis. *Psychological Bulletin, 110*, 67–85.

CHAPTER 3

Brehm, J. W. (1966). *A theory of psychological reactance.* New York: Academic Press.

Cialdini, R. B. (1996). Social influence and the triple tumor structure of organizational dishonesty. In D. M. Messick, & A. E. Tenbrunsel (Eds.), *Codes of conduct* (pp. 44–58). New York: Russell Sage Foundation.

Cialdini, R. B. (2009). *Influence: Science and practice.* Boston: Pearson/Allyn and Bacon.

Cialdini, R. B., Vincent, J. E., Lewis, S. K., Catalan, J., Wheeler, D., & Darby, B. L. (1975). Reciprocal concessions procedure for inducing compliance: The door-in-the-face technique. *Journal of Personality and Social Psychology, 31*, 206–215.

Freedman, J. L., & Fraser, S. C. (1966). Compliance without pressure: The foot-in-the-door technique. *Journal of Personality and Social Psychology, 4*, 195–203.

Littman, J. (2007). The invisible digital man. *Playboy, 54*(6), 64–66, 133–138.

Mitnick, K. D., & Simon, W. L. (2002). *The art of deception.* Indianapolis, IN: Wiley Publishing, Inc.

Mitnick, K. D., & Simon, W. L. (2005). *The art of intrusion.* Indianapolis, IN: Wiley Publishing, Inc.

Mitnick, K. D., & Simon, W. L. (2011). *Ghost in the wires: My adventures as the world's most wanted hacker.* New York: Little Brown.

Pratkanis, A. R. (2000). Altercasting as an influence tactic. In D. J. Terry, & M. A. Hogg (Eds.), *Attitudes, behavior, and social context* (pp. 201–226). Mahwah, NJ: Lawrence Erlbaum Associates, Inc.

Sagarin, B. J., Cialdini, R. B., Rice, W. E., & Serna, S. B. (2002). Dispelling the illusion of invulnerability: The motivations and mechanisms of resistance to persuasion. *Journal of Personality and Social Psychology, 83*, 526–541.

CHAPTER 4

Arnould, E. J., & Price, L. L. (1993). River magic: Extraordinary experience and the extended service encounter. *Journal of Consumer Research, 20*, 24–45.

Alter, A. L., & Oppenheimer, D. M. (2006). Predicting short-term stock fluctuations by using processing fluency. *Proceedings of the National Academy of Science, 103*, 9369–9372.

Alter, A. L., & Oppenheimer, D. M. (2008). Effects of fluency on psychological distance and mental construal (or why New York is a large city, but New York is a civilized jungle). *Psychological Science, 19*, 161–167.

Cialdini, R. B. (2001). Systematic opportunism: An approach to the study of tactical social influence. In J. P. Forgas and K. D. Williams (Eds.), *Social influence: Direct and indirect processes* (pp. 25–39). Philadelphia, PA: Psychology Press.

Cialdini, R. B. (2005). Basic social influence is underestimated. *Psychological Inquiry, 16*, 158–161.

Cialdini, R. B. (2009). *Influence: Science and practice* (5th ed.). Boston: Allyn & Bacon.

Cialdini, R. B., Petrova, P. K., Demaine, L. J., Barrett, D. W., Sagarin, B. J., Rhoads, K. L., & Maner, J. (2010). *The poison parasite defense: A strategy for sapping a stronger opponent's persuasive strength*. Hanover, NH: Tuck School of Business at Dartmouth, available at http://mba.tuck.dartmouth.edu/pages/faculty/petia.petrova/working_papers.html.

Cialdini, R. B., Demaine, L., Sagarin, B. J., Barrett, D. W., Rhoads, K., & Winter, P. L. (2006). Managing social norms for persuasive impact. *Social Influence, 1*, 3–15.

Cialdini, R. B., Reno, R. R., & Kallgren, C. A. (1990). A focus theory of normative conduct: Recycling the concept of norms to reduce littering in public places. *Journal of Personality and Social Psychology, 58*, 1015–1026.

Cialdini, R. B., & Schroeder, D. A. (1976). Increasing compliance by legitimizing paltry contributions: When even a penny helps. *Journal of Personality and Social Psychology, 34*, 599–604.

Cialdini, R. B., Wosinska, W., Barrett, D. W., Butner, J., & Gornik-Durose, M. (1999). Compliance with a request in two cultures: The differential influence of social proof and commitment/consistency on collectivists and individualists. *Personality and Social Psychology Bulletin, 25*, 1242–1253.

Fitzsimons, G. J., & Moore, S. G. (2008). Should we ask our children about sex, drugs and rock & roll? Potentially harmful effects of asking questions about risky behaviors. *Journal of Consumer Psychology, 18*, 82–95.

Fitzsimons, G. J., & Morwitz, V. M. (1996). The effect of measuring intent on brand level purchase behavior. *Journal of Consumer Research, 23*, 1–11.

Greenwald, A. G., Carnot, C. G., Beach, R., & Young, B. (1987). Increasing voting behavior by asking people if they expect to vote. *Journal of Applied Psychology, 72*, 315–318.

Hung, I. W., & Wyer, R. S. (2009). The impact of differences in perspective on the influence of charitable appeals: When imagining oneself as the victim is not always beneficial. *Journal of Marketing Research, 46*(3), 421–434.

Iyengar, S. S., & Lepper, M. R. (2000). When choice is demotivating: Can one desire too much of good thing? *Journal of Personality and Social Psychology, 79*(6), 995–1006.

Labroo, A. A., & Kim, S. (2009). The instrumentality heuristic: Why metacognitive difficulty is desirable during goal pursuit. *Psychological Science, 20*(1), 127–134.

Levav, J., & Fitzsimons, G. (2006). When questions change behavior: The role of ease of representation. *Psychological Science, 17*(3), 207–213.

Mandel, N., Petrova, P. K., & Cialdini, R. B. (2006). Images of success and the preference for luxury brands. *Journal of Consumer Psychology, 16*(1), 57–69.

McGlone, M. S., & Tofighbakhsh, J. (2000). Birds of a feather flock conjointly (?): Rhyme as reason in aphorisms. *Psychological Science, 11*, 424–428.

Novemsky, N., Dhar, R., Schwarz, N., & Simonson, I. (2007). Preference fluency in choice. *Journal of Marketing Research, 44*, 347–356.

Petrova, P. K., & Cialdini, R. B. (2005). Fluency of consumption imagery and the backfire effects of imagery appeals. *Journal of Consumer Research, 32*(3), 442–452.

Petrova, P. K. (2006a). Let's talk about it: The role of imagery in word of mouth. Paper presented at the Marketing Speaker Series, Tuck School of Business at Dartmouth.

Petrova, P. K. (2006b). Fluency effects: New domains and consequences for persuasion. Doctoral dissertation, Arizona State University.

Petrova, P. K., & Cialdini, R. B. (2009). Evoking the imagination as a strategy of influence. In C. P. Haugtvedt, P. Herr, & F. Kardes (Eds.), *Handbook of consumer psychology* (pp. 505–525). Mahwah, NJ: Lawrence Erlbaum Associates.

Petrova, P. K., & Cialdini, R. B. (2011). New approaches toward resistance to persuasion. In G. Hastings, C. Bryant, & K. Angus (Eds.), *Handbook of social marketing.* (pp. 107–122). London, UK. Sage Publications.

Petrova, P. K., Cialdini, R. B., Barrett, D., Goldstein, N., & Maner, J. (2006). Effective counter persuasion: Creating lasting resistance to a stronger opponent., *Advances in Consumer Research, 33,* 276.

Petrova, P. K., Cialdini, R. B., Goldstein, N. J., & Griskevicius, V. (2010). *Protecting consumers from harmful advertising: The role counter claim alignment in creating resistance to persuasion* Manuscript submitted for publication, available at http://www.linkedin.com/in/petiapetrova.

Petrova, P. K., Cialdini, R. B., & Sills, S. J. (2007). Personal consistency and compliance across cultures. *Journal of Experimental Social Psychology, 43,* 104–111.

Petrova, P. K., Goukens, C., & Cialdini, R. B. (2010). *Keep on talking: A dual process theory of fluency,* Working paper, Hanover, NH: Tuck School of Business at Dartmouth.

Reber, R., & Schwarz, N. (1999). Effects of perceptual fluency on judgments of truth. *Consciousness and Cognition, 8,* 338–342.

Reber, R., Brun, M., & Mittendorfer, K. (2009). The use of heuristics in intuitive mathematical judgment. *Psychonomic Bulletin and Review, 15*(6), 1174–1178.

Reber, R., Schwarz, N., & Winkielman, P. (2004). Processing fluency and aesthetic pleasure: Is beauty in the perceiver's processing experience? *Personality and Social Psychology Review, 8,* 364–382.

Reber, R., Winkielman, P., & Schwarz, N. (1998). Effects of perceptual fluency on affective judgments. *Psychological Science, 9,* 45–48.

Rothman, A. J., & Schwarz, N. (1998). Constructing perceptions of vulnerability: Personal relevance and the use of experiential information in health judgments. *Personality and Social Psychology Bulletin, 24,* 1053–1064.

Sela, A., Berger, J., & Liu, W. (2009). Variety, vice, and virtue: How assortment size influences option choice. *Journal of Consumer Research, 35,* 941–951.

Schwarz, N. (2006). On judgments of truth and beauty. *Daedalus, 135,* 136–138.

Schwarz, N., Sanna, L., Skurnik, I., & Yoon, C. (2007). Metacognitive experiences and the intricacies of setting people straight: Implications for debiasing and public information campaigns. *Advances in Experimental Social Psychology, 39,* 127–161.

Schwarz, N., Strack, F., Bless, H., Klumpp, G., Rittenauer-Schatka, H., & Simons, A. (1991). Ease of retrieval as information: Another look at the availability heuristic. *Journal of Personality and Social Psychology, 61,* 195–202.

Schwarz, N., & Xu, J. (2011). Why don't we learn from poor choices? The consistency of expectation, choice, and memory clouds the lessons of experience. *Journal of Consumer Psychology, 21,* 142–145.

Schwartz, B. (2004). *The paradox of choice: Why more is less.* New York: Ecco Press.

Sherman, S. J., Cialdini, R. B., Schwartzman, D. F., & Reynolds, K. (1985). Imagining can heighten or lower the perceived likelihood of contracting a disease. *Personality and Social Psychology Bulletin, 11,* 118–127.

Song, H., & Schwarz, N. (2008a). If it's hard to read, it's hard to do: Processing fluency affects effort prediction and motivation. *Psychological Science, 19*(10), 986–988.

Song, H., & Schwarz, N. (2008b). Fluency and the detection of misleading questions: Low processing fluency attenuates the Moses illusion. *Social Cognition, 26*(6), 791–799.

Song, H., & Schwarz, N. (2009). If it's difficult to pronounce, it must be risky: Fluency, familiarity, and risk perception. *Psychological Science, 20*(2), 135–138.

Thompson, D. V., & Hamilton, R. (2006). The effects of information processing mode on consumers' responses to comparative advertising. *Journal of Consumer Research, 32,* 530–540.

Thompson, D. V., Hamilton, R., & Petrova, P. K. (2009). When mental simulation hinders behavior: The effects of outcome-versus process-oriented thinking on decision difficulty and subsequent performance. *Journal of Consumer Research, 36*, 562–574.

Topolinski, S., & Strack, F. (2010). False fame prevented: Avoiding fluency effects without judgmental correction. *Journal of Personality and Social Psychology, 98*(5), 721–733.

Ubel, P. A., Loewenstein, G., Schwarz, N., & Smith, D. (2005). Misimagining the unimaginable: The disability paradox and health care decision making. *Health Psychology, 24*(4 Suppl), S57–S62.

Weaver, K., Garcia, S. M., Schwarz, N., & Miller, D. T. (2007). Inferring the popularity of an opinion from its familiarity: A repetitive voice can sound like a chorus. *Journal of Personality and Social Psychology, 92*, 821–833.

Winkielman, P., & Cacioppo, J. T. (2001). Mind at ease puts a smile on the face: Psychophysiological evidence that processing facilitation leads to positive affect. *Journal of Personality and Social Psychology, 81*, 989–1000.

Winkielman, P., Halberstadt, J., Fazendeiro, T., & Catty, S. (2006). Prototypes are attractive because they are easy on mind. *Psychological Science, 17*(9), 799–806.

Zajonc, R. B. (1968). Attitudinal effects of mere exposure. *Journal of Personality and Social Psychology. Monograph Supplement, 9*, 1–27.

CHAPTER 5

Alchian, A. A., & Allen, W. R. (1967). *University economics*. Belmont, CA: Wadsworth.

Baker, S. M., & Petty, R. E. (1994). Majority and minority influence: Source-position imbalance as a determinant of message scrutiny. *Journal of Personality and Social Psychology, 67*, 5–19.

Brannon, L. A., & Brock, T. C. (2001). Limiting time for responding enhances behavior corresponding to the merits of compliance appeals: Refutations of heuristic-cue theory in service and consumer settings. *Journal of Consumer Psychology, 10*, 135–146.

Briñol, P., & Petty, R. E. (2009a). Persuasion: Insights from the self-validation hypothesis. In M. P. Zanna (Ed.), *Advances in experimental social psychology* (Vol. 41, pp. 69–118). New York: Elsevier.

Briñol, P., & Petty, R. E. (2009b). Source factors in persuasion: A self-validation approach. *European Review of Social Psychology, 20*, 49–96.

Briñol, P., Petty, R. E., & Tormala, Z. L. (2004). The self-validation of cognitive responses to advertisements. *Journal of Consumer Research, 30*, 559–573.

Brock, T. C. (1968). Implications of commodity theory for value change. In A. G. Greenwald, T. C. Brock, & T. M. Ostrom (Eds.), *Psychological foundations of attitudes* (pp. 243–275). New York: Academic.

Chaiken, S. (1978). *The use of source and message cues in persuasion: An informal processing analysis*. Unpublished doctoral dissertation, University of Massachusetts-Amherst.

Chaiken, S., Liberman, A., & Eagly, A. H. (1989). Heuristic and systematic processing within and beyond the persuasion context. In J. S. Uleman, & J. A. Bargh (Eds.), *Unintended thought* (pp. 212–252). New York: Guilford Press.

Chaiken, S., & Maheswaran, D. (1994). Heuristic processing can bias systematic processing: Effects of source credibility, argument ambiguity, and task importance on attitude judgment. *Journal of Personality and Social Psychology, 66*, 460–473.

Cialdini, R. B. (2001). *Influence: Science and practice* (4th ed.). Boston: Allyn & Bacon.

Cialdini, R. B., & Trost, M. R. (1998). Social influence: Social norms, conformity and compliance. In D. T. Gilbert, & S. T. Fiske (Eds.), *The handbook of social psychology* (Vol. 2, 4th ed., pp. 151–192). New York: McGraw-Hill.

Crano, W. D., & Chen, X. (1998). The leniency contract and persistence of majority and minority influence. *Journal of Personality and Social Psychology, 74*, 1437–1450.

Erb, H., Bohner, G., Schmalzle, K., & Rank, S. (1998). Beyond conflict and discrepancy: Cognitive bias in minority and majority influence. *Personality and Social Psychology Bulletin, 24,* 396–409.

Festinger, L. (1954). A theory of social comparison processes. *Human Relations, 7,* 117–140.

Horcajo, J., Petty, R. E., & Briñol, P. (2010). The effects of majority versus minority source status on persuasion: A self-validation analysis. *Journal of Personality and Social Psychology.*

Kaufman, D. Q., Stasson, M. F., & Hart, J. W. (1999). Are the tabloids always wrong or it that just what we think? Need for cognition and perceptions of articles in print media. *Journal of Applied Social Psychology, 29,* 1984–1997.

Kelman, H. C. (1958). Compliance, identification and internalization: Three processes of attitude change. *Journal of Conflict Resolution, 2,* 51–60.

Lynn, M. (1991). Scarcity effects on desirability: A quantitative review of the commodity theory literature. *Psychology and Marketing, 8,* 43–57.

Mackie, D. M. (1987). Systematic and nonsystematic processing of majority and minority persuasive communications. *Journal of Personality and Social Psychology, 53,* 41–52.

Martin, R., & Hewstone, M. (2008). Majority versus minority influence, message processing and attitude change: The source-context-elaboration model. In M. Zanna (Ed.), *Advances in experimental social psychology.* San Diego: Academia Press.

Martin, R., Hewstone, M., & Martin, P. Y. (2007). Systematic and heuristic processing of majority- and minority-endorsed messages: The effects of varying outcome relevance and levels of orientation on attitude and message processing. *Personality and Social Psychology Bulletin, 33,* 43–56.

Moscovici, S. (1980). Toward a theory of conversion behavior. In L. Berkowitz (Ed.), *Advances in experimental social psychology* (Vol. 13, pp. 209–239). New York: Academic Press.

Mugny, G., & Pérez, J. A. (1991). *The social psychology of minority influence.* Cambridge, UK: Cambridge University Press.

Petty, R. E., & Briñol, P. (in press). The Elaboration Likelihood Model: Three decades of research. In P. A. M. Van Lange, A. Kruglanski, & E. T. Higgins (Eds.), *Handbook of theories of social psychology.* London: Sage.

Petty, R. E., Briñol, P., & Tormala, Z. L. (2002). Thought confidence as a determinant of persuasion: The self-validation hypothesis. *Journal of Personality and Social Psychology, 82,* 722–741.

Petty, R. E., Briñol, P., Tormala, Z. L., & Wegener, D. T. (2007). The role of meta-cognition in social judgment. In E. T. Higgins, & A. W. Kruglanski (Eds.), *Social psychology: A handbook of basic principles* (2nd ed., pp. 254–284). New York: Guilford Press.

Petty, R. E., & Cacioppo, J. (1986). *Communication and persuasion: Central and peripheral routes to attitude change.* New York: Springer Verlag.

Petty, R. E., & Cacioppo, J. T. (1983). Central and peripheral routes to persuasion: Application to advertising. In L. Percy, & A. Woodside (Eds.), *Advertising and consumer psychology* (pp. 3–23). Lexington, MA: D. C. Heath.

Petty, R. E., Cacioppo, J. T., & Goldman, R. (1981). Personal involvement as a determinant of argument-based persuasion. *Journal of Personality and Social Psychology, 41,* 847–855.

Petty, R. E., Cacioppo, J. T., & Heesacker, M. (1981). The use of rhetorical questions in persuasion: A cognitive response analysis. *Journal of Personality and Social Psychology, 40,* 432–440.

Petty, R. E., Haugtvedt, C. P., & Smith, S. M. (1995). Elaboration as a determinant of attitude strength: Creating attitudes that are persistent, resistant, and predictive of behavior. In R. E. Petty, & J. A. Krosnick (Eds.), *Attitude strength: Antecedents and consequences* (pp. 93–130). Mahwah, NJ: Erlbaum.

Petty, R. E., & Mirels, H. L. (1981). Intimacy and scarcity of self-disclosure: Effects on interpersonal attraction for males and females. *Personality and Social Psychology Bulletin, 7,* 493–503.

Petty, R. E., & Wegener, D. T. (1999). The Elaboration Likelihood Model: Current status and controversies. In S. Chaiken, & Y. Trope (Eds.), *Dual process theories in social psychology* (pp. 41–72). New York: Guilford Press.

Petty, R. E., Wegener, D. T., & White, P. (1998). Flexible correction processes in social judgment: Implications for persuasion. *Social Cognition, 16,* 93–113.

Priester, J. M., & Petty, R. E. (1995). Source attributions and persuasion: Perceived honesty as a determinant of message scrutiny. *Personality and Social Psychology Bulletin, 21,* 637–654.

Tormala, Z. L., Briñol, P., & Petty, R. E. (2006). When credibility attacks: The reverse impact of source credibility on persuasion. *Journal of Experimental Social Psychology, 42,* 684–691.

Tormala, Z. L., Briñol, P., & Petty, R. E. (2007). Multiple roles for source credibility under high elaboration: It's all in the timing. *Social Cognition, 25,* 536–552.

Tormala, Z. L., Petty, R. E., & DeSensi, V. L. (2010). Multiple roles for minority sources in persuasion and resistance. In R. Martin, & M. Hewstone (Eds.), *Minority influence and innovation: Antecedents, processes, and consequences* (pp. 105–131). London: Psychology Press.

Wegener, D. T., & Petty, R. E. (1995). Flexible correction processes in social judgment: The role of naive theories in corrections for perceived bias. *Journal of Personality and Social Psychology, 68,* 36–51.

Wood, W., Lundgren, S., Quellette, J. A., Busceme, S., & Blackstone, T. (1994). Minority influence: A meta-analytic review of social influence processes. *Psychological Bulletin, 115,* 323–345.

Worchel, S., Lee, J., & Adewole, A. (1975). Effects of supply and demand on ratings of object value. *Journal of Personality and Social Psychology, 32,* 906–914.

CHAPTER 6

Bernache-Assollant, I., Lacassagne, M.-F., & Braddock, J. H. (2007). Basking in reflected glory and blasting: Differences in identity-management strategies between two groups of highly identified soccer fans. *Journal of Language and Social Psychology, 26,* 381–388.

Bizman, A., & Yinon, Y. (2002). Engaging in distancing tactics among sport fans: Effects on self-esteem and emotional responses. *Journal of Social Psychology, 142,* 381–392.

Buller, D. B., LePoire, B. A., Aune, R. K., & Eloy, S. V. (1992). Social perceptions as mediators of the effect of speech rate similarity on compliance. *Human Communication Research, 19,* 286–311.

Burger, J. M. (1985). Temporal effects on attributions for academic performances and reflected–glory basking. *Social Psychology Quarterly, 48,* 330–336.

Burger, J. M., Messian, N., Patel, S., del Prado, A., & Anderson, C. (2004). What a coincidence! The effects of incidental similarity on compliance. *Personality and Social Psychology Bulletin, 30,* 35–43.

Burger, J. M., Soroka, S., Gonzago, K., Murphy, E., & Somervell, E. (2001). The effect of fleeting attraction on compliance to requests. *Personality and Social Psychology Bulletin, 27,* 1578–1586.

Chartrand, T. L., & Bargh, J. A. (1999). The Chameleon Effect: The perception-behavior link and social interaction. *Journal of Personality and Social Psychology, 76,* 893–910.

Cialdini, R. B. (2009). *Influence: Science and practice* (5th ed.). Boston: Allyn & Bacon.

Cialdini, R. B., Borden, R. J., Thorne, A., Walker, M. R., Freeman, S., & Sloan, L. R. (1976). Basking in reflected glory: Three (football) field studies. *Journal of Personality and Social Psychology, 34,* 366–375.

Cialdini, R. B., & Richardson, K. D. (1980). Two indirect tactics of image management: Basking and blasting. *Journal of Personality and Social Psychology, 39,* 406–415.

Clark, M. S., Ouellette, R., Powell, M. C., & Milberg, S. (1987). Recipient's mood, relationship type, and helping. *Journal of Personality and Social Psychology, 53,* 94–103.

Dolinski, D., Nawrat, N., & Rudak, I. (2001). Dialogue involvement as a social influence technique. *Personality and Social Psychology Bulletin, 27*, 1395–1406.

Emswiller, T., Deaux, K., & Willits, J. E. (1971). Similarity, sex, and requests for small favors. *Journal of Applied Social Psychology, 1*, 284–291.

End, C. M., Dietz-Uhler, B., Harrick, E. A., & Jacquemotte, L. (2002). Identifying with winners: A reexamination of sport fans' tendency to BIRG. *Journal of Applied Social Psychology, 32*, 1017–1030.

Finch, J. F., & Cialdini, R. B. (1989). Another indirect tactic of (self-) image management: Boosting. *Personality and Social Psychology Bulletin, 15*, 222–232.

Garner, R. (2005). What's in a name? Persuasion perhaps. *Journal of Consumer Psychology, 15*, 108–116.

Gueguen, N., Pichot, N., & Le Dreff, G. (2002). Similarity and helping behavior on the web: The impact of the convergence of surnames between a solicitor and a subject in a request made by e-mail. *Journal of Applied Social Psychology, 35*, 423–429.

Heider, F. (1958). *The psychology of interpersonal relations.* New York: Wiley.

Miller, D. T., Downs, J. S., & Prentice, D. A. (1998). Minimal conditions for the creation of a unit relationship: The social bond between birthdaymates. *European Journal of Social Psychology, 28*, 475–481.

Silva, P. J. (2005). Deflecting reactance: The role of similarity in increasing compliance and reducing resistance. *Basic and Applied Social Psychology, 27*, 277–284.

Snyder, C. R., Lassegard, M. A., & Ford, C. E. (1986). Distancing after group success and failure: Basking in reflected glory and cutting off reflected failure. *Journal of Personality and Social Psychology, 51*, 382–388.

van Baaren, R. B., Holland, R. W., Kawakami, K., & van Knippenberg, A. (2004). Mimicry and prosocial behavior. *Psychological Science, 15*, 71–74.

CHAPTER 7

Baumeister, R. F., & Vohs, K. D. (Eds.). (2004). *Handbook of self-regulation: Research, theory, and applications.* New York: Guilford Press.

Cialdini, R. B. (2003). Crafting normative messages to protect the environment. *Current Directions in Psychological Science, 12*, 105–109.

Cialdini, R. B., Demaine, L., Sagarin, B. J., Barrett, D. W., Rhoads, K., & Winter, P. L. (2006). Managing social norms for persuasive impact. *Social Influence, 1*, 3–15.

Cialdini, R. B., & Goldstein, N. J. (2004). Social influence: Compliance and conformity. In S. T. Fiske, D. L. Schacter, & C. Zahn-Waxler (Eds.), *Annual review of psychology* (Vol. 55, pp. 591–621). Palo Alto, CA: Annual Reviews.

Cialdini, R. B., Reno, R. R., & Kallgren, C. A. (1990). A focus theory of normative conduct: Recycling the concept of norms to reduce littering in public places. *Journal of Personality and Social Psychology, 58*, 1015–1026.

Cialdini, R. B., Kallgren, C. A., & Reno, R. R. (1991). A focus theory of normative conduct: A theoretical refinement and re-evaluation. *Advances in Experimental Social Psychology, 24*, 201–234.

Goldstein, N. J., Cialdini, R. B., & Griskevicius, V. (2008). A room with a viewpoint: Using social norms to motivate environmental conservation in hotels. *Journal of Consumer Research, 35*, 472–482.

Jacobson, R. P., Mortensen, C. R., & Cialdini, R. B. (2011). Bodies obliged and unbound: Differentiated response tendencies for injunctive and descriptive social norms. *Journal of Personality and Social Psychology, 100*, 433–448.

Kallgren, C. A., Reno, R. R., & Cialdini, R. B. (2000). A focus theory of normative conduct: When norms do and do not affect behavior. *Personality and Social Psychology Bulletin, 26*, 1002–1012.

Reno, R. R., Cialdini, R. B., & Kallgren, C. A. (1993). The transsituational influence of social norms. *Journal of Personality and Social Psychology, 64,* 104–112.

Schultz, P. W., Nolan, J. M., Cialdini, R. B., Goldstein, N. J., & Griskevicius, V. (2007). The constructive, destructive, and reconstructive power of social norms. *Psychological Science, 18,* 429–434.

Terry, D. J., & Hogg, M. A. (1996). Group norms and the attitude-behavior relationship: A role for group identification. *Personality and Social Psychology Bulletin, 22,* 776–793.

Terry, D. J., Hogg, M. A., & White, K. M. (1999). The theory of planned behaviour: Self-identity, social identity and group norms. *British Journal of Social Psychology, 38,* 225–244.

CHAPTER 8

Archer, J. (2006). Testosterone and human aggression: An evaluation of the challenge hypothesis. *Neuroscience and Biobehavioral Reviews, 30,* 319–345.

Balshine-Earn, S. (1996). Reproductive rates, operational sex ratios and mate choice in St. Peter's fish. *Behavioral Ecology and Sociobiology, 39,* 107–116.

Barber, N. (2001). On the relationships between marital opportunity and teen pregnancy: The sex ratio question. *Journal of Cross-Cultural Psychology, 32,* 259–267.

Barber, N. (2003). The sex ratio and female marital opportunity as historical predictors of violent crime in England, Scotland, and the United States. *Cross-Cultural Research, 37,* 373–391.

Baumeister, R. F., & Vohs, K. D. (2004). Sexual economics: Sex as female resource for social exchange in heterosexual interactions. *Personality & Social Psychology Review, 8,* 339–363.

Brown, L., Tomarken, A., Orth, D., Loosen, P., Kalin, N., & Davidson, R. (1996). Individual differences in repressive-defensiveness predict basal salivary cortisol levels. *Journal of Personality and Social Psychology, 70,* 362–371.

Burnham, T., Chapman, J., Gray, P., McIntyre, M., Lipson, S., & Ellison, P. (2003). Men in committed, romantic relationships have lower testosterone. *Hormones and Behavior, 44,* 119–122.

Buss, D. M. (1989). Sex differences in human mate preferences: Evolutionary hypotheses tested in 37 cultures. *Behavioral & Brain Sciences, 12,* 1–49.

Dabbs, J., Jurkovic, G., & Frady, R. (1991). Salivary testosterone and cortisol among late adolescent male offenders. *Journal of Abnormal Child Psychology, 19,* 469–478.

De Waal, F. (2000). *Chimpanzee politics: Power and sex among apes.* Baltimore: Johns Hopkins University Press.

Durante, K. M., Griskevicius, V., Cantu, S. M., & Simpson, J. A. (2010). *Influence of sex ratio on career trajectories and sociopolitical attitudes.* Manuscript in preparation.

Durante, K. M., & Li, N. P. (2009). Oestradiol level and opportunistic mating in women. *Biology Letters, 5,* 179–82.

Eberle, M., & Kappeler, P. M. (2004). Sex in the dark: Determinants and consequences of mixed male mating tactics in *Microcebus murinus,* a small solitary nocturnal primate. *Behavioral Ecology and Sociobiology, 57,* 77–90.

Emlen, S. T., & Oring, L. W. (1977). Ecology, sexual selection and the evolution of mating systems. *Science, 197,* 215–223.

Faruzzi, A. N., Solomon, M. B., Demas, G. E., & Huhman, K. L. (2005). Gonadal hormones modulate the display of submissive behavior in socially defeated female Syrian hamsters. *Hormones and Behavior, 4,* 569–575.

Forsgren, E., Amundsen, T., Borg, A. A., & Bjelvenmark, J. (2004). Unusually dynamic sex roles in a fish. *Nature, 429,* 551–554.

Fossett, M. A., & Kiecolt, K. J. (1991). A methodological review of the sex ratio: Alternatives for comparative research. *Journal of Marriage and the Family, 53,* 941–957.

Gangestad, S. W., & Simpson, J. A. (2000). Trade-offs, the allocation of reproductive effort, and the evolutionary psychology of human mating. *Behavioral and Brain Sciences, 23,* 624–636.

Griskevicius, V., Goldstein, N. J., Mortensen, C. R., Cialdini, R. B., & Kenrick, D. T. (2006). Going along versus going alone: When fundamental motives facilitate strategic (non) conformity. *Journal of Personality and Social Psychology, 91,* 281–294.

Griskevicius, V., Tybur, J. M., Ackerman, J. A., Delton, A. W., & Robertson, T. E. (2010). *The influence of sex ratio on saving, borrowing, and spending: An experimental approach.* Manuscript submitted for publication.

Guilmoto, C. Z. (2009). The sex transition in Asia. *Population and Developmental Review, 35,* 519–538.

Guttentag, M., & Secord, P. F. (1983). *Too many women? The sex ratio question.* Beverly Hills, CA: Sage.

Haselton, M. G., & Nettle, D. (2006). The paranoid optimist: An integrative evolutionary model of cognitive biases. *Personality and Social Psychology Review, 10*(1), 47–66.

Hermans, E. J., Ramsey, N. F., & van Honk, J. (2008). Exogenous testosterone attenuates the integrated central stress response in healthy young women. *Biological Psychiatry, 32,* 1052–1061.

Hesketh, T. (2009). Too many males in China: The causes and consequences. *Significance, 6,* 9–13.

Hesketh, T., & Zhu, W. X. (2006). Abnormal sex ratios in human populations: Causes and consequences. *Proceedings of the National Academy of Sciences of the United States of America, 103,* 271–275.

Heyman, J. E., & Mellers, B. A. (2008). Perceptions of fair pricing. In C. Haugtvedt, F. Kardes, & P. Herr (Eds.), *Handbook of consumer psychology* (p 683–697). New York: Psychology Press.

James, W. H. (1987). The human sex ratio: Part 1, a review of the literature. *Human Biology, 59,* 721–725.

Josephs, R. A., Sellers, J. G., Newman, M. L., & Mehta, P. H. (2006). The mismatch effect: When testosterone and status are at odds. *Journal of Personality and Social Psychology, 90,* 999–1013.

Kenrick, D. T., & Luce, C. L. (2000). An evolutionary life-history model of gender differences and similarities. In T. Eckes, & H. M. Trautner (Eds.), *The developmental social psychology of gender* (pp. 35–64). Hillsdale, NJ: Erlbaum.

Kim, J. S., Griskevicius, V., & Simpson, J. A. (2010, January). *Sex ratio influences satisfaction in romantic relationships.* Poster presented at the meeting of the Society for Personality and Social Psychology, Las Vegas, NV.

Kruger, D. J. (2009). Male scarcity is differentially related to male marital likelihood across the life course. *Evolutionary Psychology, 7,* 280–287.

Kvarnemo, C., & Anhesjö, I. (1996). The dynamics of operational sex ratios and competition for mates. *Trends in Ecology & Evolution, 11,* 404–408.

Kvarnemo, C., & Forsgren, E. (2000). The influence of potential reproductive rate and variation in mate quality on male and female choosiness in the sand goby, *Pomatoschistus minutus. Behavioral Ecology and Sociobiology, 48,* 378–384.

Li, Y. J., Cohen, A. B., Weeden, J., & Kenrick, D. T. (2010). Mating competitors increase religious beliefs. *Journal of Experimental Psychology, 46,* 428–431.

Licher, D. T., Kephart, G., McLaughlin, D. K., & Landry, D. J. (1992). Race and retreat from marriage: A shortage of marriageable men. *American Sociological Review, 57,* 781–799.

Magellan, K., & Magurran, A. E. (2007). Behavioural profiles: Individual consistency in male mating behaviours under varying sex ratios. *Animal Behaviour, 74,* 1545–1550.

Mazur, A., & Booth, A. (1998). Testosterone and dominance in men. *Behavioral and Brain Sciences, 21,* 353–397.

Mehta, P. H., Jones, A. C., Josephs, R. A. (2008). The social endocrinology of dominance: Basal testosterone predicts cortisol changes and behavior following victory and defeat. *Journal of Personality and Social Psychology, 94,* 1078–1093.

Mehta, P. H., & Josephs, R. A. (2010). Testosterone and cortisol jointly regulate dominance: Evidence for a dual-hormone hypothesis. *Hormones and Behavior, 58,* 898–906.

Mehta, P. H., & Josephs, R. A. (2010). Social endocrinology: Hormones and social motivation. In D. Dunning (Ed.), *The handbook of social motivation.* New York: Psychology Press.

Mills, S. C., & Reynolds, J. D. (2003). Operational sex ratio and alternative reproductive behaviours in the European bitterling, *Rhodeus sericeus. Behavioral Ecology and Sociobiology, 54,* 98–104.

Pederson, F. A. (1991). Secular trends in human sex ratios: Their influence on individual and family behavior. *Human Nature, 2,* 271–291.

Pollet, T. V., & Nettle, D. (2008). Driving a hard bargain: Sex ratio and male marriage success in a historical U.S. population. *Biology Letters, 4,* 31–33.

Roney, J. R., & Simmons, Z. L. (2008). Women's estradiol predicts preference for facial cues of men's testosterone. *Hormones and Behavior, 53,* 14–19.

Sapolsky, R. M. (1991). Testicular function, social rank and personality among wild baboons. *Psychoneuroendocrinology, 16,* 281–293.

Schmitt, D. P. (2005). Sociosexuality from Argentina to Zimbabwe: A 48-nation study of sex, culture, and strategies of human mating. *Behavioral and Brain Sciences, 28,* 247–275.

Shoal, G., Giancola, P., & Kirillova, G. (2003). Salivary cortisol, personality, and aggressive behavior in adolescent boys: A 5-year longitudinal study. *Journal of the American Academy of Child and Adolescent Psychiatry, 49,* 1101–1109.

South, S. J., & Trent, K. (1988). Sex ratios and women's roles: A cross-national analysis. *American Journal of Sociology, 93,* 1096–1115.

Stanton, S. J., & Schultheiss, O. C. (2007). Basal and dynamic associations between implicit power motivation and estradiol in women. *Hormones and Behavior, 52*(5), 571–580.

Stone, E. A., Shackelford, T. K., & Buss, D. M. (2007). Sex ratio and mate preferences: A cross-cultural investigation. *European Journal of Social Psychology, 37,* 288–296.

Sundie, J. M., Cialdini, R. B., Griskevicius, V., & Kenrick, D. T. (2006). Evolutionary social influence. In M. Schaller, J. A. Simpson, & D. T. Kenrick (Eds.), *Evolution and social psychology* (pp. 287–316). New York: Psychology Press.

Taylor, P. D., & Bulmer, M. G. (1980). Local mate competition and the sex ratio. *Journal of Theoretical Biology, 86,* 409–419.

Thornhill, R. (1980). Rape in Panorpa scorpionflies and a general rape hypothesis. *Animal Behavior, 28,* 52–59.

Van der Meij, L., Buunk, A. P., & Salvador, A. (in press). Contact with attractive women affects the release of cortisol in men. *Hormones and Behavior.*

Van Vugt, M., De Cremer, D., & Janssen, D. (2007). Gender differences in cooperation and competition: The male-warrior hypothesis. *Psychological Science, 18,* 19–23.

Weeden, J., Cohen, A. B., & Kenrick, D. T. (2008). Religious attendance as reproductive support. *Evolution & Human Behavior, 29,* 327–334.

Weir, L. K., Grant, J. W. A., & Hutchings, J. A. (2010). Patterns of aggression and operational sex ratio within alternative male phenotypes in Atlantic salmon. *Ethology, 116,* 166–175.

Wirth, M. M., & Schultheiss, O. (2006). Effects of affiliation arousal (hope of closeness) and affiliation stress (fear of rejection) on progesterone and cortisol. *Hormones and Behavior, 50,* 786–795.

Zhu, W. X., Li, L., & Hesketh, T. (2009). China's excess males: Role of sex selective abortion and the One Child Policy. *British Medical Journal, 338,* b1211.

CHAPTER 9

Adam, E. K., Hawkley, L. C., Kudielka, B. M., & Cacioppo, J. T. (2006). Day-to-day dynamics of experience-cortisol associations in a population-based sample of older adults. *Proceedings of the National Academy of Sciences of the United States of America, 103*(45), 17058–17063. doi: 10.1073/pnas.0605053103.

Akerlind, I., & Hornquist, J. O. (1992). Loneliness and alcohol abuse: A review of evidences of an interplay. *Social Science & Medicine, 34*(4), 405–414.

Beckerman, S., Erickson, P. I., Yost, J., Regalado, J., Jaramillo, L., Sparks, C., et al. (2009). Life histories, blood revenge, and reproductive success among the Waorani of Ecuador. *Proceedings of the National Academy of Sciences of the United States of America, 106*(20), 8134–8139. doi: 10.1073/pnas.0901431106.

Boomsma, D. I., Willemsen, G., Dolan, C. V., Hawkley, L. C., & Cacioppo, J. T. (2005). Genetic and environmental contributions to loneliness in adults: The Netherlands twin register study. *Behavior Genetics, 35*(6), 745–752. doi: 10.1007/s10519-005-6040-8.

Cacioppo, J. T., Amaral, D. G., Blanchard, J. J., Cameron, J. L., Sue Carter, C., Crews, D., et al. (2007). Social neuroscience: Progress and implications for mental health. *Perspectives on Psychological Science, 2*(2), 99–123. doi:10.1111/j.1745-6916.2007.00032.x.

Cacioppo, J. T., Hawkley, L. C., Berntson, G. G., Ernst, J. M., Gibbs, A. C., Stickgold, R., & Hobson, J. A. (2002a). Lonely days invade the nights: Social modulation of sleep efficiency. *Psychological Science, 13*, 384–387.

Cacioppo, J. T., Hawkley, L. C., Crawford, L. E., Ernst, J. M., Burleson, M. H., Kowalewski, R. B., Malarkey, W. B., Van Cauter, E., & Berntson, G. G. (2002b). Loneliness and health: Potential mechanisms. *Psychosomatic Medicine, 64*, 407–417.

Cacioppo, J. T., Hawkley, L. C., Ernst, J. M., Burleson, M., Berntson, G. G., Nouriani, B., et al. (2006). Loneliness within a nomological net: An evolutionary perspective. *Journal of Research in Personality, 40*(6), 1054–1085.

Cacioppo, J. T., & Patrick, B. (2008). *Loneliness: Human nature and the need for social connection.* New York: W. W. Norton & Company.

Cialdini, R. B., Cacioppo, J. T., Basset, R., & Miller, J. A. (1978). The low-ball procedure for producing compliance: Commitment then cost. *Journal of Personality and Social Psychology, 36*, 463–476.

Cole, S. W., Hawkley, L. C., Arevalo, J. M., Sung, C. Y., Rose, R. M., & Cacioppo, J. T. (2007). Social regulation of gene expression in human leukocytes. *Genome Biology, 8*(9), R189.1–R189.13. doi: 10.1186/gb-2007-8-9-r189.

Cole, S. W., Hawkley, L. C., Arevalo, J. M. G., & Cacioppo, J. T. (2011). Transcript origin analysis identifies antigen presenting cells as primary targets of socially regulated leukocyte gene expression. *Proceedings of the National Academy of Sciences, 108*, 3080–3085.

Dickens, C., & Douglas-Fairhurst, R. (2006). *A Christmas carol and other Christmas books.* Oxford: Oxford University Press.

Donaldson, Z. R., & Young, L. J. (2008). Oxytocin, vasopressin, and the neurogenetics of sociality. *Science, 322*(5903), 900–904. doi: 10.1126/science.1158668.

Dronjak, S., Gavrilovic, L., Filipovic, D., & Radojcic, M. B. (2004). Immobilization and cold stress affect sympatho-adrenomedullary system and pituitary-adrenocortical axis of rats exposed to long-term isolation and crowding. *Physiology and Behavior, 81*(3), 409–415.

Dunbar, R. (2004). *The human story.* London: Faber and Faber.

Dunbar, R. I. M., & Shultz, S. (2007). Evolution in the social brain. *Science, 317*(5843), 1344–1347. doi: 10.1126/science.1145463.

Glancy, R. F. (1985). *Dickens's Christmas books, Christmas stories, and other short fiction: An annotated bibliography.* Retrieved from http://books.google.com/books?id=d3RaAAAAMAAJ.

Goldstein, N. J. (2007). Using social norms as a lever of social influence. In A. R. Pratkanis (Ed.), *The Science of social influence* (pp.167–191). New York: Psychology Press.

Hawkley, L. C., Masi, C. M., Berry, J. D., & Cacioppo, J. T. (2006). Loneliness is a unique predictor of age-related differences in systolic blood pressure. *Psychology and Aging, 21*(1), 152–164. doi: 10.1037/0882-7974.21.1.152.

Hawkley, L. C., Thisted, R. A., Masi, C. M., & Cacioppo, J. T. (2010). Loneliness predicts increased blood pressure: Five-year cross-lagged analyses in middle-aged and older adults. *Psychology and Aging.* In Press.

Heikkinen, R.-L., & Kauppinen, M. (2004). Depressive symptoms in late life: A 10-year follow-up. *Archives of Gerontology and Geriatrics, 38*(3), 239–250.

Herrmann, E., Call, J., Hernandez-Lloreda, M. V., Hare, B., & Tomasello, M. (2007). Humans have evolved specialized skills of social cognition: The cultural intelligence hypothesis. *Science, 317*(5843), 1360–1366. doi: 10.1126/science.1146282.

House, J. S., Landis, K. R., & Umberson, D. (1988). Social relationships and health. *Science, 241*(4865), 540–545.

Insko, C. A., & Cialdini, R. B. (1969). A test of three interpretations of attitudinal verbal reinforcement. *Journal of Personality and Social Psychology, 12,* 333–341.

Kanitz, E., Tuchscherer, M., Puppe, B., Tuchscherer, A., & Stabenow, B. (2004). Consequences of repeated early isolation in domestic piglets (*Sus scrofa*) on their behavioural, neuroendocrine, and immunological responses. *Brain, Behavior, and Immunity, 18*(1), 35–45.

Karelina, K., Norman, G. J., Zhang, N., Morris, J. S., Peng, H., & DeVries, A. C. (2009). Social isolation alters neuroinflammatory response to stroke. *Proceedings of the National Academy of Sciences of the United States of America, 106*(14), 5895–5900. doi: 10.1073/pnas.0810737106.

Kiecolt-Glaser, J. K., Ricker, D., George, J., Messick, G., Speicher, C. E., Garner, W., et al. (1984). Urinary cortisol levels, cellular immunocompetency, and loneliness in psychiatric inpatients. *Psychosomatic Medicine, 46*(1), 15–23.

Lauder, W., Mummery, K., Jones, M., & Caperchione, C. (2006). A comparison of health behaviours in lonely and non-lonely populations. *Psychology, Health, and Medicine, 11*(2), 233–245.

Lovejoy, C. O. (2009). Reexamining human origins in light of *Ardipithecus ramidus. Science, 326*(5949), 74e71–74e78.

Lyons, D. M., Ha, C. M., & Levine, S. (1995). Social effects and circadian rhythms in squirrel monkey pituitary-adrenal activity. *Hormones and Behavior, 29*(2), 177–190.

Meaney, M. J. (2004). The nature of nurture: Maternal effects and chromatin remodeling. In J. T. Cacioppo, & G. G. Berntson (Eds.), *Essays in social neuroscience* (pp. 1–14). Cambridge, MA: The MIT Press.

Nation, D. A., Gonzales, J. A., Mendez, A. J., Zaias, J., Szeto, A., Brooks, L. G., et al. (2008). The effect of social environment on markers of vascular oxidative stress and inflammation in the Watanabe heritable hyperlipidemic rabbit. *Psychosomatic Medicine, 70*(3), 269–275.

Nonogaki, K., Nozue, K., & Oka, Y. (2007). Social isolation affects the development of obesity and type 2 diabetes in mice. *Endocrinology, 148*(10), 4658–4666. doi: 10.1210/en.2007-0296.

Patterson, A. C., & Veenstra, G. (2010). Loneliness and risk of mortality: A longitudinal investigation in Alameda County, California. *Social Science & Medicine, 71,* 181–186.

Penninx, B. W., van Tilburg, T., Kriegsman, D. M., Deeg, D. J., Boeke, A. J., & van Eijk, J. T. (1997). Effects of social support and personal coping resources on mortality in older age: The Longitudinal Aging Study Amsterdam. *American Journal of Epidemiology, 146*(6), 510–519.

Pressman, S. D., Cohen, S., Miller, G. E., Barkin, A., Rabin, B. S., & Treanor, J. J. (2005). Loneliness, social network size, and immune response to influenza vaccination in college freshmen. *Health Psychology, 24*(3), 297–306. doi: 10.1037/0278-6133.24.3.297.

Ruan, H., & Wu, C. F. (2008). Social interaction-mediated lifespan extension of Drosophila Cu/Zn superoxide dismutase mutants. *Proceedings of the National Academy of Sciences of the United States of America, 105*(21), 7506–7510.

Rudatsikira, E., Muula, A. S., Siziya, S., & Twa-Twa, J. (2007). Suicidal ideation and associated factors among school-going adolescents in rural Uganda. *BMC Psychiatry, 7*, 67. doi: 10.1186/1471-244X-7-67.

Russell, D. W., Cutrona, C. E., de la Mora, A., & Wallace, R. B. (1997). Loneliness and nursing home admission among rural older adults. *Psychology and Aging, 12*(4), 574–589.

Seeman, T. (2000). Health promoting effects of friends and family on health outcomes in older adults. *American Journal of Health Promotion, 14*(6), 362–370.

Steptoe, A., Owen, N., Kunz-Ebrecht, S. R., & Brydon, L. (2004). Loneliness and neuroendocrine, cardiovascular, and inflammatory stress responses in middle-aged men and women. *Psychoneuroendocrinology, 29*(5), 593–611.

Stranahan, A. M., Khalil, D., & Gould, E. (2006). Social isolation delays the positive effects of running on adult neurogenesis. *Nature Neuroscience, 9*(4), 526–533.

Tilvis, R. S., Pitkala, K. H., Jolkkonen, J., & Strandberg, T. E. (2000). Social networks and dementia. *Lancet, 356*(9223), 77–78.

Tomasello, M., & Herrmann, E. (2010). Ape and human cognition: What's the difference? *Current Directions in Psychological Science, 19*(1), 3–8.

Vallotton, C. D. (2009). Do infants influence their quality of care? Infants' communicative gestures predict caregivers' responsiveness. *Infant Behavior & Development, 32*(4), 351–365.

Weiss, R. S. (1973). *Loneliness: The experience of emotional and social isolation.* Cambridge, MA: MIT Press.

Williams, G. C. (1966). Natural selection, the costs of reproduction, and a refinement of Lack's principle. *The American Naturalist, 100*(916), 687–690.

Williams, K. D. (2001). *Ostracism: The power of silence.* New York: Guilford Press.

Wilson, D. S. (2007). *Evolution for everyone: How Darwin's theory can change the way we think about our lives.* New York: Delacorte Press.

Wilson, D. S., & Wilson, E. O. (2008). Evolution "for the Good of the Group". *American Scientist, 96*(5), 380–389. doi: 10.1511/2008.74.1.

Wilson, R. S., Krueger, K. R., Arnold, S. E., Schneider, J. A., Kelly, J. F., Barnes, L. L., et al. (2007). Loneliness and risk of Alzheimer disease. *Archives of General Psychiatry, 64*(2), 234–240. doi: 10.1001/archpsyc.64.2.234.

CHAPTER 10

Apostolou, M. (2007). Sexual selection under parental choice: The role of parents in the evolution of human mating. *Evolution and Human Behavior, 28*, 403–409.

Applbaum, K. D. (1995). Marriage with the proper stranger: Arranged marriage in metropolitan Japan. *Ethnology, 34*, 37–51.

Baier, M. E. M. & Wampler, K. S. (2008). A qualitative study of Southern Baptist mothers' and their daughters' attitudes towards sexuality. *Journal of Adolescent Research, 23*, 31–54.

Bates, A. (1942). Parental roles in courtship. Social Forces, 20, 483–486.

Cialdini, R.B. (2008). *Influence: science and practice.* Boston, MA: Allyn & Bacon.

Bateson, P. (1983). *Mate choice.* New York: Cambridge University Press.

Betzig, L. L. (1986). *Despotism and differential reproduction: A Darwinian view of history.* Hawthorne, NY: Aldine.

Buunk, A. P., & Castro-Solano, A. Conflicting preferences of parents and offspring over criteria for a mate: A study in Argentina. *Journal of Family Psychology, 24*, 391–399.

Buunk, A. P., Park, J. H., & Dubbs, S. L. (2008). Parent-offspring conflict in mate preferences. *The Review of General Psychology, 12*, 47–62.

Buunk, A. P., Park, J. H., & Duncan, L. A. (2010). Cultural variation in parental influence on mate choice. *Cross-Cultural Research, 44*, 23–40.

Clutton-Brock, T. H., Brotherton, P. N. M., Russell, A. F., O'Riain, M. J., Gaynor, D., Kansky, R., et al. (2001). Cooperation, control, and concession in meerkat groups. *Science, 291*, 478–481.

Clutton-Brock, T. H., Hodge, S. J., & Flower, T. P. (2008). Group size and the suppression of subordinate reproduction in Kalahari meerkats. *Animal Behavior, 76*, 689–700.

Courchamp, F., Rasmussen, G. S. A., & Macdonald, D. W. (2002). Small pack size imposes a trade-off between hunting and pup-guarding in the painted hunting dog *Lycaon pictus*. *Behavioral Ecology, 13*, 20–27.

Covas, R., Doutrelant, C., & du Plessis, M. A. (2004). Experimental evidence of a link between breeding conditions and the decision to breed or to help in a colonial cooperative bird. Proceedings. Biological Sciences / *The Royal Society, 271*, 827–832.

Cox, C. R., & Le Boeuf, B. J. (1977). Female incitation of male-male competition: A mechanism in sexual selection. *The American Naturalist, 111*, 317–335.

Creel, S. R., & Creel, N. M. (1991). Energetics, reproductive suppression and obligate communal breeding in carnivores. *Behavioral Ecology and Sociobiology, 28*, 263–270.

Creel, S., Creel, N. M., Mills, M. G. L., & Monfort, S. L. (1997). Rank and reproduction in cooperatively breeding African wild dogs: Behavioral and endocrine correlates. *Behavioral Ecology, 8*, 298–306.

de Moor, T., & van Zanden, J. L. (2006). *Vrouwen en de geboorte van het kapitalisme in West-Europa* [Women and the origins of capitalism in Western Europe]. Amsterdam: Boom.

Das Gupta, M. (1997). "What is Indian about you?": A gendered, transnational approach to ethnicity. *Gender and Society, 11*, 572–596.

Deady, D. K., Smith, M. J., Kent, J. P., & Dunbar, R. I. M. (2006). Is priesthood an adaptive strategy? Evidence from a historical Irish population. *Human Nature, 17*, 393–404.

Dubbs, S. L., & Buunk, A. P. (2010a). Parents just don't understand: Parentoffspring conflict over mate choice. *Evolutionary Psychology, 8*, 586–598.

Dubbs, S. L., & Buunk, A. P. (2010b). Sex differences in parental preferences over a child's mate-choice: A daughter's perspective. *Journal of Social and Personal Relationships, 27*, 1051–1059.

East, M. L., Burke, T., Wilhelm, C. G., & Hofer, H. (2003). Sexual conflicts in spotted hyenas: Male and female mating tactics and their reproductive outcome with respect to age, social status and tenure. *Biological Sciences, 270*, 1247–1254.

Emlen, S. T., & Wrege, P. H. (1992). Parent-offspring conflict and the recruitment of helpers among bee-eaters. *Nature, 356*, 331–333.

Faulkes, C. G., & Bennett, N. C. (2001). Family values: Group dynamics and social control of reproduction in African mole-rats. *Trends in Ecology and Evolution, 16*, 184–190.

Faulkner, J., & Schaller, M. (2007). Nepotistic nosiness: Inclusive fitness and vigilance over kin members' romantic relationships. *Evolution and Human Behavior, 28*, 430–38.

Fisher J., & Hinde, R. A. (1949). The opening of milk bottles by birds. *British Birds, 42*, 347–357.

Gelfand, M. J., Bhawuk, D. P., Nishii, L. H., & Bechtold, D. J. (2004). Individualism and collectivism. In R. J. House, P. J. Hanges, M. Javidan, P. W. Dorfman, & V. Gupta (Eds.), *Culture, leadership, and organizations: The GLOBE study of 62 societies* (pp. 437–512). Thousand Oaks, CA: Sage.

Girman, D. J., Mills, M. G. L., Geffen, E., & Wayne, R. K. (1997). A molecular genetic analysis of social structure, dispersal, and interpack relationships of the African wild dog (*Lycaon pictus*). *Behavioral Ecology and Sociobiology, 40*, 187–198.

Goode, W. J. (1959). The theoretical importance of love. *American Sociological Review, 24*, 38–47.

Haley, M. P., Deutsch, C. J., & le Boeuf, B. J. (1994). Size, dominance and copulatory success in male northern elephant seals, *Mirounga angustirostris*. *Animal Behavior, 48*, 1249–1260.

Hofer, H. & East, M. L. (2003). Behavioral processes and costs of co-existence in female spotted hyenas: A life history perspective. *Evolutionary Ecology, 17,* 325–331.

Kummer, H. (1992). *Weiße Affen am Roten Meer, das soziale Leben der Wüstenpaviane.* München: Piper & Co.

McNutt, J. W. & Silk, J. B. (2008). Pup production, sex ratios, and survivorship in African wild dogs, *Lycaon pictus. Behavioral Ecology and Sociobiology, 62,* 1061–1067.

Miller, G. F. (2001). *The mating mind: How sexual choice shaped the evolution of human nature.* New York: Anchor.

Murstein, B. (1974). *Love, sex, & marriage through the ages.* New York: Springer Publishing Company.

Nettle, D. (2007). A module for metaphor? The site of imagination in the architecture of the mind. *Proceedings of the British Academy, 147,* 259–274.

Park, J. H., Dubbs, S. L., & Buunk, A. P. (2009). Parents, offspring and mate-choice conflicts. In H. Høgh-Oleson, J. Tønnesvang, & P. Bertelsen (Eds.), *Human characteristics – Evolutionary perspectives on human mind and kind* (pp. 352–365). Cambridge, UK: Cambridge University Scholars.

Perilloux, C., Fleischman, D. S., & Buss, D. M. (2008). The daughter guarding hypothesis: Parental influence on, and emotional reactions to, offspring's mating behavior. *Evolutionary Psychology, 6,* 217–233.

Pinker, S., & Bloom, P. (1992). Natural language and natural selection. In J. H. Barkow, L. Cosmides, & J. Tooby (Eds.), *The adapted mind* (pp. 451–493). Oxford: Oxford University Press.

Reiss, I. L. (1980). *Family systems in America.* New York: Holt, Rinehart & Winston.

Riley, N. E. (1994). Interwoven lives: Parents, marriage, and Guanxi in China. *Journal of Marriage and the Family, 56,* 791–803.

Rusell, A. F., & Lummaa, V. (2009). Maternal effects in cooperative breeders: From hymenopterans to humans. *Philosophical Transactions of the Royal Society of London. Series B, Biological Sciences, 364,* 1143–1167.

Sprecher, S., & Chandak, R. (1992). Attitudes about arranged marriages and dating among men and women from India. *Free Inquiry in Creative Sociology, 20,* 59–70.

Spong, G. F., Hodge, S. J., Young, A. J., & Clutton-Brock, T. H. (2008). Factors affecting the reproductive success of dominant male meerkats. *Molecular Ecology, 17,* 2287–2299.

Trivers, R. L. (1974). Parent–offspring conflict. *American Zoologist, 14,* 249–264.

Wrangham, R. W., & Peterson. D. (1996). *Demonic males: Apes and the origins of human violence.* Boston: Houghton Mifflin.

Xie, X., & Combs, R. (1996). Family and work roles of rural women in a Chinese brigade. *International Journal of Sociology of the family, 26,* 67–76.

Young, A. J., & Clutton-Brock, T. (2006). Infanticide by subordinates influences reproductive sharing in cooperatively breeding meerkats. *Biology Letters, 2,* 385–387.

CHAPTER 11

Archer, R. L. (1984). The farmer and the cowman should be friends: An attempt at reconciliation with Batson, Coke, and Pych. *Journal of Personality and Social Psychology, 46,* 709–711.

Aron, A., & Aron, E. N. (1986). *Love and the expansion of self: Understanding attraction and satisfaction.* Washington, DC: Hemisphere.

Aron, A., Aron, E. N., & Smollan, D. (1992). Inclusion of the other in the self scale and the structure of interpersonal closeness. *Journal of Personality and Social Psychology, 63,* 596–612.

Aron, A., Aron, E. N., Tudor, M., & Nelson, G. (1991). Close relationships as including other in the self. *Journal of Personality and Social Psychology, 60,* 241–253.

Axelrod, R., & Hamilton, W. D. (1981). The evolution of cooperation. *Science, 211,* 1390–1396.

Batson, C. D. (1991). *The altruism question: Toward a social-psychological answer*. Hillsdale, NJ: Erlbaum.

Batson, C. D. (1998). Altruism and prosocial behavior. In D. T. Gilbert, S. T. Fiske, & G. Lindzey (Eds.), *The handbook of social psychology* (Vol. 2, 4th ed., pp. 282–316). Boston: McGraw Hill.

Batson, C. D., Sager, K., Garst, E., Kang, M., Rubchinsky, K., & Dawson, K. (1997). Is empathy-induced helping due to self-other merging? *Journal of Personality and Social Psychology, 73*, 495–509.

Batson, C. D., O'Quin, K., Fultz, J., Vanderplas, M., & Isen, A. (1983). Influence of self-reported distress and empathy on egoistic versus altruistic motivation to help. *Journal of Personality and Social Psychology, 45*, 706–718.

Brown, R. M., & Brown, S. L. (2007). Towards uniting the behavioral sciences with a gene-centered approach to altruism. *Behavioral and Brain Sciences, 30*, 19–20.

Brown, S. L. (1999). *Evolutionary origins of investment: Testing a theory of close relationships*. Tempe, AZ: Arizona State University.

Brown S. L., & Brown R. M. (2006). Selective investment theory: Recasting the functional significance of close relationships. *Psychological Inquiry, 17*, 1–29.

Brown, S. L., Brown, R. M., & Preston, S. (in press). A neuroscience model of human caregiving motivation: In S. Brown, R. Brown, & L. Penner (Eds.), *Moving Beyond Self Interest: Perspectives from Evolutionary Biology, Neuroscience, and the Social Sciences*. New York: Oxford University Press. (2)

Brown, S. L., Brown, R. M., House, J. S., & Smith, D. M. (2008). Coping with spousal loss: The potential buffering effects of self-reported helping behavior. *Personality and Social Psychology Bulletin, 34*, 849–861.

Brown, S. L., Nesse, R., Vinokur, A. D., & Smith, D. M. (2003). Providing support may be more beneficial than receiving it: Results from a prospective study of mortality. *Psychological Science, 14*, 320–327.

Brown, S.L., & Vinokur, A.D. (2003). The interplay among risk factors for suicidal ideation and suicide: The role of depression, poor health, and loved ones' messages of support and criticism. *American Journal of Community Psychology, 32*, 131–141.

Brown, S. L., Fredrickson, B. L., Wirth, M. M., Poulin, M. J., Meier, E. A., Heaphy, E. D., et al. (2009b). Social closeness increases salivary progesterone in humans. *Hormones and Behavior, 56*, 108–111.

Brown, S. L., Smith, D. M., Schulz, R., Kabeto, M., Ubel, P., Yee, J., et al. (2009b). Caregiving and decreased mortality in a national sample of older adults, *Psychological Science, 20*, 488–494.

Brown, W. M., Consedine, N. S., & Magai, C. (2005). Altruism relates to health in an ethnically diverse sample of older adults. *Journals of Gerontology. Series B, Psychological Sciences & Social Sciences, 60B*, 143–152.

Carter, C. S. (1998). Neuroendocrine perspectives on social attachment and love. *Psychoneuroendocrinology, 23*, 779–818.

Cialdini, R. B. (1991). Altruism or egoism? That is (still) the question. *Psychological Inquiry, 2*, 124–126.

Cialdini, R. B., Brown, S. L., Lewis, B. P., Luce, C., & Neuberg, S. L. (1997). Reinterpreting the empathy-altruism relationship: When one into one equals oneness. *Journal of Personality and Social Psychology, 73*, 481–494.

Cialdini, R. B., Kenrick, D. T., & Baumann, D. J. (1982). Effects of mood on prosocial behavior in children and adults. In N. Eisenberg (Ed.), *The development of prosocial behavior* (pp. 339–359). New York: Academic Press.

Cialdini, R. B., Schaller, M., Houlihan, D., Arps, K., Fultz, J., & Beaman, A. L. (1987). Empathy-based helping: Is it selflessly or selfishly motivated? *Journal of Personality and Social Psychology, 52*, 749–758.

Damasio, A. R., Grabowski, T. J., Bechara, A., Damasio, H., Ponto, L. L. B., Parvizi, J., et al. (2000). Subcortical and cortical brain activity during the feeling of self-generated emotions. *Nature Neuroscience*, 3(10), 1049–1056.

Decety, J. & Lamm, C. (2009). Empathy versus personal distress: Recent evidence from social neuroscience. In J. Decety and J. Ickes (Eds) *The Social Neuroscience of Empathy*. MIT Press: Hong Kong.

Fultz, J., Schaller, M., & Cialdini, R. B. (1988). Empathy, sadness, and distress: Three related but distinct vicarious affective responses to another's suffering. *Personality and Social Psychology Bulletin*, 14, 312–325.

Hamilton, W. D. (1964). The genetic evolution of social behavior. *Journal of Theoretical Biology*, 7, 1–52.

Hazan, C., & Shaver, P. R. (1994). Attachment as an organizational framework for research on close relationships. *Psychological Inquiry*, 5, 1–22.

Heaphy, E. D., & Dutton, J. E. (in press). Positive social interactions and the human body at work: Linking organizations and physiology. *Academy of Management Review*.

House, J., Landis, K., & Umberson, D. (1988). Social relationships and health. *Science*, 241, 540–545.

Kross, E., Davidson, M., Weber, J., & Ochsner, K. (2008). Coping with emotions past: The neural bases of regulating affect associated with negative autobiographical memories. *Biological Psychiatry*, 65, 361–366.

Lorberbaum, J., Newman, J. D., Horwitz, A. R., Dubno, J. R., Lydiard, R. B., Hamner, M. B., et al. (2002). A potential role for thalamocingulate circuitry in human maternal behavior. *Biological Psychiatry*, 51(6), 431–445.

Maner, J. K., Luce, C. L., Neuberg, S. L., Cialdini, R. B., Brown, S., Sagarin, B. J. (2002). The effects of perspective taking on helping: Still no evidence for altruism. *Personality and Social Psychology Bulletin*, 28, 1601–1610.

Manucia, G. K., Baumann, D. J., & Cialdini, R. B. (1984). Mood influences in helping: Direct effects or side effects? *Journal of Personality and Social Psychology*, 46, 357–364.

Mason, A., Schlissel, C., Canton, M., Berman, B., Saralegui, J. (Producers), & Hoffman, A. (Director). (2000). *Red Planet* [Motion Picture]. United States: Warner Brothers.

Neuberg, S. L., Cialdini, R. B., Brown, S. L., Luce, C., Sagarin, B. J., & Lewis, B. P. (1997). Does empathy lead to anything other than superficial helping? Comment on Batson et al. (1997). *Journal of Personality and Social Psychology*, 73, 510–516.

Numan M. (2006). Hypothalamic neural circuits regulating maternal responsiveness toward infants. *Behavioral and Cognitive Neuroscience Reviews*, 5(4), 163–190.

Oman, D. (2007). Does volunteering foster physical health and longevity? In S. G. Post (Ed.), *Altruism and Health* (pp. 15–32). New York: Oxford University Press.

Porges, S. (1998). Love: An emergent property of the mammalian autonomic nervous system. *Psychoneuroendocrinology*, 23, 837–861.

Post, S. G. (Ed.). (2007). *Altruism and Health: Perspectives from empirical research*. New York: Oxford University Press.

Preston, S. D., & de Waal, F. B. M. (2002). Empathy: Its ultimate and proximate bases. *Behavioral and Brain Sciences*, 25(1), 1–71.

Poulin, M. J., Brown, S. L., Ubel, P. A., Smith, D. M., Jankovic, A., & Langa, K. M. (2010). Does a helping hand mean a heavy heart? Helping behavior and well-being among spouse caregivers. *Psychology and Aging*, 25, 108–117.

Rusbult, C. (1980). Commitment and satisfaction in romantic associations: A test of the investment model. *Journal of Experimental Social Psychology*, 16, 172–186.

Sapolsky, R., Krey, L., & McEwen, B. (2000). The neuroendocrinology of stress and aging: The glucocorticoid cascade hypothesis. *Science of Aging Knowledge Environment*, 38, 21.

Schaller, M., & Cialdini, R. B. (1988). The economics of empathic helping: Support for a mood-management motive. *Journal of Experimental Social Psychology, 24,* 163–181.

Wilson, D. S., & Sober, E. (1994). Re-introducing group selection to the human behavioral sciences. *Behavioral and Brain Sciences,17,* 585–654.

Wilson, D. S., Van Vugt, M., & O'Gorman, R. (2008). Multilevel selection theory and major evolutionary transitions: Implications for psychological science. *Current Directions in Psychological Science, 17,* 6–9.

CHAPTER 12

Cialdini, R. B. (1980). Full cycle social psychology. In L. Bickman (Ed.), *Applied social psychology annual* (Vol. 1, pp. 27–47). Beverly Hills, CA: Sage.

Cialdini, R. B. (2009). We have to break up. *Perspectives on Psychological Science, 4,* 5–6.

Cialdini, R. B., Reno, R. R., & Kallgren, C. A. (1990). A focus theory of normative conduct—recycling the concept of norms to reduce littering in public places. *Journal of Personality and Social Psychology, 58,* 1015–1026.

Cialdini, R. B., & Schroeder, D. A. (1976). Increasing contributions by legitimizing paltry contributions: When every penny helps. *Journal of Personality and Social Psychology, 34,* 599–604.

Cook, T. D. (1990). The generalization of causal connections: Multiple theories in search of clear practice. In L. Sechrest, E. Perrin, & J. Bunker (Eds.), *Research methodology: Strengthening causal interpretations of nonexperimental data* (DHHS Publication No. PHS 90-3454, pp. 9–31). Rockville, MD: Department of Health and Social Services.

Cook, T. D., Shadish, W. R., & Wong, V. C. (2008). Three conditions under which experiments and observational studies produce comparable causal effects: New findings from within-study comparisons. *Journal of Policy Analysis and Management, 27,* 724–750.

Cook, T. D., & Steiner, P. M (2010). Case matching and the reduction of bias in quasi-experiments: The relative importance of pretest measures of outcome, of unreliable measurement, and of mode of data analysis. *Psychological Methods, 15,* 56–68.

Cronbach, L. J. (1980). *Towards a reform of program evaluation.* San Francisco: Jossey-Bass.

Cronbach, L. J. (with Shapiro, K.) (1982). *Designing evaluations of educational and social programs.* San Francisco: Jossey-Bass.

Evans, R. I., Rozelle, R. M., Mittelmark, M. B., Hansen, W. B., Bane, A. L., & Havis, J. (1977). Deterring the onset of smoking in children: Knowledge of immediate physiological effects and coping with peer pressure, media pressure, and parent modeling. *Journal of Applied Social Psychology, 8,* 126–135.

Fisher, R. A. (1935). *The design of experiments.* Edinburgh, UK: Oliver & Boyd.

Goldstein, N. J., Cialdini, R. B., Griskevicius, V. (2008). A room with a viewpoint: Using social norms to motivate environmental conservation in hotels. *Journal of Consumer Research, 35,* 472–482.

Helmreich, R. (1975). Applied social psychology: The unfulfilled promise. *Personality and Social Psychology Bulletin, 1,* 548–560.

Hennigan, K. M., Del Rosario, M. L., Heath, L., Cook, T. D.,Wharton, J. D., & Calder, B. J. (1982). Impact of the introduction of television on crime in the United States: Empirical findings and theoretical implications. *Journal of Personality and Social Psychology, 55,* 239–247.

Hernán, M. A., Alonso, A., Logan, R., Grodstein, F., Michels, K. B., Willett, W. C., et al. (2008). Observational studies analyzed like randomized experiments: An application to postmenopausal hormone therapy and coronary heart disease (with discussion). *Epidemiology, 19,* 766–792.

Kelley, H. H., Hommes, J. G., Kerr, N. L., Reis, H. T., Rusbult, C. E., & Van Lange, P. A. M. (2003). *An atlas of interpersonal situations.* New York: Cambridge University Press.

Kruglanski, A. W. (1975). The human subject in psychological research: Fact and artifact. In L. Berkowitz (Ed.), *Advances in experimental social psychology* (Vol. 8, pp. 101–147). New York: Academic Press.

Lewin, K. (1948). *Resolving social conflicts.* New York: Harper and Row.

Lewin, K. (1951). *Field theory in social science.* Chicago: University of Chicago Press.

Moser, S. E., West, S. G., & Hughes, J. N. (2011). Trajectories of math and reading achievement in elementary school: Effects of early and later retention in grade. Manuscript submitted for publication.

Reichardt, C. S. (2006). The principle of parallelism in the design of studies to estimate treatment effects. *Psychological Methods, 11,* 1–18.

Reynolds, K. D., & West, S. G. (1987). A multiplist strategy for strengthening nonequivalent control group designs. *Evaluation Review, 11,* 691–714.

Rosenbaum, P. R., & Rubin, D. B. (1983). The central role of the propensity score in observational studies for causal effects. *Biometrika, 70,* 41–55.

Schwarz, N., & Hippler, H.-J. (1995). Subsequent questions may influence answers to preceding questions in mail surveys. *Public Opinion Quarterly, 59,* 93–97.

Sears, D. O. (1986). College sophomores in the laboratory: Influences of a narrow data base on social psychology's view of human nature. *Journal of Personality and Social Psychology, 51,* 515–530.

Shadish, W. R., Clark, M. H., & Steiner, P. M. (2008). Can nonrandomized experiments yield accurate answers? A randomized experiment comparing random and nonrandom assignments (with commentary). *Journal of the American Statistical Association, 103,* 1334–1356.

Shadish, W. R., & Cook, T. D. (2009). The renaissance of field experimentation in evaluating interventions. *Annual Review of Psychology, 60,* 607–629.

Shadish, W. R., Cook, T. D., & Campbell, D. T. (2002). *Experimental and quasi-experimental designs for generalized causal inference.* Boston: Houghton-Mifflin.

West, S. G., Biesanz, J. C., & Pitts, S. C. (2000). Causal inference and generalization in field settings: Experimental and quasi-experimental designs. In H. T. Reis, & C. M. Judd (Eds.), *Handbook of research methods in personality and social psychology* (pp. 40–84). New York: Cambridge University Press.

West, S. G., Duan, N., Pequegnat, W., Gaist, P., DesJarlais, D., Holtgrave, D., et al. (2008). Alternatives to the randomized controlled trial. *American Journal of Public Health, 98,* 1359–1366.

West, S. G., Newsom, J. T., & Fenaughty, A. M. (1992). Publication trends in JPSP: Stability and change in the topics, methods, and theories across two decades. *Personality and Social Psychology Bulletin, 18,* 473–484.

West, S. G., & Thoemmes, F. (2010). Campbell's and Rubin's perspectives on causal inference. *Psychological Methods, 15,* 18–37.

Wilson, T. D., Aronson, E., & Carlsmith, K. (2010). The art of laboratory experimentation. In S. T. Fiske, D. T. Gilbert, & G. Lindzey (Eds.), *Handbook of social psychology* (Vol. 1, pp. 51–81). Hoboken, NJ: Wiley.

Wu, W., West, S. G., & Hughes, J. N. (2008). Effect of retention in first grade on children's achievement trajectories over four years: A piecewise growth analysis using propensity score matching. *Journal of Educational Psychology, 100,* 727–740.

CHAPTER 13

Casasanto, D. (2009). Embodiment of abstract concepts: Good and bad in right- and left-handers. *Journal of Experimental Psychology: General, 138,* 351–367.

Cialdini, R. B. (2009). *Influence: Science and practice* (5th ed.). Boston: Pearson Education.

Dijksterhuis, A., Smith, P. K., Van Baaren, R. B., & Wigboldus, D. H. (2005). The unconscious consumer: Effects of environment on consumer behavior. *Journal of Consumer Psychology, 15,* 193–202.

Knowles, E. S., & Linn, J. A. (2004). *Resistance and persuasion*. Mahwah: Lawrence Erlbaum.

Pratkanis, A. R. (2007). *The science of social influence: Advances and future progress*. New York: Psychological Press.

CHAPTER 14

Arizona State University. (2000). *Department of Psychology Self Study*.

Bickman, L. (1980). Introduction. *Applied Social Psychology Annual* (Vol. 1), 7–18. Beverly Hills, CA: Sage.

Braver, S. L., & Griffin, W. A. (2000). Engaging fathers in the post-divorce family. *Marriage & Family Review, 29*, 247–267.

Braver, S. L., Griffin, W. A., & Cookston, J. T. (2005). Prevention programs for divorced non-resident fathers. *Family Court Review, 43*(1), 81–96.

Braver, S. L., Griffin, W. A., Cookston, J. T., Sandler, I. N., & Williams, J. (2005). Promoting better fathering among divorced nonresident fathers. In W. M. Pinsof, & J. Lebow (Eds.), *Family psychology: The art of the science* (pp. 295–325). New York: Oxford University Press.

Braver, S. L., & O'Connell, D. (1998). *Divorced dads: Shattering the myths*. New York: Tarcher/Putnam.

Braver, S. L., Wolchik, S. A., Sandler, I. N., & Sheets, V. (1993a). A social exchange model of noncustodial parent involvement. In J. Bray, & C. Depner (Eds.), *Nonresidential parenting: New vistas in family living* (pp. 87–108). Beverly Hills, CA: Sage.

Braver, S. L., Wolchik, S. A., Sandler, I. N., Sheets, V., Fogas, B., & Bay, R. C. (1993b). A longitudinal study of noncustodial parents: Parents without children. *Journal of Family Psychology, 7*, 9–23.

Brechner, K. C. (1974). *An experimental analysis of social traps: A laboratory analog*. Unpublished dissertation, Arizona State University, December, 1974.

Brechner, K. C. (1977). An experimental analysis of social traps. *Journal of Experimental Social Psychology, 13*, 552–564.

Breckler, S. J. (2007, April). Rising to the challenge. *Monitor on Psychology*, p. 28.

Bush, V. (1945). *Science: The endless frontier*. Washington, DC: Office of Scientific Research and Development.

Campbell, D. T., & Stanley, J. C. (1966). *Experimental and quasi-experimental designs for research*. Chicago: Rand McNally.

Cialdini, R. B. (1980). Full-cycle social psychology. In L. Bickman (Ed.), *Applied social psychology annual* (Vol. 1, pp. 21–47). Beverly Hills, CA: Sage.

Cialdini, R. B., Bickman, L., & Cacioppo, J. T. (1979). An example of consumeristic social psychology: Bargaining tough in the new car showroom. *Journal of Applied Social Psychology, 9*, 115–126.

Cook, T. D., & Campbell, D. T. (1979). *Quasi-experimentation: Design and analysis for field setting*. Chicago: Rand McNally.

Cookston, J. T., Braver, S. L., Griffin, W. A., DeLusé, S. R., & Miles, J. C. (2007). Effects of the Dads For Life intervention on coparenting in the two years after divorce. *Family Process, 46*(1), 123–137.

Hardin, G. (1968). The tragedy of the commons. *Science, 162*(3859), 1243–1248.

Janssen, M. A., Holahan, R., Lee, A., & Ostrom, E. (2010). Lab experiments for the study of social-ecological systems. *Science, 328*(5978), 613–617.

Kelley, H. H., & Thibaut, J. (1978). *Interpersonal relations: A theory of interdependence*. New York: Wiley.

Neidert, G. P. M. (1986). *The effects of commitment, participation, and surveillance on resource management in social trap*. Unpublished doctoral dissertation, Arizona State University.

Neidert, G. P. M., & Linder, D. E. (1990). Avoiding social traps: Some conditions that maintain adherence to restricted consumption. *Social Behaviour, 5,* 261–284.

Platt, J. (1973). Social traps. *American Psychologist, 28*(8), 641–651.

Reich, J. W. (2008). Integrating science and practice: Adoptinzg the Pasteurian model. *Review of General Psychology, 12,* 365–377.

Reich, J. W., & Zautra, A. (1981). Life events and personal causation: Some relationships with satisfaction and distress. *Journal of Personality and Social Psychology, 41,* 1002–1012.

Reich, J. W., & Zautra, A. J. (1989). A perceived control intervention for at-risk older adults. *Psychology and Aging, 4,* 415–424.

Stokes, D. E. (1997). *Pasteur's quadrant: Basic science and technological innovation.* Washington, DC: Brookings Institution Press.

Thibaut, J. W., & Kelley, H. H. (1959). *The social psychology of groups.* New York: Wiley.

Zimbardo, P. (2004). Does psychology make a significant difference in our lives? *American Psychologist, 59,* 339–351.

INDEX

NOTE: In this index, page numbers followed by *f* indicate figures; page numbers followed by *b* indicate text boxes.

Breckler, S. J., 147
Briñol, Pablo, xvii, 53–54
Brock, T. C., 50
Brown, Stephanie, xviii
Burger, Jerry, xvii
Burger's Zoo, 135–137
Bush, Vannevar, 147, 148
Buss, D. M., 106
Buunk, Abraham. P., 104

Cacioppo, John, xviii
Calder, B. J., 128
Campbell, Donald, 122, 126, 149
Cantu, Stephanie, xvii
career decisions and sex ratio, xvii, 83, 85–86
caregiving behavior, 110–115
causal generalization. *See* full-cycle research
China, sex ratio in, 79
choices, difficulty in making, 45–46
A Christmas Carol (Dickens), 90
Cialdini, Robert
    on altruism and egoism, 110–111, 112,
        117–118
    Arizona State University and, xix,
        143–146, 154
    on basic/applied social psychology
        split, 133
    full-cycle model, 123–126, 132–133,
        142–143, 146, 147–148
    fundraising requests, 45
    Influence, 14–15, 26, 49, 96
    influence of, xv–xvi, xix
    interdisciplinary collaboration, 9–10
    interpersonal connections, 4–5, 12–13
    marketing of scientific results, 10–12
    methodological flexibility, 7–9
    principles of influence, 27, 32–35, 49, 96,
        136, 138
    on public service messages, 39–40
    at Radboud University Nijmegen,
        134–135
    real life observations, 5–7
    social norms, 69–71, 72, 74, 75, 77
    See also basking in reflected glory;
        full-cycle research; *specific principles
        of influence*
Clark, M. H., 132
clergy, parental influence and, 103
cognition, 53–54, 58, 94, 116
cognitive-perceptual balance, 61–62
Cohen, Adam, 145

collectivist vs. individualistic societies,
    mating patterns in, 104–105
commitment and consistency (influence
    principle), 33, 34
common resource dilemmas, 152–153
competition, intrasexual, 81, 83, 84–85
compliance
    authority and, 58n1
    with help requests, xvii, 23–25, 45
    sales techniques and, 50, 123–124
    similarity and, 64–67
computer hacking, 27–32, 38
condescension-based conflict, 19–20
connections, interpersonal, 4–5
control and well-being, 149–151
Cook, Tom, 122, 123b, 126, 128, 130
cooperative breeders, 100–102
correction of misleading information, 41
cortisol (hormone), 87–89
credibility, 30, 33, 36, 52–55, 58nn2–4
Cronbach, L. J., 121–122
"cutting off reflected failure," 62–63

Dads For Life program, 151–152
daughters, parental influence over, 105–106
Decety, Jean, 117
decision paralysis, 45–46
de Lange, Martijn, 140
Del Rosario, M. L., 128
descriptive norms. *See* social norms
de Wall, Frans, 117
Dickens, Charles, 90
difficulty/ease expectations, 44–45, 46
Dijksterhuis, Ap, xviii
discriminant validity, 122, 123b
divorced fathers, 150–151
door-in-the-face technique, 33, 37
Dubbs, Shelli. L., 104
Dunbar, R. I. M., 93
Durante, Kristina, xvii
dynamic social impact theory, 5

ease/difficulty expectations, 44–45, 46
Edison, Thomas, 148
egoism and altruism. *See* altruism vs.
    egoism debate
Eisenberg, Nancy, 145
elaboration likelihood model (ELM), 51
elephant seal reproduction, 99–100
emotions, 22–23, 25–26
empathy-altruism hypothesis, 111, 112, 117

empirical interpolation/extrapolation, 123b
Epley, N., 17–18
Erdös, Paul, xvi, 3
estradiol/estrogen (hormone), 87–89
Evans, R. I., 122
"even a penny helps" strategy, xv, 45
evolution
    altruism and, 113–115, 117
    human reproduction and, 103–104, 107
    of human sociability, 92–96, 108
    individual decision making and, 5
    See also sex ratio
expectations, future, 43–44
experimental methods
    non-randomized studies, 127–130, 128f, 131f, 132
    randomized studies, 125–126, 130, 132

fame, consequences of, 7
Feyerabend, Paul, 8
field studies, 7–9, 119, 121, 125–126, 132–133, 146
financial decisions and sex ratio, xvii, 82–83, 85–86
Finch, J. F., 63–64
Fisher, Ronald, 120
fitness interdependence, 114
Fleischman, D. S., 106
fluency
    expected effort and, 44–45
    familiarity, risk and, 41–43
    familiarity, social consensus and, 40
    future expectations and, 43–44
    liking and, 46–47
    making choices and, 45–46
    processing style and, 47–48
    truth and, 41
Flynn, Francis, xvii
focus theory of normative conduct, 69–71, 78
    See also social norms
fonts (typography), 44–45, 46, 47
"fox" behavior, 9–10
full-cycle research
    basic vs. applied research and, xviii, 119–123, 132–133, 145–148, 154
    Cialdini on, 142–143
    example studies, xviii, 135–139, 149–153
    generalization and experimental methods, xviii, 123b, 125–132
    overview, xvi, 123–125

Pasteur's Quadrant and, 123, 147–148, 154
    in social psychology programs, 143–146
future expectations and fluency, 43–44

Garcia, S. M., 40
Garner, R., 66
generalizable causal effects, xviii, 123b, 125–132
    See also full-cycle research
genes and genetics, 92–96, 97, 106–107, 112, 113–115
Gilovich, T., 17–18, 25
Goldstein, Noah J., xvii, 74, 77, 124
grandparents, 104–105, 107
Graziano, William, xviii
Griskevicius, Vladas, xvii, 74, 77, 124
group/multilevel selection, 93, 117

hacking (computers), 27–32, 38
Hamilton, W. D., 112
Hansen, W. B., 122
harshness bias, 17–18
Havis, J., 122
Hawkley, Louise, xviii
health, 91–92, 115–116, 135–136
Heath, L., 128
"hedgehog" behavior, 9–10
Heider, Fritz, 61–62, 65
helping behavior, 110–115
help-seeking
    alignment of asker/helper goals and, 22–23
    favorable impressions of help-seeker, 19–20
    as form of influence vs. weakness, 15, 20–21
    harshness bias and, 17–18
    memory of negative outcomes, 18–19
    non-alignment of asker/helper goals, 23–25
    regrets about not asking for help, 25–26
    similarity and compliance, 64–66
    underestimation of helpfulness, xvii, 15–17
Hennigan, K. M., 128
Hernán, M. A., 132
heterogeneous irrelevancies, 123b
heuristic mechanisms, xv, xvii, 37, 49–51, 53, 55–57
heuristic-systematic model, 51

Murphy, Gardner, 146
"My Big Break" (documentary), 3, 7

Nagoshi, Craig, 145
naked mole-rat reproduction, 102
National Forest Service, 39
Neidert, Greg, 152, 153
Netherlands, 134–141
Neuberg, Steven L., xvi, 6, 10–11,
    12–13, 145
Nolan, J. M., 74
nonequivalent dependent variables
    (observational studies), 131–132f
non-randomized studies, 127–130, 128f,
    131f, 132
norms, social. *See* social norms
Novemsky, N., 46
nudges, help requests as, 22

observational studies, 129–130, 131–132f
oneness and altruism, 112, 113
oxytocin, 115

parental influence on reproduction, 99,
    103–107
parent-offspring conflict theory, 106–107
Pasteur, Louis, 148
Pasteur's Quadrant, 123, 143, 146–148, 154
*Pasteur's Quadrant: Basic Science and
    Technological Innovation* (Stokes),
    146–148
peer review, 144–145
penetration (PEN) testing, 35
Perilloux, C., 106
perspective taking, 111, 112, 116, 117
persuasion
    historical background, v–vii
    misgivings about, 17
    non-alignment of asker/helper goals
      and, 23–25
    scientific study of, vii–viii
    tools for, 14–15
    See also social influence
Petrified Forest National Park, 39, 72–73
Petrova, Petia, xvii
Petty, Richard E., xvii, 53–54
pilot tests, 139, 140
Pinker, S., 98
Platt, J., 152
politeness norms vs. security roles, 36–37
political participation study, 138–140

polyandry, 100
polygynously mating mammals, 99–100
Preston, Stephanie, 117
pricing strategies and sex ratio, 86–87
primary cognition, 53–54, 58
processing style and fluency, 47–48
program evaluation, 149
progress, linear model of, 146–147
propensity scoring, 129, 130, 132
provincial descriptive norms, 77
    See also social norms
proximal similarity, 123b
public image, 4, 12
    See also basking in reflected glory
public policy, xviii, 43, 147
public service messages, 39
pure science. *See* basic vs. applied research

randomized studies, 122, 125–126, 130, 132
real world vs. laboratory experiments, 7–9,
    119–125, 132–133, 145–146, 149
reciprocal obligation (influence principle),
    33, 34–35
reframing of messages, 73
regression discontinuity study
    design, 127, 128f
regret, 25–26
Reich, John W., xix, 143, 149–150
religiosity and sex ratio, 83
Reno, R. R., 124, 126
reproductive behavior
    animal social control over, xviii, 99–102
    human social influence and, 102–107
    sex ratio and human mating patterns,
      80–81, 84–86, 88
resistance, acknowledgment of, 139
Reynolds, K. D., 39–40, 130
Rice, W. E., 35
right hand bias, 137
risk, 24, 25, 38, 41–43, 82–83, 86
romantic love, 104
Rosenbaum, P. R., 129
Rozelle, R. M., 122
Rubin, D. B., 129
Russo, Nancy, 145

Saenz, Delia, 145
Sagarin, Brad J., xvii, 35
Sandler, Irwin, 150–152
Savitsky, K., 17–18
saying no, costs of, 16–17

scarcity (influence principle), 33, 34–35,
    50–52, 136
    See also sex ratio
Schaller, Mark, xvi, 3–4, 7–8, 10, 12–13
Schroeder, D. A., 45, 124
Schultz, P. W., 74, 93
Schwartzman, D. F., 39–40
Schwarz, Norman, xvii, 40, 42
Science: The Endless Frontier (Bush), 147
scientific influence principles
    interdisciplinary collaboration, 9–10
    interpersonal connections, 4–5, 12–13
    marketing of scientific results, 10–12
    methodological flexibility, 7–9
    real life observation, 5–7
scientific progress, 146–147
secondary cognition, 53–54, 58
security roles vs. politeness norms, 36–37
selective investment theory, 114–116
the self, 112, 113, 117
self-esteem, 4, 22–23, 63–64
self-presentation to others, 61–63
self-regulation, 75–76
self-validation persuasion mechanism,
    54, 56–57
Serna, S. B., 35
sex ratio
    background research, xvii, 80–81
    economic and social behavior
        and, 82–84
    hormones and, 87–89
    individual differences and, 84–87
    influence on relationships, 81
    See also scarcity (influence principle)
Shadish, W. R., 122, 126, 130, 132
Sherif, Muzafer, 146
Sherman, S. J., 39–40
Shiota, Lani, 145
similarity and compliance, 64–67
Simpson, Jeff, xvii
sociable weaver (bird), 100
social bonds, 114–116
social engineering
    attack on Motorola, xvii, 28–32
    attacks against individuals, 37–38
    defenses against attack, 34–37
    defined, 27
    vulnerability to attack, 32–33
social exchange theory, 151
social impact theory, dynamic, 5
social influence

alignment of asker/helper goals
    and, 22–23
Cialdini's principles of, 27, 32–35, 49, 96,
    136, 138
fluency and, 48
help-seeking as a form of, 15, 20–21
language and, 98, 108
misgivings about, 17, 21
multiprocess theories of, 51–52
non-alignment of asker/helper
    goals, 23–25
sex ratio and, 84
    See also persuasion; scientific influence
        principles; *specific principles of influence*
social isolation/loneliness, 91–92, 95–96
social networking, 37–38
The Social Neuroscience of Empathy
    (Decety), 117
social norms
    descriptive and injunctive norm
        functioning, 75–76
    effective use in messages, 71–74
    focus theory of normative conduct,
        69–71, 78
    identification of, 40
    "operators are waiting" example, 68–69
    security role disagreement with, 36–37
    similarity and conformity, 76–77
    social proof and, 55
social proof (influence principle), 55–57,
    58n4, 139
Social Psychological Research Institute
    (SPRI), 144–145
social psychology
    as academic discipline, 133, 143–146,
        148–150, 153–154
    basic vs. applied research, xviii, 119–123,
        132–133, 145–148, 154
    experimental methods, 7–9, 125–132
social status, 87–88, 104, 105, 107
social structure evolution, 92–94
social support research, 116
Society for the Psychological Study of Social
    Issues (SPSSI), 147
software, malicious, 35–36, 37, 38
Song, Hyunjin, xvii, 42
sons, parental influence over, 105–106
source attractiveness, 57
source credibility. *See* credibility
spotted hyena reproduction, 100
Stanley, Julian, 149

Steiner, P. M., 132
stock market risks, 42–43
Stokes, Donald, 146–148
Stolba, Alex, 98–99
Sunstein, Cass, xv, xvi
Szot, Colleen, 68–69

testosterone (hormone), 87–89
Thaler, Richard, xv, xvi
thinking
    authority principle and, 53–55
    scarcity principle and, 51–52
    social proof principle and, 55–57, 58n4
Thoemmes, F., 130
time, 126, 127–128, 133n
Tormala, Z. L., 53–54
treatment effects, 127, 128*f*
Trivers, R. L., 104, 106
truth and fluency of processing, 41, 47

underestimation effect, xvii, 15–17
unit relationships, 61–62, 65–66
Units, Treatments, Observations and
    Settings (UTOS), 121–122, 124
University of Nijmegen, xviii, 134
U.S. Bureau of Land Management, 152

us/them distinctions, 60, 62, 63

validity of experiment results, 122, 124–125,
    127, 130
van Baaren, Rick, xviii
van Hooff, Jan, xviii
vulnerability to social engineering, 32–33,
    35–36

Weaver, K., 40
websites and social engineering attacks, 38
well-being and control, 149–151
West, Stephen, xviii, 129, 130, 145
Wharton, J. D., 128
white fronted bee-eaters (bird), 101
Williams, George, 92–93
willpower, 75–76
Wilson, David Sloan, 117
Wolchik, Sharlene, 150–152
Wong, V. C., 130
Wu, W., 129

Zajonc, R. B., 46
Zimbardo, P., 147
zoo restaurant study, 135–137
Zuatra, Alex, 149–150